The Right Women

*A Journey Through the Heart
of Conservative America*

Elinor Burkett

A LISA DREW BOOK

SCRIBNER

A LISA DREW BOOK / SCRIBNER
1230 Avenue of the Americas
New York, NY 10020

Set in Spectrum
Designed by Brooke Zimmer
Manufactured in the United States of America

10 9 8 7 6 5 4 3 2 1

Library of Congress Cataloging-in-Publication Data
Burkett, Elinor.
The right women: a journey through the heart of conservative
America / Elinor Burkett.
p. cm.
Includes bibliographical references.
1. Anti-feminism—United States. 2. Feminism—United States.
3. Conservatism—United States. 4. Liberalism—United States.
5. Sex discrimination against women—United States. I. Title.
HQ1426.B847   1998
305.42'0973—dc21   97-29501
CIP

ISBN 0-684-83308-5

In Memory of Anna and Bernard Cohen,
who gave me the gift of a skeptical mind.

For Emily and Rebecca,
and the women they are becoming.

Acknowledgments

Writing a book is a lot like building a stone wall. You lay the base well before you understand the shape of the rise. You can never be sure whether the row you are beginning will be the final course, or just another step toward the top.

For me, *The Right Women* began decades before I even considered the possibility of becoming a writer. I could never have written it had I not spent years as an academic: studying history, helping to found a women's studies program and teaching hundreds of students about the struggles of women, and men, to make America a more just society. So I am grateful to the women at the University of Pittsburgh who shared with me that stunning moment of discovery that was the founding of the women's history program, and to my students at Frostburg State University both for their fascination and for their skepticism.

My research for this book was dependent on the willingness of dozens of women to speak openly and candidly with me, despite the fact that I presented myself honestly as a liberal feminist. Without them, obviously, this book would not exist. I offer my heartfelt thanks to them all, and most especially to Carol O'Dowd, Whitney Adams, Representative Helen Chenoweth, Judy Jefferson, Nona Brazier, Cori Johnson, Dina and Amanda Butcher, Adelle Kirk, Marianne Reid, Kim Barghouti, Linda Holscher, Wendy Kaiser, Michelle Grothe, LaRee MacRae, Michelle Cote, Jackie Bradbury, Carolyn Trochman and Kay Sheil.

In the course of writing this book, I was blessed with the wisdom, the insights and the cooperation of a group of women I have learned to call friends. Barbara Ledeen smashed a thousand stereotypes in a single afternoon, and left me infinitely richer. April Lassiter shared her heart, her soul and her personal journey, helping me to understand both the young woman

I once was and the older woman I now am. Amy Holmes led me through her own odyssey from liberalism to a new conservatism. And Lauren Maddox and Karen Johnson offered me the trust and cooperation without which I could never have cracked the arcane world of Capitol Hill. I am deeply grateful to them all.

The women in my life were forced to endure regular quizzings, frequent interviews and endless reality checks. For their good humor and boundless support, I thank Rose Anderson, Pat Millette, Sky Cappucci, Ruth LaMothe and Deborah Sontag. Two other women offered concrete assistance, as well as good humor and support. Lisa Bankoff, agent extraordinaire, believed in this book even before I did, and Lisa Drew of Scribner gave me the opportunity to make it a reality.

Finally, the men in my life, for if I have learned one lesson that has dramatically changed it over the past two decades, it is that my world would be poorer if it were exclusively female. No matter how many books or articles I pen, I cannot fail to thank Frank Bruni, my sometime coauthor, my frequent cothinker, my perpetual friend, for being a one-man Dial-a-Lede and a perennial Dial-a-Title. Ivan Bernstein promised me skepticism, and never let me down. Joel Rapoport, Robin Haueter, Robert Jones, Paul Millette and Bruce Conroy helped me stay sane and avoid taking myself too seriously.

My gratitude lingers on Dennis, my sweet and wise husband, my greatest booster and harshest critic, for keeping me grounded enough to think and energized enough to dream.

Contents

Introduction: Through the Looking Glass   15

PART I The New Recruits

The Babes   27
A Digression into a Mad Hatter's Tea Party   45

The Abolitionists   52
A Digression into the World of Soccer Moms and Gender Fissures   75

The Outlaws   83
A Digression into Cooking Up Trouble   115

The Apostates   124
A Digression into a Posse of Pistol-Packing Mamas   139

PART II The Old Faithful

The Holy   149
A Digression into Faith of a Different Fabric   171

The Operators   176
A Digression into the Strong Arms and Stronger Spirits of Frontierswomen   200

The Ideopreneurs   205
A Digression into the Mind of a Femi-Newtie   228

The Weary   229

Epilogue: Everything Has a Moral, If Only You Can Find It   248
Notes   259
Index   279

"They're dreadfully fond of beheading people here:
the great wonder is, that there's any one left alive!"

LEWIS CARROLL, *Alice's Adventures in Wonderland*

The Right Women

Introduction

Through the Looking Glass

It wasn't until the congressional elections of 1994 that I squarely confronted any serious chinks in my feminist mythology. That year, women's history of an unexpected—almost shocking—sort was made, or remade, virtually without notice. I might have missed it myself had I not happened to tune into C-Span one night when it was broadcasting a seminar for freshman members of the 104th Congress sponsored by two right-wing think tanks. Among those freshmen gathered at the Orioles' stadium in Baltimore were seven women—by far the most Republican women ever elected to Congress in a single year. Yet they weren't waving feminist banners over this milestone. Rather, they were crumpling any such banners and stomping on them. "There's not a femi-nazi among us!" crowed Rep-elect Barbara Cubin of Wyoming. She was making that boast to Rush Limbaugh, whom she had praised as her ideological muse. She had just handed him a plaque designed for him by the seven neophytes. It read "Rush was Right."

Who were these women, and how had they swept into power with so little fanfare? The latter question was easy to answer. Their stealth ascendance could be attributed to the fact that feminists were horrified by them and had no desire to train a spotlight on them, while the liberal news media were too busy noting the sharp falloff in new congresswomen from the Democratic party, the supposed haven for all things female, to try to explain the less tidy, opposite phenomenon happening on the other side of the political divide.

Indeed, these Republican congresswomen confounded expectations not only in their numbers, but also in their postures. They were not moderate Republicans, centrists in pumps and pearls reaching out from the right to grab hold of the same middle ground that Bill Clinton was grasping from the left. Quite the opposite. The group included Helen Chenoweth of Idaho, who advocated the abolition of the Internal Revenue Service and insisted on being called "Congressman." Linda Smith of Washington denounced the League of Women Voters, which she called the "League of Women Vipers," as too liberal. Sue Myrick of North Carolina, who proposed the creation of modern-day concentration camps for drug dealers while mayor of Charlotte, regularly invoked God's wrath against her adversaries. With the exception of Sue Kelly of New York, the distaff freshmen disdained the Congressional Women's Caucus, although they insisted that they would find time for freshman weekly Bible study.

I was tempted to follow feminist tradition and write these women off as pawns of men or unenlightened slobs trying to force all females but themselves back into the kitchen. Alas, truth intervened. These women were independent enough to buck even the males of their own party, and—even by feminist standards—they were positively spunky. Cubin once treated her male colleagues in the Wyoming state legislature to homemade cookies baked in the shape of penises. Enid Waldholtz of Utah arrived at the Capitol pregnant and promptly set up a nursery in her office. When Chenoweth's congressional opponent ran a series of Thelma-and-Louise ads accusing her of extremism, she countered with spots vowing to "show those boys in Washington a thing or two."

To a woman who came of age during the heyday of modern feminism, it didn't make sense. In my mythology—mainstream feminist mythology, it's fair to say—women like Chenoweth, Cubin, Myrick and company seemed like natural feminists; yet they actually bragged about their aversion to the very movement that had helped blast open the doors of Congress to them.

The contradiction nagged at me. What was going on in America? I wanted to pass these women off as an anomaly, but I had already become uncomfortable at the frequency with which feminists were writing off distasteful realities as anomalous. So I took off my rose-colored feminist glasses and began a survey of the landscape of American womanhood, without blame, wishful thinking or disdain. Suddenly, I found women challenging feminist mythology everywhere. Young women, twentysomethings who'd been raised with all the advances of feminism and whose parents had eschewed all manner of blue and pink distinctions, were marrying young, and taking their husbands' names. Their older sisters, who had broken new ground for women, were giving up six-figure salaries to stay home and raise their children. Christian women who were supposed to exercise those homemaking skills were lobbying on Capitol Hill against a broad range of feminist-supported liberal programs. Bright, energetic women were joining the staffs of the American Enterprise Institute, the *American Spectator* and other bastions of the far right to work for causes I'd always believed no self-respecting independent woman could support. Black women claiming Malcolm X as their inspiration were running for Congress as Republicans. And, as the American economy bred anxiety from Maine to California, women who had spent decades doing battle for women's rights and progressive causes were suddenly questioning whether the old answers even belonged among the multiple-choice options on the new test.

This wasn't the way it was supposed to happen.

MY MOTHER, Anna, was the woman Betty Friedan had in mind when she wrote *The Feminine Mystique* in 1963. One of the first female graduates of the University of Pennsylvania, Anna was bright, curious and bored out of her mind staying home to raise her two daughters. She kept herself busy helping my father in his business and working with various civic groups, but I always wondered why she hadn't followed her early dream and gone to medical school. She refused to satisfy my curiosity. "I guess it just wasn't important enough to me," she responded dismissively whenever I broached the topic. My father was equally unhelpful. All he could say was that my mother had never brought up the idea in the years after the depression, when they could have afforded the luxury.

The question hung over our household as my sister and I grew up, and it was resolved, in an odd way, when we came of age, and headed for the type of career my mother had forsaken. I thought I was following the advice my father had given me explicitly: Don't worry about getting married and having children. Go to school. Find a career. Make something of yourself. Only years later did I understand that I was also following the advice my mother had given me less overtly: Don't end up like me.

Entering college in 1964, I joined a wave of other women who had also tasted their mothers' frustration and forged it into a weapon against a nation that had forgotten its own women. Simply by asking the question "What about women?" we reimagined America and stormed Washington, Bismarck, Sacramento and every possible political center with scores of demands, from equal wages to safe streets. We created a new language and wove it into the lives of the next generation. We rewrote the nation's understanding of its past in the hope of reshaping its future.

The shape of that future seemed absolutely, glaringly clear to us: Women would discover their potential, throw off the shackles of outmoded roles and oppressive stereotypes and take their rightful places in politics, science, business and the arts. Men might balk and struggle to retain their supremacy, but in the end, they would either grow to appreciate the richness of equality or be vanquished by the power of national sisterhood. Young women and their brothers would grow up in a world in which Johnnie would feel free to dance to Stravinsky and Susi could gravitate toward welding. And with women in a position of full equality, women's nature—women's sensitivity and intuitiveness—would make America a kinder and gentler place.

Certainty was at the heart of our movement, as it is at the heart of every revolutionary, or would-be revolutionary, tide. Young, educated, privileged white women, we never questioned our authority to speak for all American women. We never asked ourselves whether the Bastille we were attempting to storm might be a living room which some woman had lovingly decorated, or a church that offered her comfort.

That certainty radically redefined how women are seen in America. Three decades after Betty Friedan touched a national nerve with *The Feminine Mystique,* girls are no longer consigned to home economics while boys trudge to woodworking and shop. No newspaper would dare divide its Help Wanted section into male and female categories. No university would refuse to promote a faculty member simply because she was a woman.

Today more bachelor's and master's degrees are awarded to women than to men. In 1996, women made up more than half the freshman class at Yale Medical School and 45 percent of the graduating class of its law school. In the past ten years alone, the number of female executive vice presidents of businesses has more than doubled, while the number of female senior vice presidents rose 75 percent. Women now own 40 percent of all retail and service businesses, employing a staggering 15.5 million people. The year Friedan published her seminal work, only fourteen women served in the United States Congress; by 1996, the number had risen to fifty-six, and female candidates are winning their races for political office at the same rate as their male counterparts.

Violence against women has hardly disappeared, but it is no longer the sort of taboo which made the women who appeared at the first speak-out against rape in New York feminist heroines. Dozens of laws that kept women from credit, divorce, control over their own bodies and choices in housing or employment have vanished into the dustbin of history. And virtually no one questions what three decades ago seemed like revolutionary doctrines: equal pay for equal work and equal access to jobs.

While no rational person could claim that a female nirvana has been created in Peoria or Seattle, American women think differently about their lives now than they did in the 1950s, and so do American men. Few girls grow up without the widest sense of personal options in the world. Few grown woman don't know that they have the right to get angry, get a job, or get divorced. Measured against three millennia of women's history, the progress has been breathtaking.

Yet the same certainty which fueled that progress seems to have distanced feminism from the very women it purports to serve. While more than half of the nation's women believe that a strong women's movement is important to their lives, two-thirds refuse to call themselves feminists. Even young college women shy away from the label, only one-fifth expressing any willingness to be identified with the movement. In the public mind, feminists have become grotesque caricatures: man-hating harridans trying to divorce women from full partnership with the men they love. American women have tarred feminism with every negative from "doctrinaire" to "irrelevant."

It was this fact that kept tugging at me in the months after the 1994 election, as I began to think about the new Republican congresswomen, as I tried to make sense of the fact that corporate executives and bankers are giving up their jobs to raise their children, and that GenX-ers are hailing Newt Gingrich with the enthusiasm my generation reserved for Che Guevara. I knew what the pat feminist explanation was: None of that is true; it's all an invention of woman-hating researchers and reporters. Or, alternatively: Yes, it's true; look how male supremacists have squashed all the progress we'd won.

Both answers seemed glib. Both answers seemed clichéd. Statistical analyses told me nothing; the numbers have been twisted so often that they are more useful as patterns for fried snacks than for information. I decided to go on the road and check the pulse of the American woman.

BEFORE I began this quest, I had never actually talked to any woman who refused to call herself a feminist, and conservative women were more remote from my experience than were, say, women journalists and academics in Paris, Tokyo or Buenos Aires. Everyone I knew criticized the government, but always for being too inactive, never for being too big. Everyone I knew believed in affirmative action, rigid separation of church and state and gay rights. No one I knew seriously considered the possibility that abortion should not be an inviolable right.

I was aware that there were people who disagreed with these views, but I also knew that they were the pawns and playthings of the "ruling class," and were indifferent to the plight of the poor, intolerant of diversity and willing to level entire countries to maintain American hegemony over the world. I didn't actually know any of this firsthand, of course, because America is not so much a heterogeneous society as a patchwork of homogeneous societies living together cheek by jowl yet remarkably isolated from one another.

But I was arrogant enough to be sure I knew what to expect when I entered the offices of the Independent Women's Forum to meet Barbara Ledeen. After all, I'd done my homework, both about the woman and about the group, which billed itself as a political home for women uncomfortable at either Phyllis Schlafly's or Gloria Steinem's end of the mythical spectrum. Ledeen had worked in the Pentagon under Reagan, and her husband Michael had been one of the architects of Reagan's foreign policy. She supported Virginia Military Institute's single-sex policy and the abolition of affirmative action. She opposed the Violence Against Women Act and a wide range of special educational programs targeted to young girls. So predicting what Barbara would be like hardly seemed like rocket science. Pearls and pumps, I assumed. Country club. Haughty superiority.

The woman who burst from the warren of rooms in the basement of the townhouse off Dupont Circle was wearing an Indian cotton dress and black boots. Her graying black hair was fashionably wild. She looked more like me than most of the women with whom I've marched arm in arm down Pennsylvania Avenue at rallies for abortion rights, the Equal Rights Amendment and a dozen other liberal causes.

Her resume was straight out of the same New Left handbook as mine. Fed up with racism and imperialism, Ledeen had given up on America by 1970 and took off to look for a "civilized country." She didn't see much alternative. An internship at the *Washington Post* had soured Barbara on journalism. ("The cozy establishment relationship with the media pissed me off," she said. "They went to the same parties. They slept with each other's wives. It was disgusting.") Although she'd been a prelaw student in college, she knew she couldn't possibly enter the bar. ("I couldn't swear to uphold laws that were horrible and racist.")

So Barbara flew off to Europe with a backpack and an empty wallet, convinced the worst crime in the world was hypocrisy—and that remaining in a country she found abhorrent would be hypocritical. She sold paintings in the market in Zagreb, fled Edinburgh when it got too cold and wound up teaching English in Milan. She avoided other Americans, pretended she was Canadian and got herself engaged to a Spanish communist who was going to take her away with him to Cuba.

A cliché of the 1960s.

A leader of the conservative 1990s.

"I don't get it," I muttered weakly. I had dressed for our encounter. I looked down at my pumps and pearls with distress. "I was a radical then and I'm a radical now," she responded. "A real radical. Remember, today's establishment used to be antiestablishment. I still am."

I spent hours listening to Ledeen talk and absorbing her pointed attacks on women like me. "Liberal women pretend that they are so concerned about poor women," she said to me one afternoon. "Give me a break. Blue-collar women don't want to put their kids in day care at 6 A.M. They would like to take care of them. They want the choice. The women's movement was supposed to be about choice, but it has never done anything to give these women choices. 'Choice' is our word, not theirs. Choice is not just about abortion. It's about single-sex schools and school choice. It's about having a home-based business so that you can take care of your kids, or having the flexibility to work part-time. Liberals say that affirmative action is about creating opportunity and choice, but affirmative action has never really helped poor people. It's white women who've benefited the most from affirmative action because we were poised to take advantage of it. To the poor we've said, 'Multiply and you'll get government help.' That's not opportunity, and that's not choice."

For Barbara, feminism's emphasis on work outside the home as the sine qua non of fulfillment is nonsense. Most women, and most men, never have a chance to do fulfilling work. Marriage and children form the center of most women's lives, she argued, and feminism had held such occupations and preoccupations in contempt. "I admit that I'm obsessed," she said repeatedly, "but someone has to stand up and say that marriage is important to civilization and that children need two parents."

Barbara agreed with feminists that women were victims; she disagreed only about who was playing the role of victimizer. "Sure some women are victims," she said. "So are some men. But most women don't think of themselves as victims of their husbands or their sons or their boyfriends. They feel victimized by taxes they can't pay and teachers who don't teach and government regulation that penalizes employers who would like to give them flex time."

Predictably, Ledeen and the Independent Women's Forum had been dismissed out of hand by a litany of feminist leaders. In fact, they had been roasted alive. In an article called "The Judas Wives" in the *Washington Feminist FaxNet,* a weekly newsletter, Martha Burk called them "a pack of she-wolves." Trish Wilson Antonucci dismissed the women involved as "residents of expensively-furnished ivory towers," as if Gloria Steinem and Betty

Friedan lived in hovels. Susan Faludi, who used her book *Backlash* to warn of the existence of a low-level conspiracy against women's rights by virtually every segment of American society, called IWF members "pod feminists" and the group part of a "media-assisted invasion of the body of the women's movement: the Invasion of the Feminist Snatchers."

I admit that I was saved from falling into such stereotyping by the quip from Faludi, who is the mistress of the *ad feminen* attack and has a prodigious talent for disapproval. The gospel according to Faludi, enshrined in her tome, taught that conservative Christian women "always played by their men's rules." Women who were burnt-out, or single and lonely, were victims of the counterassault. Even while declaring that the goal of feminism is "to win women a wider range of experience," she spent 460 pages arguing that any woman who chose experiences of which Faludi herself disapproved had been duped, co-opted or brainwashed.

As I found myself starting to dismiss Barbara Ledeen, I heard in my own thoughts a nasty, patronizing and holier-than-thou arrogance I had always considered the province of Faludi, or at least Rush Limbaugh. I slipped several rungs on my own moral superiority ladder—and started listening, and remembering. I kept flashing back to a *New Yorker* cartoon from the late 1960s, a drawing of two well-dressed women talking on the phone about the importance of consciousness-raising groups—and how glad they were that their maids could work late on Wednesday nights. The truth of that depiction had stung me at the time. It stung me still.

I love feminism like I love an old friend whose flaws I understand thoroughly and intimately. We are bound up by nostalgia and by my respect for a glorious past. But neither blinds me to its flaws. And, to me, nothing reeks more strongly of antifeminism than petty name-calling that does nothing to engage the issues. (As when Gloria Steinem branded Kay Bailey Hutchinson of Texas a "female impersonator" during Hutchinson's campaign for the Senate.) Nothing exposes the hypocrisy of feminists more than a Faludi-esque lack of respect for women they don't agree with, for women who don't work outside their homes, who aren't liberal, alienated from traditional religion, pro-choice and overtly feminist. Feminism "asks that women be free to define themselves—instead of having their identity defined for them, time and again, by their culture and their men," Faludi wrote in 1991. But she, and all too many other self-styled feminist luminaries, refuses to grant women the same freedom from definition by feminists.

I concluded that the only way for me, as one person—as a writer—to grant American women that freedom, and the only way to understand why so many women had distanced themselves from feminism, was to listen carefully to their voices, to pay attention to their lives, their needs and daily concerns, to try to find myself in the brash conservative women of Generation X, to approach women like Helen Chenoweth with respect, to meet America's women on their own ground and take their pulse.

So, over the past two years, I have traveled across America listening to the voices of women on ranches in North Dakota, in logging towns in Idaho, in congressional offices in Washington, D.C., and on college campuses in Ohio. I've interviewed female candidates at the Libertarian Party convention, followed Republican women on the campaign trail, partied with self-styled hip female GenX-ers and watched Muslim women transform themselves with head coverings. I've quizzed beauticians in Montana about feminism, militia-women in Missouri about abortion, mothers about their struggles with their children's schools and young women with pierced belly buttons at a Christian rock festival in Illinois about affirmative action. I learned, gradually, to listen.

THIS BOOK is my account of that journey.

It is neither an attack on feminism nor a defense of antifeminism, but a travelogue through the lives of women who are living, and rewriting, feminism—rarely with protest marches or political tracts, but rather with the choices they make about careers and marriage and child rearing, about balancing family and work, about what they wear, who they watch on television and the last names they use to identify themselves.

What you will see is a stunning, and absolutely ignored, burst of exuberant independence by which, one by one, American women are configuring and reconfiguring their own personal balance between tradition and non-tradition. They are forging new relationships to institutions feminism has written off as hopelessly patriarchal. They are rejecting prepackaged doctrines—religious, secular or feminist—and treating all ideologies as smorgasbords of ideas and influences, selecting the morsels that fit into their lives and rejecting those that cause them discomfort.

No matter what they call themselves—feminist or antifeminist, conservative, liberal, independent, religious or secular—they are rarely eschewing feminism itself. Instead they are repudiating feminism's relentless insistence on theoretical consistency and purity because their lives are messy composites of work and relationships, responsibilities, loyalties, dreams and desires that don't fit neatly into theoretical straitjackets. Feminists preach that the patriarchy oppresses women and gives advantage to anyone with a penis; the women in these pages look at their husbands working on construction crews and in dreary offices, and then at Oprah Winfrey and Katherine Graham, and wonder what reality feminists inhabit. Feminism teaches that men and women are natural antagonists; the women who shared their thoughts with me look to men for comfort when they're lonely or sick or aging. The women's movement urges them to have it all; American women are saying that the price for having it all is simply too high.

But American women are not turning their backs on the ideals of the women's movement, the heart of feminism. Quite the opposite. They are living up to those ideals by deciding for themselves what creates a rich life, by refusing to march in lockstep with anyone—even their so-called sisters. They might be undermining the feminist dream of a united American sisterhood speaking in a single clear voice, but they are carrying forward the torch at its center, and that flame burns bright in their refusal to live the lives their feminist forebears prescribed for them.

 PART I

The New Recruits

The Babes

No one had ever before tried throwing a public party for young conservative women, so April Lassiter and her friends were caught between giddy excitement, stage fright and a touch of naughtiness as they stood at the top of the steps to the Eighteenth Street Lounge on February 29, 1996. Their invitation—an entreaty to "Merge Right"—had been an immediate hit in the nation's capital. The phones had been ringing off the hook. Word was that people were coming in from out of town and that all the television networks were sending their reporters.

Lassiter was running late, as usual, caught up in last-minute legislative negotiations in her office in the Capitol, where she worked as a policy adviser to House majority whip Tom DeLay. After a long meeting with Newt Gingrich's assistant on women's affairs about a plan to increase the visibility of Republican congresswomen, she'd had just enough time to whip off a quick interview with CNN before racing over to the Dupont Circle hot spot they'd rented for the evening. She ran directly to the bathroom to throw off her not entirely sedate work clothes and emerged in a silvery-pink minidress and dark makeup that lent her the air of 1960s chanteuse Petula Clark, whose name meant nothing to her. Then she pulled out a cigar—the emblem of the bad girls of the Republican revolution—perused the room and smiled with the naively precocious arrogance of a young person who knows she's at the center of the action and assumes she'll wind up at the vanguard. Everything looked perfect: the homemade cookies decorated with traffic signs proclaiming No Left Turn, the centerpiece elephant with its squash nose and bottles of champagne stacked on a table by the bar lest anyone attending forget they had happened on an EVENT.

By 8 P.M., hundreds of young women and scores of young men who knew where that evening's action would be were lined up outside the front door. Inside, Chris Ardizzone, a top assistant to Phyllis Schlafly, the Antichrist of American feminism, was poised on the edge of a couch in a skirt that barely covered what her mentor would undoubtedly call her "private parts." She too puffed on a cigar as she bantered about the importance of abstinence-promoting sex education in schools.

In the back room, Kellyanne Fitzpatrick, who had just declared herself the nation's only truly conservative pollster, was sipping champagne with Grover Norquist, a conservative gadfly who was one of the intellectual architects of Newt's revolution. A lawyer who had apprenticed in the political circus with pollster Frank Luntz, Kellyanne had just opened her own company and had already snared as clients the national weekly edition of the *Washington Times*, the Republican candidates for a New Jersey senate seat and several upstart neoconservative groups, like Norquist's Americans for Tax Reform and the Competitive Enterprise Institute. Not bad for a 29-year-old.

Kellyanne was on the cusp of becoming a media darling, and enjoying every moment of her celebrity as one of the poster children of the Republican revolution. "The liberals have no new ideas," she said cockily. "Conservative principles have truth." She'd been profiled in *George*, John Kennedy's faux journalistic attempt to make life inside the Beltway look glamorous. The *National Journal* had declared her a "poll star in the Republican galaxy," and she had just signed a contract with CNN to provide commentary on the forthcoming election. No wonder, given her brassy certainty and the fact that she managed to make a business suit look sexy—a skill she'd been practicing since she ran for Blueberry Princess in New Jersey, where she grew up.

"For us, there's been no galvanizing event to connect us to the government; therefore we don't trust or need it," Kellyanne said as the crowd became a crush. "We grew up in car seats while Ma and Dad pumped gas on odd and even days. We watched *Challenger* blow up. We were the children of no-fault divorces. When I was 17, I watched Geraldine Ferraro accept the vice presidential nomination at the Democratic convention, and thought it was interesting. Then I listened to Ronald Reagan and saw someone four times my age, of a different gender and from a different coast, who was communicating a message that appealed to me as a young adult. Being liberal is no longer fashionable. It went out with bell-bottoms. We're never going to be Stepford Democrats. Most of us make Ayn Rand look like a leftist."

Genevieve Wood, a talk show host for Paul Weyrich's NET, Political Newstalk Network, sauntered through the crowd, beaming. She'd lived and worked behind the Liberal Curtain for so long that she still seemed almost shocked to be surrounded by so many like-minded people. Genevieve had studied at Baylor University in Texas and at the College of Charleston, then began her adult life working on the 1988 presidential campaign of Jack Kemp. But she crossed the invisible frontier when she took a job at NBC in New York City. "Suddenly I was the token conservative surrounded by liberals," she said. "Everyone there was from New York and Miami, and they weren't quite sure where Kansas City was. One girl actually told me, 'You know, you're the first girl I've ever met who was pro-life and you're really cool.' "

At 27, Genevieve was still trying to figure out how the Republicans had gotten it wrong on key social issues for so long. "I always say to my parents, 'You complain about LBJ and the Great Society, but where were you? Where were *your* answers?' "

Amy Holmes wandered more shyly through the crush in the uniform of the evening: a black dress with dark stockings. But hers was almost the only black skin in the room. Holmes had begun as a "thinking liberal" when she went to work for Barbara Ledeen at the Independent Women's Forum straight out of Princeton, where she had resisted both the conservatives and their message. In Washington, however, she gradually began moving toward the right, skipping over mainstream Republicanism entirely and catapulting herself into the center of the conservative revolution. "Contrary to the caricatures paraded on TV on the six o'clock news, conservatives aren't Bible-thumping weirdos," she explained. "After you're exposed to the people and the ideas, you realize that a lot of them make sense. Conservatives may not have all the answers, but at least they have some new approaches. The old ones certainly aren't working."

By 9 P.M., the club was jammed with policy wonks, writers and would-be political wizards as the Hill rats—that horde of ambitious, idealistic and underpaid young people who work as press secretaries and floor assistants in congressional offices, as researchers at think tanks and public relations companies and as rising associates at law firms and in special-interest lobbies—poured in. The only woman in the crowd with a nose ring was behind the bar waiting for tips. These were not stalwart Republicans, whom Wood derisively calls "the status quo." The idea of joining the Federation of Republican Women, the mainstream Republican club, flatly repulses them. "Dinosaurs," Wood describes them. "We don't need tea parties. We need to be tough."

These young women see themselves as the generation that will wrest the Republican Party away from the country club set. So, by day, the group plots insurrection against the Bob and Elizabeth Doles. By night, they do exactly the same thing. The music blared, but it barely dented dozens of earnest conversations about welfare reform and flat-tax proposals. "There are no economic issues, there are only social issues," one young woman lectured a small group of men listening raptly. It was unclear whether the attraction was the woman or her political analysis.

An NBC correspondent was grabbing the highest-profile partyers for interviews. "What about Pat Buchanan?" he asked Lassiter. She groaned. "I will not allow this party to be about Pat Buchanan," she said, seemingly convinced she had the power to effect that reality. "The problem isn't so much the message as the delivery. Women like candidates who don't scream."

Between sound bites, Lassiter bubbled about the design for the cover of the new CD her rock band, Honey Lake, was releasing. The plan was to photograph her drenched in honey. April was titillated at the irony of that look for a serious political and social conservative. At the age of 27, she reveled in defying expectations. But the irony she preferred was her membership in an informal study group of Jewish conservatives, black Republicans and pro-life women who called themselves the Self Haters.

That evening's party was a fund-raiser for the Independent Women's Forum, Barbara Ledeen's group, and Ledeen and a group of her friends mingled conspicuously through the chaos. It wasn't just their gray, or graying, hair that put them out of step in the Eighteenth Street Lounge. Even in such an ideologically consonant circle, a generation gap was inescapable. Thirty years earlier, old leftists studied with disapproval the young upstarts cutting their teeth on Marx and Gramsci, dismissing them as undisciplined, arrogant, too willing to offend the wider society. Young conservative activists elicit strikingly parallel reactions from many of their ideological forerunners. Older Christian women are horrified by the young women's short skirts, a flaunting of sexuality that borders on the amoral. Secular conservatives like the members of the IWF are less shocked by the flaunting than amused by the flouting of liberal presuppositions about what conservatives wear, how they dance, what they do with their free time. Looking about the crowd in that room filled with smoke and long, exposed legs, Ricki Silberman, a former vice chair of the Equal Employment Opportunity Commission and IWF activist, kept shaking her head in amusement. "In my day young Republicans didn't look like this," she quipped. "If they had, maybe we would have liked them."

But even among the secular conservatives, the difference in the historical baggage each age group carries creates an often dramatic schism. The older conservatives grew up at a time when America was discovering its own injustices, and many of them still struggle with a pair of long-held liberal assumptions: that equal protection under the law means protecting groups rather than individuals, and that government inaction breeds or perpetuates social injustice. They might reject those assumptions intellectually, but their lives and politics have been indelibly marked by them. The younger women, in contrast, came of age at the height of identity politics, with the culture of victimhood being explored ad nauseam on daytime television. They have emerged as rampant individualists who eschew the rhetoric of group empowerment for the philosophy of self-empowerment. They don't struggle with that critical pair of liberal assumptions; they struggle against them.

The generation gap is widest on abortion, which the older conservatives are more likely to support than their political progeny—which is hardly surprising. For the older women, whose view of abortion was shaped by the debate over a woman's right to control her own body, abortion speaks to a woman's most fundamental rights. For younger women like April and Kellyanne Fitzpatrick, however, the central issue is not privacy—a woman's right to control her own body—but visibly moving fetuses that they believe to be fully human. "We're pro-life," Fitzpatrick says. "We grew up with sonograms. We know life when we see it. The fetus beat us."

More importantly, perhaps, for these younger women, issues like abortion and affirmative action, which defined the politics of the older generation, have never been galvanizing issues. What defines their generation is less what they believe in than what they don't believe in: government. In their world, the federal government doesn't foment positive change; it foments problems. In post–Cold War America, the federal government has replaced the Soviet Union as the enemy.

Women's issues? April dismisses the very concept of issues that are of peculiar concern to women as passé, the vestige of some paleolithic era. "There is no such thing as a women's issue. Men worry about their families and kids and women worry about the economy and national defense."

Feminism? "Feminists started out doing important things, but they went too far and fell into a victim mentality, demanding that women need special privileges. They are telling women that they can't make things right for themselves, that someone else has to do it for them. Maybe I was blessed. I grew up listening to 'Free to Be You and Me,' so I know my ideas are as good as any man's.

"I have no problem with different roles for men and women; different doesn't mean lesser to me. In fact, differences are erotic. Sure there are still problems, but legislation is not the answer. I think feminism has provoked so much fear and resentment that it has actually impeded progress.

"I'm not a feminist. I love my ovaries. I'm proud that I can be soft and sensual and then turn around and play hardball with the best of them. I don't like any word that defines me foremost as a woman. I'm a conservative who happens to be female."

April was not schooled in these positions by Republican June and Ward Cleavers. Her mother, who teaches nursing at Howard University, is a committed liberal; her father, who runs a mental health and substance abuse program, is decidedly pro-choice. Politics was not, in fact, a very strong force in her life, even when she entered the University of Virginia, one of the bastions of the new conservatism. Instead, April found herself pulled toward religion, as she wrestled with the angst of a young person trying to find meaning in a world in which the structures and values of two centuries had crumbled. "It's only logical that it would be a different struggle for us," she explains, "because we grew up when there was a movement away from community, from *gemeinschaft,* to *gesellschaft.*" Rather than throw herself into politics, April struggled to find such community, and she lived it as a leader in the Christian youth group Young Life. "Kids are desperate to find a loving God. They just want to believe. My generation might not go to church, but we're deeply spiritual."

When she finished college, April moved away from the fundamentalist community, which she found too insular, into politics and, ultimately, a job on DeLay's staff. That move was less an affirmation of Republican Party principles ("I've never been a hard-core Republican trying to promote capitalism," she says) than an attempt to become a player in a society debating the issues that intrigued her: the role of government, the breakdown of values, the creation of community. In the process, she has become one of the darlings of the Republican right. She dates single Republican congressmen, is a popular guest on *The Youngbloods*—a television talk show hosted by Genevieve Wood, a sort of *The McLaughlin Group* meets MTV—and is one of the party's favorite speakers at the continuous round of civics programs Congress sponsors for the nation's high school students. Lassiter knows how to push "the message" like a true pro.

"Stats on you show that you are more likely to believe in UFOs than that social security will be around when you retire," she told a group of high school students who were spending a week in the nation's capital learning about American democracy firsthand. The Democrats had sent an earnest young man who wore a formal suit and spoke flawless Beltway-ese to debate her. April showed up in a black mohair sweater and dark pinstriped trousers. Her lipstick and nail polish were dark. The boys in the audience drooled; the girls looked her over carefully for fashion tips. The format was question-and-answer.

Welfare? "It's become a hammock instead of a springboard," she said. "We should tell people that they can do it, and that we'll help them. Instead, we're saying, 'You're a loser, so we have to support you forever.' "

Affirmative action? "Would you want to get a job just because you had boobs? We need to work for a society that is color-blind and gender-blind. But we can't end racism and sexism with special programs for people."

Moral responsibility for the poor? "We have a moral obligation for each other, but I don't believe that the federal government should be the agent. After forty years of government spending, illegitimacy rates are up, suicide rates are up. These programs don't work. Money doesn't solve problems. People do. A big part of the solution is you and me, not the government."

Abortion? "This is a very personal matter to me because my birth mother was raped when she was 15 years old and was offered an abortion. She opted for adoption instead. It is my personal view that life begins at conception, that abortion is murder. I know women are faced with difficult decisions, and if the mother is in danger, I think we should save her. But that's it. We can't keep hurting each other. We have to respect life."

As I DROVE back from Washington to New York after the "Merge Right" party and a round of interviews with female GenX rebels, I fantasized telling my friends about my evening. I could hear their reactions: "Jeane Kirkpatrick in a miniskirt"; "Selfish, privileged trendoids." I knew just what names they would call the group: arrogant, stupid, naive, hypocritical, vicious, opportunistic and greedy. I wasn't omniscient; I could recall precisely what I would have said about these young people before I actually met them.

Then I stopped and began to tremble. I pulled over to the side of the road and sat wondering how many of those same adjectives my parents and their friends used to describe me when I was 27. "Wait a second, wait a second," one friend actually said when I shared this observation with her. "We weren't selfish, greedy and intolerant." I thought back to what *we* said about people who were religious, about our parents—about poor dumb schmucks whose only crime was to get drafted.

These Young Turks' intolerance was frighteningly reminiscent of my own, and that was not the only similarity between April, Kellyanne and their friends and those of us who were the self-styled radicals of the 1960s. I'd like to think that we were "better," but in fact, we too were cocky and judgmental. Our worldview left no room for ambiguity: we were right and everyone else was wrong. There was no possibility of legitimate disagreement. We had a similarly overblown sense of our own wisdom, our understanding of people and the issues. We also were convinced that we had the power to remake the world. Spending time with this new group of rebels was embarrassingly nostalgic.

That realization forced me to look again at the young conservatives, and I concluded that as much as I abhorred their politics, at least they weren't guzzling beer and partying all night. They were reading, studying and almost frantically discussing politics and morality and truth. They were incredibly earnest in their concern for the future of the nation. Earlier generations had been incited to social consciousness, to activism and rebellion by concrete events: the Great Depression, World War II, segregation and lynchings in the South, the war in Vietnam. This generation has had no such defining event. Instead they are defined by the widespread belief that they will be the first generation in the nation's history to have less of a shot at the American Dream than their parents did.

The precariousness of their future can't be salvaged by a romantic movement in which they idealistically fling their bodies across the White House steps, or choose jail over paying taxes. Pop singers might express their angst, but they would find it hard to write folk songs about the end of social security. So if April Lassiter and her friends want to be the Mario Savio or Angela Davis of the 1990s—heralds of a movement that will speak to the needs of their generation—they can't launch a Free Speech movement, call for sit-ins or fling their bras into garbage cans. They have to do the nerdy work of policy wonks, to tear apart budgets and scrutinize bureaucratic regulations, to use every skill they developed as the first generation of Internet whiz kids. To them, there is no choice, as there was none for those of us stirred by the horrors of lynchings and poverty. In their minds, without change there simply is no future—and they trust no one in government to protect their tomorrows.

That distrust is what most reminded me of my generation. In their voices, I heard the same suspicion of government that I had chanted and ranted for decades, a disdain for the Republicans ironically parallel to what my friends and I had had for the Democrats and an anarchist tendency that was in every way familiar. Women of my generation felt suffocated by a world that our parents and grandparents had hopelessly screwed up. Racism and sexism were so woven into the very fabric of the society—into the legal system and the economy, the culture, the very mind-set of the populace—that they seemed ineradicable without a total social overhaul. American imperialism had given the power- and money-hungry freedom to rape the world at will. American democracy had been undermined by money, by the imposition of the interests of the ruling class on ordinary citizens, to the point that those ordinary citizens couldn't discern where their true interests lay. The government propped up the system, and the Democratic Party, although pretending to concern for the poor and oppressed, was an integral part of the problem. Traditional institutions, from church to family, were too caught up in preserving social order to become forces for good. Our rallying cry: "No more halfway measures. Revolution now."

April and Kellyanne also feel suffocated by a world rife with racism and sexism, despite three decades of liberal programs designed to eradicate them. Drug abuse and crime are so rampant that they grew up afraid to walk the streets of their own neighborhoods. Traditional institutions—from church to community—have collapsed as a force for social integration. The national debt is so large that their future looks mortgaged, yet they are maligned, alternately, as a disinterested and self-interested generation. The government remains committed to business and politics as usual, and the Republican Party, dominated for decades by the bluebloods and their allies, has been too busy defending big business and the prevailing social order to push for any of the drastic measures necessary to alter the nation's course. They have no effective institutions to turn to. Their rallying cry: "No more halfway measures. Revolution now."

Our revolution was against our parents and grandparents, of course. Theirs is against baby boomers, which, for a generation that grew up thinking of ourselves as "outsiders" in the political system, is a difficult shift. It rankles to hear some well-dressed 25-year-old accuse us of being members of the establishment. Our identities were formed as rebels. We might be middle-aged homeowners with new cars and healthy bank accounts, but we still think of ourselves as the long-haired, blue-jean-clad, VW-driving protesters the establishment derided. We still want to think of ourselves as the people our parents warned us about, rather than the parents doing the warning.

So we dismiss young conservative women as pseudorebels idolizing Newt as a new brand of cool—ignoring all those old posters of Che Guevara that decorated our walls. We accuse them of being ideologues—forgetting that every generation of young falls in love with ideology, perhaps as a substitute for experience. The only difference is that today it is Ayn Rand and Thomas Jefferson rather than Adam Smith, Karl Marx or Gramsci. We deride them as privileged brats indifferent to suffering—despite the class origins of our old heroes, from Abbie Hoffman to Fidel Castro.

The problem is that most critics simply refuse to trust the sincerity of young women like April, dismissing their protestations of idealism—of concern for the poor and minorities—as covers for basic selfishness. They can't believe that someone who advocates the abolition of welfare as we know it could care about any group but the affluent, or that an opponent of affirmative action could be a supporter of women's rights. They refuse to consider the possibility that old concerns might surface with new rhetoric in a different generation.

That suspiciousness has created a deep well of resentment against baby boomers, which in turn has evolved, mutatis mutandis, into pride at their estrangement from the dreaded establishment—which means the dreaded liberals, who have pretty much run things in America during their lifetimes. So every expression of horror and outrage that appears in the *Washington Post* or the *New Republic* becomes proof of their ethical, or at least ideological, purity. The embarrassment of their parents ("Oh God, how can I tell my friends that my daughter is actually a fan of Newt Gingrich?") becomes a badge of honor.

And they revel in their war stories of being treated as revolutionaries on the nation's college campuses. Kellyanne Fitzpatrick is quick to talk about her arrival at Trinity College, a Catholic women's college in the Washington area, and how her efforts to start a Republican Club were thwarted not by student disinterest but by the refusal of faculty members to serve as its adviser. Everyone has a story about run-ins with feminist faculty members over abortion, affirmative action and the "stupidity" of women's studies.

It's not just the faculty and administrators. Today's liberal students greet campus conservatives with the warmth Columbia University's football players showed radical demonstrators during the 1968 campus strike. Conservatives are shunned, mocked and flayed alive on liberal campuses, and they parade their scars as proof of the hypocrisy of liberalism and the righteous of their own quest. Ask Corinne Johnson of Albion College.

Cori arrived at the small private college in a small town west of Detroit from Michigan's Upper Peninsula in the fall of 1995. Albion seemed just right to her, exuding the air of a conservative campus, which is precisely what she was looking for. Although her parents aren't very political—and her mother is "sort of liberal"—Cori says she's been a committed Republican since the age of 7, when Ronald Reagan fired her political imagination. Cori hadn't been on campus two weeks before she ran into trouble. For years, Albion had been tapping into its general funds to offer special diversity awards of $4,000 to each African-American student on campus. Two conservative students had asked the student senate to ask for the elimination of the award. On September 18, 1995, practically the entire student body filtered into the senate meeting to debate the issue.

Cori had no intention of speaking until she heard the handful of students opposed to the award apologizing for their position. She stood up, all five feet two inches of her. "I'm not apologizing for my beliefs," she exploded, shaking. She was, after all, a new kid on campus. "I don't believe it is fair to use general funds—our tuition—to give awards on the basis of skin color, or any other born characteristic that everyone does not have the opportunity to achieve. If someone wants to raise private money for awards that can only be given to African-American students, that's fine, but general funds should only be used to make awards based on merit." As Cori began speaking, a group of black students started chanting against her. White students joined them. Cori was booed off the floor. She hadn't realized that opposing affirmative action meant being branded a racist. That was her first college lesson.

Things got worse the next semester when Cori was appointed as a representative to the student senate and a member of its student affairs committee. On March 19, 1996, a student organization called Break the Silence asked that committee to endorse a letter they had written to the members of the Michigan state legislature in support of same-sex marriage, in reaction to pending legislation which would negate the legality in Michigan of such marriages performed in other states. With that endorsement, Break the Silence could ask the full senate for its support. But Cori's committee turned them down.

That alone might have been enough to ruin Cori's reputation, but she and her boyfriend Jeff, president of the college Republican Club, then upped the ante, sending out a press release headlined "Albion College Students Say 'No' to Gay Marriage." The text reported accurately that the student affairs committee of the student senate had rejected a resolution to denounce pending legislation to ban "homosexual marriage." But the quiet, almost bucolic, campus of fifteen hundred exploded, with students convinced that the headline misrepresented the situation at Albion.

"Who the fuck do you think you are, ignorant bitch," one student wrote Cori by e-mail. "How dare you speak for me and the rest of the student body and senate by releasing such a ridiculous, homophobic, closed-minded letter. . . ." H. Milligan, a few months away from his graduation, added—in his own spelling: "The only thing scarier than a facist biggot is a facist biggot in power. The only thing scarrier than that is an innocent looking little girl who is a facist biggot and is in power."

Cori tried, without much success, to clarify her position. "I'm not anti-gay," she explained. "I have gay friends. My position on homosexuality has nothing to do with how I feel about individual gay people. I don't like drinking but I have friends who drink. But I'm against gay marriage because I'm concerned with the moral breakdown of society. Marriage is an institution for procreating a family." Few were willing to listen. Those who did were hardly mollified by her words.

Students growled at Cori as she walked from class to class. People stopped talking to her entirely. Finally, terrified, she began venturing out only if accompanied by a male friend. Cori and Jeff were then called up for "review" by the executive board of the student senate, which charged her with violating senate rules by passing herself off as an official spokesperson of the student body. On April 1, at the request of Cori and Jeff, the student senate held a public hearing on the executive board's recommendation that the two be expelled from the student senate. The campus was plastered with flyers announcing the event, which was scheduled to be held in the largest lecture hall on campus. Even so, it was standing room only by 9 P.M. when Cori arrived. College Republicans from around the state crowded around her waving placards and posters proclaiming their support for free speech. Scores of Albion students and faculty arrived wearing pink ribbons, a show of support for same-sex marriage. The state press treated the event like the showdown at the PC Corral. The decision was a foregone conclusion: the student senators voted overwhelming to expel Cori and Jeff from office.

The student senators insisted that their decision was the only appropriate response to misuse of office, but Cori didn't buy it. "I don't think I did anything to violate the Constitution," she said. "This wasn't about the Constitution. This was a political lynching."

The senate decision was not the end of the young woman's nightmare. Members of Break the Silence, the group which had originally asked the student representatives for the endorsement on their letter supporting same-sex marriage, went to the Albion police and accused Cori and Jeff of distributing Ku Klux Klan materials, defaming gay students and threatening violence. A group of students began pushing for judicial charges to be brought against Cori for disturbing or distressing other students. The charges raised the possibility that Cori would lose her $15,000-a-year scholarship.

"I spent weeks with stomach trouble," Cori said. "There I was, just a freshman, and I'd already been removed from the senate and had hate crimes charges filed against me. So much for liberal tolerance, so much for liberal belief in free speech."

Today, Cori is an avowed enemy of everything liberal, and predictably, feminism isn't spared her attacks. Yet, oddly, even as she rails against feminism's confusing equality with sameness, against its cult of victimhood and indifference to the family, she speaks and fights for what she believes and stands firm for her principles, with a sense of self which is an unwitting endorsement of the most fundamental principles of feminism. Cori is being her own person, defining her own life—and social pressure be damned. She is refusing to be silenced by anybody.

This observation struck me again and again as I traveled the country talking to young women: the assumptions and victories of feminism permeate their lives so thoroughly that they are the movement's clearest descendants, even as they are its greatest critics. To members of a different generation, the notion of a conservative woman who is spunky and independent is an oxymoron. Not to Cori and her counterparts. They simply take that spunk and independence for granted.

"Growing up, I never had any sense of limitations because of my gender," she says. "I've always wanted to be a prosecutor and it never occurred to me that being a girl would stop me. I've never felt any bias. I think about my high school. There were five valedictorians in a class of 187 and all five of us were girls. Some men have poor opinions of women, but it is no longer societally enforced, and it certainly won't stop me.

"When I was young I read a biography of Amelia Earhart. She's my heroine. What she did was totally unheard of. But I can't go along with the feminist movement, and I don't see why I should. Feminism is trying to blur the genders. It has absolutely nothing to offer me or anyone I know."

UNLIKE Cori Johnson, Amy Holmes doesn't find feminism irrelevant. She just thinks it's stale and dangerously dated, which is feminism's loss, since Amy is precisely the kind of young woman—smart, articulate, political and entirely determined—who fueled the success of the women's movement in the late 1960s. In fact, her attitude toward feminism is a recent development. When Amy graduated from Princeton in 1994, she was still a "thinking liberal": she thought feminism had done a pretty good job for American women and assumed it was continuing in that vein.

Then she moved to Washington, D.C., and threw herself into the major social issues of the day. It never occurred to Amy to do anything else. The daughter of a white American mother and a black African father, she was raised with a deep social consciousness that made any thought of finding work that would just be about paying the rent, or buying nice clothes, inconceivable. Gradually, during the two years she has worked in the capital's conservative circles, Amy has come to the conclusion that feminism has committed political and social femicide by beating dead horses, or beating live horses with the wrong stick. She gives feminists credit for advancing the status of women—to a point. But she is convinced that progress can continue only if feminism is willing to connect with the women it purports to serve.

"Feminists keep worrying about equality for women and they measure it by counting the number of women who are running Fortune 500 companies," she says softly, but firmly. "You know what I say to the idea of women running 50 percent of those companies? So what? I'm not saying that women shouldn't have the opportunity to run Fortune 500 companies if that's what they want. But that doesn't do anything for most women.

"What women want and need in their work lives is flexibility. They don't need more government help; they need less." Amy points to federal labor laws that require employers to pay workers overtime even if those workers prefer to take compensatory time instead, a luxury only federal employees enjoy. She argues that feminists, who are closely allied with the labor movement, which opposes this sort of change in the Fair Labor Standards Act, seem indifferent to how much it would help parents, especially women, juggle the competing demands on their lives. Home-based work is another sore point for Amy, since a growing number of mothers with small children are looking for ways to work at home so that they can earn money without having to spend it on child care. She points to a host of regulations written to correct injustices from a different era—on "cottage industries" and piecework, in particular—that close off this option for women.

"If feminists really cared about women, about ordinary women, these are the issues they'd be screaming about. But they don't want to do anything to make it easier for women to stay home with their children because they are afraid that this will send the wrong message to the market, that a lot of women care more about their families than about careers. It's selfish. They want to make sure that companies aren't afraid to promote women like them to high positions, so they ignore the interests of most of the women in this country."

Few young women devote that much energy to worrying about feminism's impact on women and work, of course. Where most younger women break with feminism is much closer to home. And that break strikes at the heart of feminist theory, which defines participation in the workplace as the sine qua non of human fulfillment, and at the growing disagreement of younger women with that belief.

I know that many feminists will read these words and take umbrage at the suggestion that they turned their backs on their sisters who are full-time mothers and homemakers. I can even anticipate the rejoinder: the reminder that feminists long supported public funding of child care centers and family leave acts. But such protestations are disingenuous. Most of those programs were designed to help women "liberate" themselves from household responsibilities, not to help them handle them more easily. Furthermore, what support feminism has offered "traditional" women could never compensate for the hostility early feminists planted in the heart of the movement toward women who refused to follow their lead. Remember the language Betty Friedan used to describe the life of educated housewives in *The Feminine Mystique:* "waste of a human self" and "parasite." Helen Gurley Brown wrote in *Cosmopolitan* in 1965 that a housewife was "a scrounger, a sponger." And even as late as 1970, Gloria Steinem was calling homemakers "dependent creatures who are still children" in *Time.*

Friedan, Brown and Steinem thought they were striking a blow for the liberation of women trapped in suffocating roles. But many of the women in those "suffocating roles" liked the air they were breathing. They felt degraded not by their husbands or their sons, but by feminist leaders unable to conceive that any woman would choose to be a housewife. The overzealous rhetoric was understandable in a moment when feminists were struggling so hard to break women free from confining traditions. But it alienated and demeaned tens of thousands of women who found those traditions fulfillingly spacious.

Today's young women were raised outside of those confines, or at least with clear role models of women living far beyond those walls. They grew up with children's stories about women who were doctors and firefighters. They saw women journalists and politicians on the nightly news. Their female college professors taught them that they could, and should, have it all. But many simply aren't buying it. They are looking at the unmentioned costs of having it all, and, with the same pride and confidence with which we broke down the walls of domesticity, they are declaring that the price is too high.

At least that is what Adelle Kirk is doing. Adelle is a feisty 26-year-old who is constitutionally incapable of not speaking her mind. She is bawdy and funny and nobody's idea of a wallflower. She had little choice, actually, since her three older brothers were good students, great athletes and social dreams. It was do or die for the baby sister, who was unwilling to be left behind. She graduated from private school in California and headed for Princeton supremely confident that she could run as fast, jump as high and succeed as thoroughly as her brothers Mark, Frank and Harry. No one ever suggested otherwise.

Today she still exudes that same confidence. "I'm just as smart as any man, just as strong—except in terms of brute strength—and my opinions are just as valid," she says. Then she adds the kicker repeated by scores of women of her generation: "There's no reason I can't feel all that and still be a wife and mother."

For Adelle, being a wife meant donning a white wedding veil at the age of 24, and being a mother means raising her own children. It's not that she's without alternatives. She's already a successful retail marketing consultant advising companies like Nike and Talbot, and she knows that she's poised for a career as high-powered as that of her brothers. But Adelle also knows that she wants to have children, and she has clear ideas about what that decision means. "What's the point of having kids and letting them be raised by a nanny?" she insists. "That's totally selfish. Feminism took careerism way too far."

Her plan is to cut back her work schedule to three days a week once she has kids, and she fully expects that to be hard. "I know I'll be pissed off when someone gets a promotion I could have gotten," she says. "But I want to have influence over my kids' development. I won't let them be raised by someone who might turn them into ax-murderers."

Ironically, Adelle has the flexibility she wants because feminism won. Her company routinely allows female employees to adjust their schedules to their family circumstances, and it is hardly unique these days. One of feminism's most unsung victories—unsung, perhaps, because leaders of the movement aren't entirely comfortable with the reality it reflects—is the revolution in corporate willingness to accommodate the needs of working mothers. Chase Manhattan Bank, the largest banking company in the country, with a workforce which is 62 percent female, offers employees the option of working flextime, of sharing jobs or compressing their workweeks by putting in four ten-hour days instead of five shorter ones. At USAA insurance, ten thousand employees are working such compressed weeks so that they can spend three days a week at home with their kids; seventeen hundred are working from home, leaving only 23 percent of their workers on a five-day-a-week, nine-to-five, go-to-the-office routine.

Such arrangements are not confined to the domains of white-collar workers. AlliedSignal, a New Jersey company that manufacturers jet engines, offers on-site child care and compensates employees for the cost of in-home child care when their children fall ill. Ridgeview, Inc., a hosiery mill in North Carolina, not only provides day care for $46 a week, but arranges with the local public schools to have guidance counselors come into their plant to meet with working moms.

Young women like Adelle, then, live with both the confidence and opportunity that women of earlier eras lacked, and they are rewriting feminism to conform to that new reality. Despite years of being warned about divorce, about spousal abuse and the traumas of combining marriage and a career, women of her age group are marrying young—and with full idealism. They aren't agonizing about choosing between careers and families. They are finding ways to combine the two without shirking their responsibilities in either realm. So it's hardly surprising that Adelle would declare: "My generation is better off. We've struck a better balance. We've kind of gone beyond feminism, so we've got a lot more choices, and we're accepting responsibility for them."

Curiously absent from Adelle's discussion of her dreams, of the opportunities she's enjoyed and choices she's made, is any acknowledgment of how she got them. It is an omission that almost all young women like her make. Enjoying the fruits of feminism, they spend little time thinking about who tilled the soil and grew the crop. And that may be what drives feminists so crazy about them: they have never said thank you.

Frankly, my first instinct was to grab these young women and start screaming: "Look, before you put feminists down for being wrongheaded or shortsighted or irresponsible to children, blue-collar women or whoever, go somewhere you can get a taste of what it used to be like. How would you feel if you were looking for a job and there was a separate set of newspaper listings for men and women—and you were the wrong gender for all the jobs that paid enough to cover the rent? How would you feel if you'd been told you had to go to the state university because your parents were overburdened paying tuition at Duke for your brother, whose grades were never as good as yours? Maybe we made mistakes. I'm sure we did. But, excuse me, they don't obliterate what we've given you."

In my fantasy, the target of my rage is shattered, and confesses her sin. Which is what makes it a fantasy. Most young women are unlikely to see feminists as much more than ideology police, or feminism as more than a religious order with a prescribed set of dogmas and regulations. They could never understand that for many of us feminism instead is an ideology designed to ensure that women have the right to think their own thoughts, to dream their own dreams—and the opportunity to translate those thoughts and dreams into their own vision of the future. They can't see this as ideology. To them, it is normal. It is as natural as breathing or voting or driving a car.

So they watch Gloria Steinem on television or read articles by Karen DeCrow and wonder precisely what these women are talking about. "Feminists have moved into a sort of post-discrimination feminism, which sounds like an oxymoron to me," is Stephanie Herman's explanation. The Denver woman, a writer and stay-at-home mom, says that she has "never, ever" suffered gender discrimination. "In my little corner of the world, nobody has these problems." Feminism, then, "becomes this whole thing about striving for female expression and defining female identity. NOW seems to define feminism as a movement for some collective. A collective based on gender seems, to me, unnatural."

For women who've spent decades struggling for women's rights, who still bear the scars of rejection and derision, the lack of gratitude, or even of simple acknowledgment, rankles. It hurts our pride in the primary accomplishment of our lives. In the most basic way, it hurts our need to feel important and relevant. Ironically, it forces many feminists even further into the cult of victimhood, entrenching them deeper into a stubborn refusal to recognize how many battles they've won.

But what are young women to do? Wake up every morning and thank Susan B. Anthony for the vote? Sing a psalm of gratitude to Margaret Sanger whenever they have sex? Write an ode of appreciation to Earle Haas every time they change a Tampax? Bend their knees in tribute to Betty Friedan after each raise? The concept is laughable, because gratitude of this sort is not natural. It might even be dangerous, because gratitude would propel these young women into our pasts, at the expense of their own futures.

A Digression into a
Mad Hatter's Tea Party

On the evening of the Fourth of July, 1996, I sat on the Mall in Washington, D.C., listening to patriotic tunes, watching fireworks light up the sky and thinking about gratitude. I was not suffering an overdose of patriotism; I was in the full throes of the aftereffects of fourteen hours of interviews with female delegates to the presidential convention of the Libertarian Party. They'd all spoken passionately and eloquently about living without freedom. But they weren't referring to the plight of peasant women in Uganda or Bosnian Muslims in Srebrenica. They were talking about themselves—middle- and upper-middle-class white women from Kansas City, New York and San Francisco.

Kate O'Brien, a 43-year-old civil engineer from Menlo Park, California, had bemoaned the drug laws, the Internal Revenue Service and the sales tax as measures of her oppression. Jackie Bradbury, a 27-year-old student from Nebraska, had griped that she and her peers had been forced to become a "generation of janitors" to clean up the mess left by the baby boomers, a mess that includes everything from the minimum wage, poorly conceived immigration policy, a soaring national debt and gun control to a litany of measures that impinge on the operation of the free market system. At a workshop on home schooling, delegates had decried taxation as a form of slavery and public education as a means of recruiting citizens into dependency.

Sitting on the Mall, then, I couldn't help but think about gratitude, and how infrequently it is expressed by women on the left or the right or on any of those continua that exist in the alternate realities so many Americans create. While feminist tracts make it sound as if women in this country share the indignities of their sisters in China or rural Africa, Libertarians—both male and female—dismiss American freedoms out of hand and picture themselves as living under the iron heel of federal fascism. I wasn't looking for an all-girl rendition of "America the Beautiful," but some acknowledgment—of suffrage, of equal pay laws, even the absence of clitoridectomies—would have appeased me. But it appears that in the era of competition for Most Victimized, and the attendant rewards, both material and psychic, which that status conveys, even an iota of appreciation is hopelessly passé.

The Libertarians are an odd mélange of hippies incensed by antidrug laws and militia crazies worried about guns; of Christians convinced that God demands libertarianism since only he can offer salvation; and of Jewish intellectuals enthralled with theorizing about Ayn Rand. They are the idols of many of the young conservative women. As they gathered in the belly of the beast—amid all those Depublicans and Remocrats who control the nation's capital—they espoused three overarching principles: "individual freedom, personal responsibility, and freedom from government on all issues at all times." That means that they hate the Democrats because the party loves to meddle in other people's business. They despise the Republicans because they aren't really all that different from the Democrats. They aren't impressed with Ross Perot since he wants to make government more efficient, rather than nonexistent. And they are grateful for absolutely nothing about America.

How could they be, delegates asked, when they have been enslaved by the behemoth on the Potomac that sends IRS agents to spy on law-abiding citizens, that tells them how to work, what to eat, smoke, drink and drive, and under what circumstances? They will be grateful only when they and all Americans are liberated from the tyranny of the NEA, EPA, HUD, FBI, DEA, IRS, BATF and every other alphabet-soup agency created in the last one hundred years.

"Government is force," declared Harry Browne, their presidential candidate, "and I want to minimize the use of force in solving social and political problems."

As I wandered the halls of the Hyatt-Regency on Capitol Hill, I wondered at the scarcity of women. The Libertarian Party convention made the Republican convention look like an exercise in gender equity. But every organizer I found pointed to the female leadership of the party with a pride that seemed ironic for people who insist they are not "gender-defined." The party's first vice presidential candidate, who ran in 1972, was Tonie Nathan, the first American woman ever to win an electoral vote, they all said, never failing to add that she was available for interviews. The 1996 vice presidential candidate was also female: Jo Jorgensen, a divorced mother of two from South Carolina. Every female delegate I bumped into could recite the list of Libertarian women who have been elected to public office or achieved high positions in the party. No one omitted Ayn Rand, the Virgin Mary of Libertarians, whose "objectivist" philosophical writings are the movement's Holy Grail.

But none of that changed the reality that the crowd of contrarians was overwhelmingly male. "We have a lot of trouble recruiting women," acknowledged Jackie Bradbury, who chairs the Nebraska chapter of the party. Jackie, her hair short and punk, was a Violent Femmes and Depeche Mode fan and the hippest-looking delegate to the convention. "The problem is women's attitudes. Men prize independence, which pushes them toward libertarianism, while women are invested in interdependence, which inclines them toward socialism. When men see infants, they see potential. When women see infants, they see needs to be satisfied. So it is only natural that men relate to the concept of freedom while women have bought into the glorification of need."

Jackie and the other female delegates didn't seem particularly over-wrought at the absence of women in their party. In fact, they said they couldn't care less, since they are convinced that the number of women in the group is irrelevant. Libertarians, they explained, "have declared an armistice in the gender wars." Such a declaration is, in fact, a necessary pretense for women who think of themselves as freewheeling individualists, who flaunt a kind of macho (or is it macha?) pride in their self-reliance, and walk with an I-don't-need-nothing-from-nobody swagger. What other choice do they have? After all, it's not easy to fight gender wars when you are unwilling to buy arms from Big Government.

"What makes me mad is that the liberals in the government and the feminist establishment are putting women back on a pedestal," said Jackie. "I am not a fragile little creature. Whatever I want to achieve, I'll achieve. They're always implying that we're not good enough, smart enough, that we don't have enough internal fortitude to do it for ourselves, so the government has to do everything for us. Well, don't tell me that. That's an insult. Their insistence that we have to have help galls me."

Libertarians are tough characters intent on enshrining their bravado in social policy. Marianne and Paul Smith of the Oregon delegation, for example, are home schooling their son because they don't want him to be obedient, to say the Pledge of Allegiance, to sit still and speak only when spoken to. They don't want any kid trained that way, which explains their support for the abolition of "government" schools. Kate O'Brien opposes any measure that hints at Big Brother taking care of her, or anybody else. She's stood in front of abortion clinics to defend doctors and patients from abuse, but she doesn't want the government joining her. That would be unwarranted interference by the central state. She dislikes hard-core pornography, but hates the idea that any authority would protect her, or anybody else, from it. That would be stepping on the First Amendment.

Given this bent, it was surprising to find the party in the midst of a major

feud about abortion, and even more surprising to realize that they were trying to hide their disagreements. The press was barred when Jo Jorgensen led
delegates in a discussion of the contentious issue. Nobody, male or female,
wanted to admit that Libertarians were having trouble agreeing to disagree.
So there they were, a bunch of self-styled anarchists with advanced degrees
in hairsplitting, trying to decide what Ayn Rand would think about the termination of pregnancies. Doris Gordon, leader of the Libertarians for Life faction, had spent years arguing that Rand would have been appalled at this
deviation from Libertarian purism. "We charge that abortion is unjust homicide," she said, a violation of a fetus's inalienable rights. Her opponents had
countered with rants about pregnancy police and pulled out the favorite libertarian argument, "Let's get the government out of our lives."

The abortion wars had heated up at the 1996 convention because the
party's presidential candidate seemed to be antichoice. In libertarian terms
that doesn't mean that Harry Browne wanted the federal government to
prohibit abortions, but he seemed willing to allow individual states to do so,
which was sufficient to send the Association of Libertarian Feminists on a
tear, refusing to endorse Browne and condemning him and his supporters as
substandard libertarians.

"A basic tenet of libertarianism is that if you must ask permission before
exercising a right, you are not free," argues Christine Krof Shock in commu-
niqués to the other Libertarian Feminists. "Libertarians are demeaned when
they have to beg to carry a gun. Shouldn't Libertarians be just as demeaned
when women have to beg for an abortion? . . . When joining the party, members sign a pledge not to use government coercion to achieve personal, ethical or religious goals. Nor should members be compelled to tolerate force
against a specific right, just because it is unpalatable to our candidates or our
party."

Shock and company never invoked feminism or women's rights in their
attacks on Browne because, at heart, they are acutely uncomfortable with
talking about women's rights. Libertarians, after all, pride themselves on
defending everyone's rights. Singling out one gender doesn't make much
sense in an anarchist fantasy. So it seemed perversely logical that the institution female Libertarian delegates seemed to loathe almost as much as the federal government—and nobody loathes institutions more thoroughly, or
with more panache, than libertarians—was feminism. "I can't stand to listen
to feminists talk," Jackie said dismissively. "All I hear are a bunch of rich
white mothers talking about how angry they are. Why are they so angry?
They've coasted all their lives. They'll never be satisfied. They want the gov-

ernment to solve all their problems. You could eliminate all the men from the planet and they'd still find a way to blame all their problems on them.

"My motto is, 'Don't whine about it. Do it.'"

The intellectuals and would-be intellectuals who dominate the philosophical wing of the libertarian movement—many of whom reject the Libertarian Party since it is, in the end, an institution—offer a more analytical critique of the women's movement. "Feminist is a label that has been owned by socialist-oriented feminists for so long that for most people it implies a political agenda I'm not comfortable with," said Karen Michaelson, a rock musician, novelist and member of the Association of Libertarian Feminists, in a movement publication. Karen's use of the word "socialist" seems oddly out of place since there is little indication that Gloria Steinem or Susan Faludi, for example, advocate the redistribution of their wealth. But Libertarians have a nasty habit of using the word "socialist" as a catch phrase for those who support a large central government. "Several years ago I got sick of feeling I had to redefine the word every time I used it, by starting sentences with, 'I'm a feminist, but' . . . 'I'm a feminist but I also support the right to bear arms.' 'I'm a feminist but I'm a First Amendment absolutist and believe pornography is protected speech,' etc. All of which only resulted in people telling me I wasn't *really* a feminist."

Karen isn't *really* a feminist because she's a rampant individualist who abhors the idea of some patriarchal state interfering or intervening in her life, even in the guise of helping or protecting her. Unlike many members of the Independent Women's Forum, who reject the feminist movement as too preoccupied with individualism—and thus insufficiently concerned with family and community—Karen and her philosophical allies in the Association of Libertarian Feminists criticize the movement for its lack of respect for individualism, for what they see as a shocking tendency to paint all women with the same brush and to turn to the state for the collective redress of their grievances.

In so doing, they dismiss out of hand the basic notion of feminism, expressed succinctly by Catharine MacKinnon: "since a woman's problems are not hers individually but those of women as a whole, they cannot be addressed except as a whole." The concept that there might be a point of view, a set of concerns, problems or tendencies shared by women as a group is, to libertarians, innately subversive to, and thus destructive of, individual differences. But if that idea drives libertarians to distraction, liberal feminist demands elicit an even stronger reaction from women who are ideologically opposed to federal funding of day care centers or abortions, federal regulations mandating equal pay, wage and hour protections or legal rights for pregnant women, and any federal action to end sex discrimination; "feminism's roots are radically individualistic, anti-political, and anti-State," said Wendy McElroy, editor of a bible of libertarian feminism, *Freedom, Feminism and the State.* "Arising out of the pre–Civil War anti-slavery movement, the early women's movement recognized clearly that government was the real obstacle preventing women from achieving freedom and equal rights."

Libertarian feminists love to invoke the early feminists to remind women that the mothers of their movement—from Susan B. Anthony to Charlotte Perkins Gilman and Margaret Sanger—agreed that the true enemy of women was the state, no doubt as a way to bolster their argument that the liberation of today's women is equally dependent on redrawing their relationship to government. But resting their demand for a return to that philosophy and strategy on our foremothers places it on a shaky foundation. Obviously, the state was the enemy in the era of Anthony, Gilman, Sanger and company, since they lived at a time when the government gave women fewer legal rights than 9-year-olds. They could not vote, own property or sign contracts.

However, for all the whining and moaning of feminists—mainstream and libertarian—the status of women has improved enough since then that those legal restrictions, and more, have been lifted. If women nonetheless continue to suffer from discrimination, it is difficult to place the blame on state policy or anti-female laws. But that doesn't stop today's libertarian pretenders to feminist truth from doing so, from insisting that women's liberation can be achieved only by dismantling all government interference in citizens' economic or personal lives, whether that interference keeps women from voting, as it once did, or protects them from being fired because of their gender, as it does now. If the Big Brother state is oppressive, Big Sister is no improvement. "For feminists to discover in the state the new 'Mr. Right,' and to wed themselves thereby, for better or for worse, to a public identity inseparable from the exigencies of state power and policy would be a mistake," wrote Jean Bethke Elshtain, a leading libertarian theoretician.

The feminist movement that is left after libertarians strip away any possibility of government involvement bears little relationship to what leading antifeminist intellectuals Elizabeth Fox-Genovese and Christina Hoff Sommers, on the one hand, or mainstream feminist leaders like Patricia Ireland or Gloria Steinem, on the other hand, imagine. No lobbying for "family-friendly" laws, no demands for new affirmative action programs. No laws or programs of any kind. Instead, they hold out a vision of strong, independent women committed to their own sacred individuality banding together to solve whatever problems they might share. "We will have to rely on ourselves and on each other," writes Joan Taylor Kennedy, the mother superior of the libertarian feminism. "Because we still need to expand our own options, to make our lives a little easier, to learn even more to help each other."

It's a glorious fantasy of sisterhood that makes Martin Luther King's dream of a color-blind society seem eminently practical. Millions of women will magically and mysteriously have the tools to take care of themselves and will join hands in cooperation and mutual support—if that darned central government will only get out of their lives. Then, and only then, freed from the tyranny of their only oppressors, will American womanhood live happily ever. And then, and only then, will there be gratitude.

The Abolitionists

"Are you a real Republican?"

It's the first question Judy Jefferson was asked as she drove through the empty Mississippi Delta from town to town, church to church, meeting to meeting, through the winter of 1996. Among the dozen possible retorts that came to mind:

- Why can't an African-American be a real Republican?
- Why can't a woman be a real Republican?
- Did black folks fight and die in the civil rights movement for the right to be Democrats?
- Do you seriously expect me to join the party that brought us George Wallace, Orville Faubus and Bull Connor?

Depending on the moment, Judy, 44, and with the mouth of a tough sister from Chicago, was capable of uttering any of those responses. They were all disingenuous, of course. Living in a region where Democrats didn't even need to bother campaigning, Judy couldn't help but know that she's an anomaly. Her congressional district—the second poorest in America—had been carved out in the 1980s to ensure a black representative, and, as she is fond of saying, "black folks are loyal." That loyalty usually gave the Democrat a pretty automatic 60 percent of the vote. So Judy knew she was bucking tradition when she threw her hat in the ring to represent her district in Congress as a Republican. But, what the hell, she was a Republican.

"This country is out of control," she said. "The people are out of control, the government is out of control. We've reached the point where people—

common folks, black people, white people, rich, poor—want to return to the strong values that have sustained us in troubled times. The Democratic Party has completely moved away from any discussion of Christian values, of morality, of rights and wrongs. That puts them totally out of step with the way people think.

"Conservative means doing a lot with a little. Black folks have been doing a lot with a little forever. We're natural conservatives."

Judy Jefferson wasn't quite a natural; she grew into being a conservative. During her childhood in Chicago she never thought twice about being a liberal and a Democrat. She didn't need to know the meaning of the word "oxymoron" to know that it described a black Republican, even a black conservative. A few years at Spelman College in Atlanta did nothing to shake those assumptions, which passed for convictions. Then she landed at Graceland College in the middle of nowhere in Iowa, lured by a hefty Ford Foundation grant. Judy knew she wasn't in black America anymore her first morning in the dorms. She emerged from the shower to the spectacle of two white girls staring at her unabashedly. "Can we touch your hair?" one asked. "Not this morning," Judy muttered, before she fled back to her room.

Iowa taught Judy to deal with all kinds of people, planting some seeds of political doubt and dissonance. But it still didn't convert her. When she finished school, she saved some money, planning to leave the country and renounce her citizenship as quickly as possible. Then her father, who had retired to Mississippi, got sick, and Judy decided to take one last trip home before her final departure. The boat sailed without her, and two weeks became twenty-four years. Judy loved to tell the story on the campaign trail. "People don't come to Mississippi," she quipped, "they leave Mississippi. I'm a Mississippian by choice."

Politics wasn't even a distant passion at that point in her life. Judy hung around at her parents' house, then scrambled to find a way to make a living. She wound up teaching elementary school and working in a program for ex-offenders, which meant she was broke and wrung out like a dishrag. In 1984, she was pulled into a local Republican political campaign and began writing copy for a series of radio dramas, using her second-, third- and fourth-grade pupils as her focus group. The Harrisons, the black family she created for those spots, became part of Mississippi lore as voters listened to Christine Harrison dress down her husband George for handing over his vote to the Democrats as if it were some old shoe he'd found on the street. With the success of the Harrisons under her belt, Judy turned professional and took voters in North Carolina into Smitty's barbershop ("For blacks, barbershops are what country clubs are for white men," she says), where the candidates kept dropping by and the Republican made more sense than the Democratic toady.

Suddenly, Judy found a calling, and a cause. She started her own production company, filling in the spaces between candidates with commercial advertising work. Then, in 1995, she looked around and realized that she couldn't face two more years of Representative Bennie Thompson, her local liberal Democratic congressional representative. "The Democratic Party is dominated by anti-fetus feminists and self-absorbed homosexuals," she says. "Our government has failed us. Our schools have failed us. And we don't want to acknowledge it, but even our clergy has failed us."

Judy didn't believe that the solutions to the problems of black America could come from Washington. Washington is the problem, she insisted, the force that had reduced a proudly self-reliant community to a bunch of whimpering beggars waiting for a handout from the Man. "We used to believe in our own community and in ourselves," she said. "We had no choice until the 1960s, and we might have been poor, but our businesses thrived and our community thrived. Now everyone drives past the old black business areas to get to Wal-Mart. Now we have churches that are empty all day when we need day care centers, but nobody thinks we can build any unless we get government grants.

"The empowerment of local communities is the rebuilding of America. We need to rebuild America one family, and one community at a time."

Judy realized that she had run out of people she wanted to support as Republican candidates. Black people still refused to break the umbilical cord that tied them to the Democratic Party. The clergy preached morality and responsibility on Sunday, but danced for the Democrats the rest of the week. ("The Moral Majority doesn't represent the majority and there's a big question as to exactly how moral it is," she quipped, including both black and white churches under that umbrella.) So Judy turned to her husband, and they prayed. "This is entirely too hard to do unless you feel a call from God," she said. She heard that call and realized that politics was what her mother had reared her to do. "This is why she sacrificed to give me music lessons. This is why she was always nagging at me to stand up straight."

Judy's logic was persuasive. "There are only two ways to beat a Democrat in this state," she concluded. "It would take a sports hero or a black woman. In Mississippi that means Jerry Rice or Walter Payton, and since neither of them has filed, I'm the best shot." For the next four months, she and her husband drove their battered baby blue 1985 Bonneville across the Delta, talking at a Republican women's club one day, and the membership rally of the Southern Christian Leadership Conference the next. In December 1996, she boldly went where no black woman had ever dared go before: into the heart of the beast, the annual Coon Dog Day of Mississippi politicians.

She and her husband followed the back roads out of town until they were "so far out into the country they had to pump daylight in." Judy was nervous; her ground rule was that they would be out by dark. "I wasn't entirely sure they didn't pull out the sheets when the sun went down," she says, not entirely joking. They parked their car on the narrow country road and climbed up the hill into a field filled with white folks. Dozens of men in aprons were gathered around enormous barbecue pits—"so big they had to be raised and lowered with hydraulic jacks. I thought for a second, Oh, okay, this is where they used to put us after they skinned us."

Judy clapped politely as the governor speechified. Then she worked the crowd with her mixture of urban sassiness and rural irony, digging for contributions, enjoying every minute of the discomfort her presence provoked in the white boys. "I never pretend there's no difference between whites and me," she says. "America is a racist country with a racist past and a racist present. We have to acknowledge that and build bridges."

She didn't quite make it out before dark. By the time she and her husband made it to their car, deep shadows had already fallen over the road, and the good old boys were ready to let their coon dogs loose to howl at the moon. But Judy couldn't resist a little last-minute politicking. "A big white guy, with white hair and that ruddy complexion that rednecks have, was just arriving with a bunch of people," she recalls. "Suddenly, this black woman jumps out of the dark at him and says, 'Hi, I'm Judy Jefferson and I'm gonna beat Bennie Thompson in November.' The man never stopped walking. He reached into his pocket. I almost ran. Then, never pausing for a second, he handed me a $100 bill and wished me luck."

Everywhere she traveled—from Bolton to Como—Judy preached the gospel of independence, self-reliance and old-fashioned morality. She attacked welfare, proclaiming, "Those who can't do for themselves have to be taken care of, but the purpose of government is to support the citizenry, not to deliver life on a silver platter." She openly supported prayer in schools: "There are people praying in schools every day. The students pray, 'Please don't let anybody jump me in the bathroom.' The teachers pray, 'Please let my car still be in the parking lot when I get out of class.' "

Judy hoped to tap into the deep conservatism of the black community, a conservatism long at odds with the community's allegiance to the Democratic Party. She had jumped ship back to the party that had held the loyalty of black voters from the Civil War through the 1930s. Frederick Douglass had told his followers that "The Republican Party is the ship, all else is the sea," and they had listened as the party of Abraham Lincoln freed the slaves. Even in the 1940s, former congressman Oscar DePreist lashed out at blacks who were being lured by the sweet talk of Franklin Delano Roosevelt and the New Deal into deserting the party that had taken the vote away from southern white Confederates and given it to newly freed slaves: "There is a melancholy fate for any man who compromises with the devil," he said.

Loyalty, however, crumbled as the Democrats under FDR and beyond remade themselves into the party of ordinary Americans, of the working man and woman, of the poor and forgotten. By 1940, black Americans were equally divided in their support for the two parties; by 1968, the Republicans had managed to hold on to a mere 10 percent of that vote—and things have not changed much since.

Today, in attitudinal surveys and opinion polls, African-Americans sound more like Pat Buchanan than like Jesse Jackson. Two-thirds identify themselves as either conservative or moderate. Most disapprove of mandatory busing, two-thirds believe affirmative action needs to be reformed, nearly 60 percent favor the death penalty and almost three-quarters support school vouchers. Yet almost 90 percent of black Americans seem to forget those values when they choose a political party, preferring the perceived racial openness and sensitivity of the Democrats to the message of traditional morality and bootstrap perseverance spouted by the Republicans.

"Suddenly a light is going on in the black community because we've been pushed to the edge," Judy explains. Like most black conservatives, she makes a habit of paying more attention to the latter statistics than to the former. It was almost two months before the primaries and she was excited by the crowds, the attention, the hope. "Our children are scared at school and they are scared to be at home alone. Adults are frightened to go out shopping, and also frightened to stay home. There are no man-made solutions. We need divine intervention to deal with these problems. The problem is that if you talk this way, you're labeled a conservative. Those titles scare people. For those of us living in the real world—working-class people, particularly black people in the South—you can't separate religion and politics. That's my message, and I think people are beginning to listen."

Judy pasted together her campaign on a wing, a prayer and a lot of $5 contributions that still only added up to $3,000. She rode around in her old car eating stale sandwiches she had made at home two days earlier, using every dime she could collect for gasoline and posters. She had no money for the kind of hip radio spots she knew how to produce. Television wasn't even a distant fantasy. In the middle of the campaign, she was so broke that she found herself seventy miles from home with $3 worth of gasoline in her tank.

"It's particularly tough running as a woman," she explained one evening after she returned from three days on the road. "You have to convince people that you can handle the job while being a wife and mother. You have to convince them you're savvy enough to hang with the big boys. And you have to convince them that you are concerned with issues beyond the family, as if there are such things, since agriculture, defense and business *are* family issues."

Judy's goal was to reach the black women in her district, to talk to them about government policies that were destroying their families, about how families work and how that work molds and changes lives. Women, she thought—not the anti-fetus white feminists of the North but hardworking, self-respecting black women in the South—would respond. She wasn't naive. She knew that black women were even more loyal to the Democratic Party than were their husbands and sons; but they were also even more firmly entrenched in their churches, in traditional religious beliefs about family and responsibility. The black women she met every day weren't followers of Betty Friedan or Gloria Steinem. Judy thought she could win them over by appealing to their pride, to their concerns about their children, to their concern for morality and values.

She often brought along her 80-year-old mother and spoke about how her mother and father had sacrificed everything to raise her right. Her mother had worked days and her father nights so someone would always be home. It was her father who cooked her supper when she came home from school. "There was no woman this and man that," she said. "They believed that families work together." The women listened and, Judy thought, were moved. "The men are enthusiastic but they stand back, they keep telling themselves they have to clear their heads," she said. "Women are more openly enthusiastic. They have more faith in their guts."

In donning an elephant hat, Judy wasn't tilling entirely virgin soil. In 1994, Dorothy LeGrand was the Republican candidate for Congress in Minneapolis, running against an eight-term white male Democrat who had a reputation as a consummate Washington insider. While he was wheeling and dealing on Capitol Hill, Dorothy, the granddaughter of a tobacco sharecropper who was the first freed slave in her family, was working her way up from clerk, to maid, to real estate saleswoman, waitress and law clerk before becoming a lawyer. A conservative whose libertarian instincts led her to support both abortion and gay rights, Dorothy preached individual responsibility, exhorting constituents to "get off your back and go to work." Her opponent skated back to Washington, but Dorothy garnered an amazing 38 percent of the vote.

In Massachusetts, Patricia Long, a Boston attorney, took on the Democratic establishment at the same time, becoming the first African-American woman in the state's history to run for Congress. Pro-choice and a firm supporter of state control over welfare, education and the environment, she received 30 percent of the vote. In 1996, in what Judy hoped was a nascent movement, black women ran as Republicans for Congress in Texas, Georgia, Minnesota, Connecticut and Massachusetts, for governor of Washington and for secretary of state in Colorado.

Only the latter won. Judy Jefferson's black male opponent in the Republican primary left her in the Delta dust, with just 20 percent of the vote.

BLACK MISSISSIPPIANS didn't vote against Judy Jefferson. They reaffirmed their position on a seventy-five-year-old struggle that was black America's greatest political debate, the historic clash between W. E. B. Du Bois, a Harvard-educated historian, and Booker T. Washington, a former slave. At that bleak moment in history, black Americans suffered the tyranny of segregation, the violence of lynchings and the hopelessness of economic marginalization. Washington, the cofounder of Tuskegee Institute, warned blacks not to look to whites for liberation from their despair. Work hard, pull yourself up by your bootstraps, rely on yourselves and each other, he preached. Gain economic solidity, and social equality will inevitably follow. To the followers of Du Bois, the cofounder of the NAACP, Booker T. was the quintessential Uncle Tom. You don't have to earn white respect, Du Bois countered. It's your constitutional and human right. Demand legal rights and legislative changes, he insisted. Gain social equality under the law, and economic parity will inevitably follow.

The black community turned its collective back on Washington's message of self-help and, for decades, channeled its considerable energy and meager resources into the struggle for an end to legally enforced discrimination, to the backs of buses, to segregated restaurants and to inferior all-black schools. By the mid-1960s, those restaurants, buses and schools had been integrated. Black citizens were lining up to vote even in the most retrograde communities in the South. And, gradually, the force of law was brought against employers and Realtors and governors who continued to deny black Americans equal rights and equal access.

Economic improvement, however, did not follow as promised. The disappearance of legalized discrimination, together with affirmative action programs and an economic boom, swelled the ranks of the black middle class, but the remainder of the black community was left behind in misery. In 1970, about one in three black Americans was poor; in 1993—after decades of federal programs—30.7 percent still lived below the poverty level. Black male unemployment rose from 5.4 percent in 1969 to 23.4 percent in 1982. In fact, 80 percent of the economic progress achieved by the black community between 1940 and 1980 was made before 1965, the year that Lyndon Baines Johnson signed the Voting Rights Act, the year after the Civil Rights Act became the law of the land.

Few young women who grew up in the heady days of those civil rights triumphs—days of mortal risk and dazzling success—realized that their sweet victories would turn as sour as today's economic realities suggest. Nona Brazier, however, had no other expectation. As she watched the Freedom Rides and sit-ins on television, she was underwhelmed. "Why would you want to go to the counter where the man who fixed the meal had on a Klan robe the night before?" she wondered. "Eat someplace else. Better yet, start your own restaurant."

The daughter of a command sergeant major in the U.S. Army, Nona was born in Japan but grew up in Texas. Her family had been business owners and teachers in Louisiana, and Nona was expected to live up to family tradition. She still remembers crying hysterically when she got her only *B* in school. She was never allowed to use lethargy, or racism, as an excuse. "My parents taught me not to give racism power," she says, quickly adding that it wasn't always easy. Nona still stiffens when she recalls how white people would come up to her, pat her on the head and say, "'My you're articulate,'" as if they were surprised that a horse could talk. "But I was raised to realize that there was racism, and that there probably would be for a long time, and that meant I had to be twice as good, that I had to keep fighting and pushing."

Politics was not an abiding passion in her family, but Nona's father, a supporter of Eisenhower, made no bones about his view of the Democrats. "They held Democratic functions one day of the week and Klan rallies the next," she recalls. "That's the Democratic Party I remember." Nona's skepticism about the civil rights movement was rooted in her instinctive belief in the philosophy of Booker T. Washington. If she was unimpressed with sit-ins and Freedom Rides when she studied black history in college and graduate school, she was enthralled with the National Business League, which built whole towns, started its own railroads and factories to stimulate the economy of black America, and the early black Odd Fellows chapters, which offered mortgages and educational loans to members.

"Doing it on our own without asking anybody for anything," she thought in excitement. She soon learned that other black students thought Booker T. was a sellout, that his approach implied that black folks were inferior to whites. That wasn't how Nona heard the approach, which pulled at every muscle of tradition her parents taught her about at the principles of Kwanza: family, self-determination and cooperation. In her mind, Du Bois's alternative—his emphasis on "Litigate, Legislate and Integrate"—was already forcing black people to look outside their own community for strength, for solutions. It might help the "talented tenth," she thought, but it wasn't likely to do much for the hardworking nine-tenths.

The only modern voice Nona heard that spoke to her beliefs, and to her conviction that black self-sufficiency held the key to black liberation, was that of Malcolm X. At first blush, it might seem odd that Nona was drawn into the Republican Party because she was so deeply influenced by the philosopher-king of the militant wing of modern black activism. But Malcolm's image has received more publicity than his teachings. "The American black man should be focusing his every effort toward building his own businesses and decent homes for himself," Malcolm said in a sermon that Clarence Thomas enjoys quoting. "As other ethnic groups have done, let the black people, wherever possible, however possible, patronize their own kind, and start in those ways to build up the black race's ability to do for itself. That's the only way the American black man is ever going to get respect."

For Malcolm, that didn't mean rallying, demonstrating and demanding that white society compensate black Americans for years of enslavement, servitude and discrimination. "This is no revolution, this is a beg-o-lution," he said of the civil rights movement. "You 'Toms' are asking the white man for a cup of coffee at a lunch counter. Holding hands with white people and singing 'We Shall Overcome' is laughable.

"The so-called Negro has to stop the sit-in, the beg-in, the crawl-in, asking for something that is by rights already his. The so-called Negro has to approach the white man as a man himself."

Malcolm taught that being a man didn't mean sitting around heaping blame on whitey. It meant learning about your oppression, acknowledging white evil and moving on by accepting your own measure of responsibility. Poverty, he said, is no excuse for ignorance, any more than is history. Ignorance breeds poverty; it's not the other way around. "How many dictionaries and reference books do you suppose we would collect if we went through a black housing project in New York?" he once asked. "Enough to fill a car trunk or van? Or maybe a suitcase? We can't blame the white man for the dictionaries black children don't have.

"You can blame a person for knocking you down, but you can't blame that person if you refuse to get back up. . . . However much slave history taught us about the injustice and misery we as a people had suffered, it did not excuse us from assuming responsibility for ourselves and each other by altering its course."

Those words thrilled Nona, who saw in them her own unformed vision of a bold black America pulling itself up by its own initiative and saying, to the white world: Here we are, look at what we can do and have done despite your discriminatory laws and your racist attitudes. No more enfeebling dependence on the Great White Father State. No more meaningless confrontation when self-sufficiency could serve as a vaccine against discrimination. But, despite Malcolm X, black America seemed to be moving in the opposite direction. Instead of forging solidarity to rebuild community, black leaders seemed to be forging solidarity to coerce benefits from "the system." They were so intent on forcing white America to atone for its sins that they allowed the tradition of black self-help to evaporate, and forced the community to become dependent on whites.

Nona points to the strategies other ethnic groups in America—Asians, Cubans, Jews—followed to build themselves up, often against formidable odds. "People need commerce, not programs," she concludes. "You don't build a community with programs. The black leadership has ignored that most basic principle of nation building."

After Malcolm X was killed, and the community turned its back on his teachings by throwing its lot in with Democratic Party promises, Nona gradually became disillusioned with the politics of black America "The black leadership in this country is gagging gnats and swallowing camels with all this fussing around about whether blacks have a certain percentage of jobs," she now says.

Nona couldn't do much to turn the tide, since her personal life was a shambles. She became pregnant when she was 16 years old and refused to go through with the abortion her mother arranged for her across the border in Mexico. Instead, she married the baby's father and they struggled as she finished her college degree at the University of Texas. Then, just as Nona was beginning to catch a glimpse of a normal, middle-class life, her husband

returned from Vietnam and committed suicide. Their son was 4 years old.
Nona walked to a local bridge and threw her ring into the water. Her youth
was over.

She took off for Los Angeles, where she worked as an insurance claims
adjuster. In her spare time, she tried out her ideas about self-help and self-
reliance by working with a community alternative school and a community
food cooperative. When she remarried and moved with her husband to Seattle in the mid-1970s, she felt, once again, that she was finally firmly on track.
Once again, her world collapsed when that marriage ended in divorce. "He
believed he was a victim of a racist society," she says, "and I had no patience
with that." Left now with three children, Nona floundered until she married
her current husband, Martin Brazier, in 1983, and added his four children to
her menagerie. Gradually, they carved out their place in that progressive
city, opening a grocery store and then parlaying that experience into a
garbage-hauling business.

That, ironically, was the beginning of Nona's political career. Suddenly
she was swamped by regulations and paperwork, choked with taxes and
threatened simultaneously by union demands and lack of capital. Trying to
practice what she had always preached by opening a business and hiring from
within her community, Nona was about to go under because the government made small business impossible. She declared war on the Democrats.
"Who are you going to support, the party that takes 43 percent of your hard-
earned money or the party that wants to cut down the size of government so
that you can keep it?" she asked anyone who would listen. "How can black
people support a party that throws so many regulations in your path and
takes so much of your money that you can't possibly build yourself up?"

Nona threw her lot in with the Republican Party, quickly rising to the
position of party chairwoman in the Seattle area. By 1995, when Linda Smith,
a white congresswoman, decided against running for governor of Washington, Nona concluded that she had no alternative: she could support no one
in the race, or she could run herself. When the Republican Party convened
for its state convention in Bellevue in June 1996, two thousand delegates
rose to their feet and cheered the 46-year-old women. But she refused to
pander to their sensibilities. Ellen Craswell, her leading opponent and the
darling of the state's formidable Christian right, was using the visage of
George Washington on her campaign signs. Nona, unimpressed with empty
patriotic symbols, could not resist reminding her fellow Republicans that
Washington had been a slave owner.

Nona quoted Malcolm X at meetings of the Rotary Club and spoke against affirmative action at synagogues. She proposed an overhauling of the state's Department of Social and Health Services, which she called a bureaucracy designed to "warehouse the poor," and went so far as to suggest that elected officials should receive no pensions. For ten months, she preached her version of the Contract with America to anyone who would listen: zero-based budgeting to force state agencies to justify each year's spending, a charter school initiative that would allow citizen groups to establish their own publicly funded schools and the death sentence for the rape of virgins.

Although two of her opponents were female, Nona, like Judy Jefferson, counted on women voters for victory—not out of any feminist sense of solidarity, but because she's convinced that women are more flexible, more practical, more sensible than men. Her base in the women's community was an organization she and other female business owners fed up with the prevailing definition of "women's issues" had founded several years earlier. The founders of the Pushy Broads Association, the prototype for what later became the Industrial Strength Women, were the female Booker T. Washingtons and Malcolm Xs of the women's movement in Seattle.

Their response to "women's issues" was identical to Nona's reaction to the civil rights movement: Get over it. Their message was simple: The feminist movement has degenerated into the cult of victimhood and done more to turn women into whimpering victims than any man. Want to start a "nontraditional business"? Don't whine about how women have been locked out of certain fields; just do it. Think your gender is holding you back at work? Sue or find another job. Worried that "women's issues" are being ignored by the legislature? Get over it. All issues are women's issues, from the budget to taxation to the nation's defense strategy. "What do women need?" Nona asks. "The same thing that men need: strong marriages, the ability to produce and the chance to pass their principles and produce on to their children."

Nona has little patience for feminist complaining and bemoaning. When other women talk about the importance of organizing to keep up the pressure for women's rights, she interrupts with a story about the time a group of women in the state began talking about establishing a Republican women's group. You can't have a women's group, male Republican leaders responded, women are already in charge. Jennifer Dunn is in the House of Representatives, there are powerful women in the state house and senate, and a local businesswoman is serving as ambassador to New Zealand. "I mean, really, won't these women ever declare victory?" Nona almost giggles.

But she worries that feminists aren't simply wasting energy and spinning their wheels, that they have actually disempowered women, not only just by turning them into whiners, but by encouraging them to turn their backs on the one realm of power over which they have long had exclusive control. "Feminists don't want to admit it, but it's true that the hand that rocks the cradle can be the hand that rules the world," she says. "Instead of forgetting about rocking the cradle, women—real women out there in the real world where I live—have learned how to turn that rocking into power."

On the second Tuesday of September, the women, and men, of Washington endorsed much of Nona's message, but they rejected her candidacy in favor of Ellen Craswell, whose conservative Republican values and strong stand against abortion paralleled Nona Brazier's. No one was really surprised. Nona, who had entered the race late because of business problems and a bout of ovarian cancer, had raised only $50,000. Craswell outspent her by $300,000.

FOR DECADES, conservative black women huddled in obscurity, ignored by black leaders, who dismissed them as traitors, tokens or opportunists—subsumed, in the eyes of white society, by the Carol Moseley-Brauns and the Faye Wattletons. They maintained their own think tanks and policy groups, wrote their own political analyses—which were widely ignored—and quietly plotted an alternative course for their community, and their nation. They were the black community's dirty secret, a small band of Aunt Thomasinas and sellouts to the Reagans and Bushes.

Then Clarence Thomas was nominated to the Supreme Court, and they were catapulted into national prominence. The furious opposition of the judge's detractors, who were legion, was a predictable report for a hungry media. The existence of his supporters—of black men and women who disavowed every liberal social program from affirmative action to welfare, and every important black leader from Jesse Jackson to Kweisi Mfume—was a delicious story for journalists who thrive on the exotic and the ironic. Suddenly, the voices of women like Anne Wortham, a professor of sociology at Illinois State University, and Constance Newman, director of the Office of Personnel Management, were broadcast to a nation that had long believed, or had long been led to believe, that all black people worshiped at the altar of the NAACP.

And then Anita Hill emerged quietly out of the flatlands of Oklahoma in a blue-green suit, impeccably understated, hesitantly angry and unashamedly Republican. For liberals and feminists of all races, the Hill-Thomas hearings were a morality play about the war between the sexes and the often subtle horrors of sexual harassment. For conservatives, they were a three-ring circus of political correctness. For conservative black women, however, they were exquisitely personal. Counterbalancing the ecstasy of their newfound visibility was the agony of watching one of their own attack another member of their tiny clan, and the humiliation of having their "blackness" questioned by arrogant white liberals on the Hill and in the press. Ultimately, Anita Hill was thrown to the wolves, painted as Satan collaborating with a horde of liberal devils to steal the nation's highest judicial prize from the great conservative black hope. Both that portrayal and the gratuitous senatorial lectures on the black experience left deep scars.

For white Americans glued to their television screens for the senatorial version of *As the World Turns,* the Thomas hearings provoked little of this emotion. They were, instead, the ultimate theatrical revelation with a cast of unlikely characters emerging, seemingly, out of the thin air. Few Americans had ever seen such a large group of impressively educated black Americans in one place at one time. Few had ever heard so many articulate black Americans disagreeing about so many things. The myth of a monolithic black America came crashing down as Yale University–trained lawyers disavowed affirmative action, a stance that totally confused millions of Americans who presupposed that those lawyers would never have gotten to Yale without it.

That confusion was a sure sign of the growing threat the black anti–affirmative action crowd posed to the united front that had made those programs sacred cows. An occasional strident critique from a prominent black male conservative like Thomas, Walter Williams or Glenn Loury was one thing. A full-blown attack by prominent black women was another. That was double treason in the land of identity politics and its attendant censoriousness, a stamp of approval on the conservative agenda from the very people who were supposed to despise it.

Yet those traitors boldly declared themselves once Thomas's nomination came under attack for his opposition to affirmative action, or any other "race-based solutions." During the worst of the fray, Phyllis Berry Myers, who had run the congressional affairs office at the Equal Employment Opportunity Commission during Thomas's chairmanship, stood up and announced: "You may kill this nomination, you may even kill this man, but so many of us will take up this banner."

Teresa Doggett watched the show from Austin, Texas, and cringed while Thomas was crucified as a turncoat—an affirmative action success story rejecting the very programs that had propelled him from poverty to prominence. Teresa quietly agreed with the judge, although she had never been poor, had never needed affirmative action. Which was precisely the point.

The daughter of a psychiatric social worker and a postal worker, Teresa was born into a black family with deep roots in the middle class. Her grandfather was the first black graduate of Washburn Law School, and one of the first black attorneys to practice in Kansas. She was the paragon of a middle-class adolescent of the 1950s: ballet, piano and violin lessons, high expectations, and few excuses. "I was expected to be great at everything," she says. "I was told there was nothing I couldn't do if I worked hard enough."

After graduating from Wichita State University and Creighton University Law School, Teresa fled the Midwest for the action of Washington, landing at her cousin's house without a job or contacts. She spent a year trying out life as a tax attorney and then moved into the federal bureaucracy. Four years at the Department of State and the Department of Agriculture hooked her on public policy issues, and she headed to the Kennedy School at Harvard University for graduate studies.

Life outside of Kansas was a shock for Teresa. She'd never rebelled against her parents' middle-class values. She'd never met a liberal. Until she landed in Washington, she hadn't even known she was supposed to be one. When she found out, she called her mother on the phone and screamed, "Why didn't you warn me!" But even Washington didn't prepare her for the Kennedy School, a bastion of liberal thinking. "Everybody made such a big deal out of the fact that I was a Republican," she says, laughing. It didn't seem funny at the time. "I'm from Kansas, and they were *Harvard*."

From Cambridge, Teresa migrated into international banking, where she remained until she married John Doggett and moved with him to Austin. There she ran a mentor program that matched working women with displaced homemakers, unwed mothers and women on welfare. By the time Clarence Thomas was nominated to the Supreme Court, she had left that position to work with her husband in their own international import/export firm.

Teresa knows that during that journey through school, through government service and banking, she could have taken advantage of a dozen affirmative action programs, and that concept enrages her. She can't imagine why anyone should have given special preference or consideration to a person who had been born with at least a silver-plated spoon in her mouth just because she was black and female. "I have no trouble supporting special programs to help those who have limited opportunities and advantages," she says. "But basing these programs on race or gender makes no sense at all."

Perhaps she would have stayed immersed in the import/export business, keeping those thoughts to herself, but the Clarence Thomas fiasco inter-

vened. During the three-day Hill-Thomas hearings, her husband—a Yale
Law School classmate of Hillary Clinton's and an old acquaintance of Anita
Hill's—was called to testify before the Senate Judiciary Committee. The
lanky, bearded attorney was almost stunningly verbose in his post-midnight
testimony, parading his credentials—his degrees from Yale and Harvard
Business School, the dozens of countries where he had worked. His attempt
to gain credibility backfired, turning him into a National Lampoon caricature of egomania. Teresa sat at his side and fumed.

They flew home to Texas to shouts of "Uncle Tom" and threatening
phone calls, and to suggestions that John should run for political office.
He declined, but as Teresa watched the attacks on the black people she
admired—the men and women who shared her views on affirmative
action—something started festering in her, a powerful confluence of "I'll
be damned if they can shut me up" and "I'll show those so-called black leaders." That unformed thought, of course, was about elected office, but Teresa
resisted. "How could I run for office when I think politics stink," she says of
her attitude then, and now. Then she concluded that that opinion might be
her greatest qualification.

In 1994, Teresa tested the political waters by running for state comptroller against a Democratic incumbent. She was caught between sexism
(remember, she says, this is Texas, where the trophy wife mentality still isn't
dead) and feminism—dogged by the party's pro-choice women, although
she was mystified as to why they should care if the state comptroller was
opposed to abortion. But she had the time of her life. "I love being a conservative, campaigning as a conservative and getting conservatives to be reasonable," she says. "Conservative" was the only label Teresa attached to herself
during the campaign. "I never brought up in the race that I was a woman or
an African-American. Everybody is sick of those labels."

Teresa raised almost $300,000 without any help from the Republican
National Committee or the state party, which were unwilling to invest in
what seemed like a losing battle. On election night, then, they were startled
when she walked away with 45 percent of the vote. The most optimistic pre-
diction she'd been given had her at half that figure.

By 1995, she was ready to try again, this time against Representative Lloyd
Doggett (no relation), a well-financed Democratic incumbent. If that didn't
make the odds against Teresa daunting enough, their district had never sent
a Republican to Congress. But Teresa seems to enjoy butting heads with
tough realities. "Politics is a very ugly game, and running for Congress is no
picnic," she says. "But I am a warrior, and Congress is my calling." On other

occasions, she explains her attitude even more personally: "I'm blessed. I'm stupid enough not to think that I have any limits."

Teresa campaigned as a no-nonsense pragmatist bent on injecting some common sense into a sea of ideologues, both conservative and liberal. She proposed a two-tier flat-tax plan with a 15 percent rate for low-income earners and double that for the more affluent. Targeting Austin's growing high-tech community—called "Silicon Gulch" by the locals—she talked up tax credits for companies that trained new employees, suggesting that such a plan would encourage those companies to hire more local workers. She followed the party line on handing control over education and welfare to the states. And when asked about affirmative action, she said, succinctly, "Scrap it. The solution is to change the system."

The second time around, the Republican Party still didn't give her any money, but a who's who of Republican luminaries flew in to campaign with her: House Majority Leader Dick Armey and onetime presidential contender Steve Forbes, former United Nations Ambassador Jeane Kirkpatrick and Representative Sue Myrick of North Carolina. Everyone agreed that Teresa was the party's only chance to pick up the seat since, as one columnist said, a "cookie-cutter white man" had no chance at all.

Even liberal black leaders were impressed by Teresa and her campaign. "She is a role model for women everywhere," Akwasi Evans, editor of a weekly black newspaper in East Austin, told the press. "She has gone where men normally go, and she has achieved success. She has an economic platform that appeals to a wide constituency, and she has an innate sensitivity to the problems of the African-American culture."

But Teresa was plagued by a series of predictable problems. Austin is a pro-choice town, and Teresa never wavered from her pro-life stance. Feminists who weren't repelled by that position were horrified by her critique of affirmative action. And the Republican country club set wasn't entirely comfortable with a dignified black woman, no matter how conservative. At one fund-raiser, she overheard a group of wealthy Republicans talking about the welfare system, about black families with all their illegitimate children. She couldn't resist. She sidled up to the group and interjected, sweetly, "Hey, I'm African-American and I have a father and my brothers are fathers."

In fact, Teresa made no bones about any of the problems she had with her party of choice and some of its constituencies. She berated antiabortion activists for being "pro-life but not pro-people." When party leaders tried to consult her about welfare reform, she snapped, "Don't ask me. I've never been poor. Ask people who got off welfare." And she made no apologies for those criticisms. "My job is not to be the black Republican. My job is to be Teresa Doggett."

She didn't do that job well enough to gain a seat in Congress, but she takes solace in the fact that she fought Lloyd on the issues, that she campaigned as she thought everyone should: as gender- and race-neutral as possible in a race- and gender-obsessed world. No appeals to the "women's vote." No parading of her "special status" as an African-American. Her detractors might see the gesture as futile, since voters could not help but notice the color of her skin and the curves in her anatomy. But in a nation in which politicians play any card they can pull out of the deck, Teresa held back her aces, claiming no special privilege because she believes she deserves none. That was her answer to every question she had ever been asked about affirmative action, and a statement of a new approach to preferences in America.

Affirmative action was the brainchild of the Lyndon Baines Johnson White House, where the notion of the "shackled runner" was born. In LBJ's vision—or what was publicly presented as his—it wasn't enough to remove the legal shackles that had kept black Americans from competing in the race. Doing so might help the talented and privileged few, he believed, but it would do nothing to help those who were so far back that they couldn't even see the starting gate. Johnson proposed that America provide the newly unshackled with a reverse handicap to move them from outside the arena, so to speak, onto the field.

White liberals embraced the concept enthusiastically, but some black civil rights activists were ultimately skeptical. Martin Luther King Jr., for example, was a firm supporter of the concept of compensatory justice. "A society that has done something special *against* the Negro for hundreds of years," he wrote, "must now do something special *for* him." But he nonetheless opposed a special bill of rights for blacks, insisting that simple justice required that similar protections be offered to all the disadvantaged, of whatever race. King feared that any program of racial preference that ignored the white poor would turn out to be a bargain with the devil, that it would breed racial tension, resentment and stigmatization. Tear down legal barriers and reshape the economy to provide full employment, he argued. Improve education and training. But remember that poverty and degradation know no color line.

Thirty years, and billions of dollars, later, King's warning about the potential price of programs of racial preference seems prophetic. White men are convinced they are getting the shaft, white women look at black professionals with suspicion and blacks can never be entirely sure if they have earned their positions. If that weren't bad enough, Teresa argues, affirmative action hasn't even worked. Twice as many black families are members of the middle class today as they were thirty years ago. The number of black corporate managers has risen 50 percent and the number of black professionals 75 percent. But that was what everyone expected would happen to the best and brightest when barriers against their advancement were lifted.

But while those privileged few might have become more numerous, and more prosperous, poor blacks are further behind than they were when their shackles were first removed. In 1971, the median income of America's black families was 61 percent of that of whites. Today that figure stands at 54 percent. While women and Asians still enjoy regular employment gains, for more than a decade such gains among blacks have either stagnated or declined.

Liberals look at these figures and conclude that we need more: more programs, more preferences, more affirmative action. Teresa looks at them and scoffs: affirmative action has reinforced, not reversed, the trend Johnson feared; the end of legal discrimination siphoned off the cream of the black community and left behind a bereft underclass. She and her ideological allies delight in reminding their liberal opponents that if you add up the cost of administering all the nation's affirmative action programs, both private and public—the cost of training, research and monitoring compliance—you'd have enough money to pay every black family of four $25,000 a year, surely a greater boon than affirmative action.

The problem, as Teresa sees it, is that affirmative action is indiscriminate; programs are applied equally to all members of "protected" groups rather than to the individuals who really need help. The businesses that benefit from federal set-aside programs created to help young, shaky, minority-owned businesses are usually ones that are already as stable and profitable as their white competitors. The women and blacks who get preferential hiring at universities and newspapers are those who already have Ph.D.'s. Even federal programs specifically designed to remove barriers to opportunity that hamper only the poor have been so twisted that they offer benefits to anyone who happens to be of the correct race or gender.

The leaders of the black and feminist communities have thrown up roadblocks against any attempt to reshape affirmative action toward its original purpose. For too many, conservatives say, these programs have turned into some perverse form of number crunching in which numerical equality, rather than economic justice, has become the measure of success. They have been transformed into compensatory justice, reparations for past wrongs, rather than a strategy for lifting the poor out of their misery.

Those conservative critics are not entirely incorrect. When liberals look at affirmative action and consider "the problem" they want it to correct, they are thinking about parity and equality, so compensatory justice makes sense. But when conservatives look at affirmative action and consider "the problem" they want it to correct, they aren't worried about parity; they are thinking about poverty. In that case, compensatory justice is pretty much beside the point. That clash in definitions provokes the bitterest resentment, on both sides, over the question of affirmative action for women. Liberals demand the inclusion of women in order to foster equality. Women like Teresa Doggett say, "Please, white women with college degrees hardly make my heart bleed." She would never deny that women have been locked out of a score of professions, denied advancement and underpaid in relation to their male coworkers. But she is just as certain that privileged white women, even privileged black women, can get to the top without government help—thank you very much. And if they can't, well, society has more serious problems.

In essence, the fight is an ironically reversed dispute over the "trickle-down" theory. Liberals endorse it, insisting that if private business and government agencies are forced to hire and promote women and blacks to executive positions, the racist culture of companies like Texaco or the sexist environments of companies like Hooters cannot survive. Teresa rejects that notion out of hand. Women and middle-class black people have benefited from affirmative action for thirty years because they were poised for employment and advancement. They've received raises. They've gotten promoted. Racist and sexist cultures have begun to change. How has that filtered down into Watts or rural Alabama? she asks.

Teresa doesn't advocate abolishing all programs of preference and advantage. She just doesn't have enough faith in the trickle-down theory to want to concentrate her efforts at the top. When she's talking to black people about affirmative action and they ask, "What's the choice? How else can we help the poor?" Teresa has a short and direct response: Cancel all programs that give preference to middle-class black men and comfortable white women. Cut out the pork barrel of giveaways based on historical injustice. Revamp the basis of affirmative action from race and gender to class so that it will serve the truly needy, not the merely aspiring.

That's blasphemy in many circles, of course, and true believers react to blasphemy by covering their ears. Teresa and her allies are written off as liars, as greedy, self-interested elitists who've gotten their own and are only pretending to give a damn about the poor. ("It seems part of the wider success of the right wing in persuading voters to accept their myths," Virginia Held, a prominent feminist philosopher, wrote.) The Teresa Doggetts of America smile, and wonder who's calling whom an elitist.

IT'S LONELY being a politically conservative black woman. White women don't even try to call you sister. Black men know that you're a traitor. And the Republican Party isn't exactly running to your part of town to invite you to supper.

Even Faye Anderson, an eternal optimist, couldn't put any other spin on the reception held by the Council of 100, a coalition of African-American Republicans, during the Republican National Convention in San Diego in 1996. Faye, the group's executive director, hovered by the door of the roof garden of the Doubletree Hotel for hours, greeting guests and answering questions. Teresa and John Doggett arrived early and swept Faye up into the excitement of Teresa's campaign. A few white women from the party's beleaguered pro-choice faction stopped by to express solidarity with the other most beleaguered group. Clare Alale, who calls herself "one of Arkansas's homegrown eccentrics," was still gushing from Colin Powell's speech that same night. Everyone was hoping that Powell would stop by. If not Powell, at least Representative J. C. Watts of Oklahoma, or Jack Kemp, or one of the other white glitterati whose presence would be proof that black Republicans had arrived.

The members of the Council of 100 had been waiting for their day to come for more than twenty years. That night, they were still waiting. Year after year, election after election, they predict that black voters will finally come to their senses and opt for the party that reflects their traditional values. Year after year, election after election, black voters return to the Democrats.

Anderson struggles with an explanation. She blames Barry Goldwater for opposing the Civil Rights Act. She blames black Americans' willingness to sell their votes cheap and to neuter themselves politically by putting all their eggs in the Democratic Party basket. She blames Ronald Reagan and his talk about "welfare queens," and George Bush, who hauled out an evil-looking Willie Horton to scare voters away from Michael Dukakis. She blames the white religious right for finding racism in Christianity and the black clergy for forgetting their own Sunday morning sermons. Mostly, she blames the Republican Party leadership.

"What are they doing?" she repeats my question. "Nothing. And as Fannie Lou Hamer used to say, 'I'm sick and tired of being sick and tired' of this party doing nothing and squandering real opportunities."

Faye Anderson sees those opportunities everywhere: In the conservatism of black churches and neighborhoods. In the community's discomfort with abortion, which claims almost half of black children conceived. In the growing number of black votes cast for Republican governors and congressmen—22 percent for Senator Kay Bailey Hutchinson of Texas, 20 percent for Senator Connie Mack of Florida, 40 percent for Governor George Voinovich of Ohio. And especially in the Million Man March, where no demands were made of the government or white people, where black participants committed themselves to the Republican values of self-sufficiency and self-help.

"It's incredible," she says, "the lack of understanding of the role of blacks in the Republican Party, not just among African-Americans, but among Republicans who think that somehow we are the interlopers and that they are the true Republicans."

That's precisely how the Republican convention looked, even to someone trying not to have a jaundiced eye. Only 60 of the country's more than 8,000 black officeholders identify themselves as Republicans, and most weren't in San Diego. Only 54 of the 1996 delegates were black—a decrease from 1992, when there were 107—which explained a great deal about the sparse turnout at the council's reception.

"I can't recruit black votes," says Clare Alale. "Whites have to do that. When they hear I'm going to a Republican convention, my friends at home say, 'Home girl, you got to be courageous to immerse yourself in a world of whiteness.' I tell them, 'If you believe in Farrakhan and Malcolm X, you have to be a Republican.' But they won't listen to me. They need to hear it from somebody white."

Clare's attention is diverted by a group of women complaining about newspaper stories that painted black delegates as a group of fat cats. "Where do they live?" she asks with a solid *hrrumph.* "In some run-down ghetto or a country hovel? My grandparents paid poll taxes. My mama was a schoolteacher, and I'm just getting by."

In that sense, Clare wasn't very different from the other black delegates, or even the black Republicans around the country, who refuse to fall into the kind of neat categories the press craves. Black conservatives are as likely to be 60 as 35, to be teachers as businesswomen. The only characteristics that seem to bind the group together is that they are unlikely to hail from the Northeast, they are likely to be religious and they are more likely to be female than male. Judy Jefferson and Nona Brazier knew what they were doing, after all. "What else would you expect?" Clare asks. "Women are the keepers of the family, the keepers of the community and the keepers of the faith. Republicans are about making sure we have something to keep."

Clare looked weary. By then she and the core group at the event had been standing around for almost three hours. Most of the trays of roast beef and egg rolls and gourmet pasta salads had begun to wilt. Colin Powell had not shown up, but a celebrity finally did walk through the door. It was Marion Barry, the Democratic mayor of the District of Columbia, smiling and gladhanding and heading directly for the chicken.

🖋 🖋 🖋

A Digression into the World of Soccer Moms and Gender Fissures

In September 1996, I decided it was time to interview some of those soccer moms who seemed to be all the rage with the media and both political parties. I was intensely curious, since I knew dozens of moms—working moms, farming moms, home-schooling moms, neurotic moms, overbearing moms—but not a single mom of the soccer variety. So I spent hours driving through suburban New Jersey, Kansas City and Detroit searching for harried white women in four-wheel-drive sports vehicles filled with rambunctious children decked out in shorts with high black socks and cleats. Alas, nary a soccer mom in sight, which was hardly surprising. The mythic soccer mom who became the oracle of the 1996 election was mainly a computer-generated construct—like those mathematical models built to tell us precisely what "average" looks like, which turns out to be like no one at all. There are, of course, a few certifiable soccer moms, although no two observers have been able to agree on exactly how many. Soccer officials say that 5 million kids are playing on their teams, but, alas for the punditocracy, they also say that 90 percent of the parents who coach and crow and harass at games are fathers. And when you figure that most of these kids have parents who are too busy working, mowing the lawn or sleeping to show up regularly, there can't be more than a hundred to two hundred thousand members of this arcane subculture.

Most of the few I found were either "wrong"—wrong age, wrong race, wrong religion or wrong socioeconomic stratum—or had been interviewed so frequently by NBC, CBS, CNN, ABC, their local television stations and the entire print press corps of at least five nations that they spewed out more practiced sound bites than womanly political wisdom. I finally concluded that I didn't really need to meet a soccer mom face-to-face, since I'd already heard all of them interviewed. Anyway, the only reason I wanted to meet them in the first place was so that I could understand the gender gap, and listening to them made me realize that they didn't understand it either. So I decided to read every interview, every analysis, every statistic and every speculation I could possibly locate instead and try to figure it out for myself.

I admit it was a major challenge since few phenomena have been dissected so frequently, and at such great length, without shedding any light on what is really happening. The gender gap, I concluded, must be incredibly complicated, sort of like astrophysics, or at least electricity. But after weeks of study, I was able to boil it down into plain English in five points:

1. The gender gap emerged in 1980 because women hated Ronald Reagan.
2. The gender gap reflects the fact that American women are more liberal than American men.
3. The gender gap exists because American women and American men have fundamentally different values. Women are more compassionate, more idealistic and more likely to believe that the federal government should have a substantial role in their lives.
4. If the Republicans would change their position on abortion, the gender gap would narrow.
5. If the Republicans ran more women candidates, the gender gap would narrow.

Now all of this sounds perfectly reasonable—especially when it is nicely illustrated with graphs and tables and thoroughly scientific-looking pie charts—until you begin . . . to think.

1. As enjoyable as the thought might be, old Ronnie was not the founding father of the gender gap. It reared its ugly head even before he was born (okay, maybe not quite that long ago, but certainly before Bob Dole's conception), when women fought to maintain Prohibition. Anyway, it might be true that women preferred Jimmy Carter in 1980, but they hardly treated Reagan like Attila the Hun; he won 49 percent of their votes. And four years later, 55 percent of American women embraced him enthusiastically, which suggests that their alleged hatred for his policies didn't run very deep.

But that's just minor quibbling. The more serious problem is that the gender gap that was provoked by Reagan had less to do with female dislike for the Gipper than with male passion for him, which is an important distinction. Women didn't desert the Republican Party in droves when Reagan was nominated. They stayed right where they'd been for years, with the Democrats. But men—those angry white men—would have followed Reagan anywhere, and he seduced them away from the majority party that had long held their loyalty into the Republican camp.

2. Pundits seem to have a hard time distinguishing between Democrat and liberal, or Republican and conservative. So proof of the "liberalism" of

American women is that they are more likely to call themselves Democrats than are men. But that hardly is the definition of liberalism. Black women routinely identify themselves as conservative, but virtually every black female in the country who goes to the polls casts her vote for a Democrat. Older white women say that they are conservative, but they are the very women most decidedly against the GOP during elections. And, when asked about their party affiliation, a remarkably high percentage of self-defined hard-core conservative Christian women swear their lifelong allegiance to the Democrats.

3. The values numbers were paraded out almost daily before the November 1996 election: 58 percent of adult men said that government was part of the problem, while only 38 percent of adult women agreed. Women were more interested than men in social programs, in an effective social safety net, in finding leaders who would reaffirm our values and in civility. They worried about health care and education, while their husbands were fanatical about the budget deficit and taxes. All this means that in 1996 women loathed Newt Gingrich and were desperate to kick out the Republican Congress and give someone else a chance. We knew this because women said so on scores of polls.

Or so the pollsters who designed the questions and interpreted the results concluded. But in making their predictions, they ignored the fact that people don't necessarily vote their values, and they don't necessarily do what they say they intend to do. So the values argument worked during the polling season when that group of well-paid statisticians and pundits got to pretend that they knew what the rest of us were thinking. But the minute the election results came in, their argument fell to earth like a deflated balloon. The same gender gap that they described as the result of a difference in values not only elected Bill Clinton, but handed the Congress back to the dreaded Republicans led by the despised Newt Gingrich running the government according to that horrible Contract with America—none of which could have happened if women had really believed that Republicans were some kind of bogey monsters.

4. The problem with the abortion argument is that it is based on the assumption that women—the masses of women who live in places like Salina, Kansas; Pharr, Texas, and my own backyard, Hobart, New York—care so deeply about abortion that they will tailor their votes accordingly. The corollary assumption is that men and women think differently about the subject. Neither assumption has any basis in fact. Men and women agree on abortion, and only one woman in ten says that a candidate's position on abortion is relevant to her vote. Jobs, crime, education, sure. But abortion is at the bottom of almost every priority list—for men and for women. On one poll in which women were asked if abortion was their priority in selecting a candidate, only one of the 850 women surveyed said yes, and she was pro-life.

5. Believing that women candidates can influence the gender gap is deliciously wishful thinking—and Geraldine Ferraro and hundreds of other losers are living proof that it is sheer delusion. Time and again politicians confuse "the women's vote" with women candidates, despite all evidence to the contrary. While Independents and Democrats say they trust Republican women more than they trust Republican men, being female simply isn't enough. In the 1990, 1992 and 1994 elections, for example, most women chose the Democratic candidate regardless of gender, although women swung even more heavily Democratic when the candidate was female. When the Republican was female, the Democratic advantage shrank, though it did not disappear. Celinda Lake, a Democratic pollster, concludes that the novelty of female candidates—and the advantage it once conferred—has simply worn off.

The bottom line is that the gender gap is really more of a gender fissure, if you will, which, like any other fissure, opens up and lets off steam from time to time, then closes up and lies dormant. Some physicist who has spent a lot of energy timing the opening and closing of fissures in places like Yellowstone might understand why actual fissures behave this way, but nobody has yet unraveled the mysterious behavior of gender fissures. Yet several things seem abundantly clear. First, the greatest irony of the gender gap is that while pollsters find that women are more likely to believe in the federal government than men, their votes suggest that they distrust it enough that they don't mind maximizing the possibility of gridlock. Had women voted as enthusiastically for Democratic aspirants to Congress as they did for Bill Clinton, after all, Newt and the boys would have spent Christmas 1996 emptying their congressional offices.

Second, while the gender fissure might occasionally be real, the only *gaps*—the Old Faithfuls of gaps—are race, religion, income level, education and marital status, and this is hardly a new phenomenon. While the gap between men's and women's votes for Clinton was 10 percent, the gap between the votes of blacks and whites was a walloping 40 percent—which is about what it has been for years. In fact, the black vote was far more critical to Clinton than the female vote: Dole won the white vote by 2 percent; he lost the black vote by 72 percent. Or, try it a different way: Clinton doesn't owe his election to women; he owes it to Jews (80 percent), Catholics (53 percent) and atheists (57 percent), whose support for the president compensated for his loss among Protestants. Or: he won because voters without any higher education liked him enough to offset Bob Dole's victory with college graduates—which is another way of saying that the poorest Americans voted most heavily for Bill Clinton.

What the gender gap probably teaches most clearly is that the leaders of the Jewish, black, welfare and Catholic communities have lacked the political acumen of feminists, who have exploited any and all evidence of a difference between male and female voters as a wedge to influence both the Democratic and the Republican Parties. Pro-choice Republicans have pointed to gender gap numbers to bolster support for a change in their party's antichoice plank. Women of both parties have paraded the numbers to persuade their male colleagues to back female candidates and sponsor new legislation. They've played hardball with the best of them, using whatever cards they could find hidden in the deck, and they have been remarkably successful.

But the strategy reeks of hypocrisy. The same feminists who have long insisted that women and men are the same—same abilities, same work ethics, same needs—turn around and argue the opposite in order to gain political advantage. Naomi Wolf, a leading neofeminist who happens to be married to a presidential speechwriter, advised President Clinton to advertise himself as the Great White Father in order to gain women's votes in 1996— although she has spent a lifetime condemning the very patriarchy such an image bolsters. Feminists have played the gender card to persuade politicians to support a broad range of programs—from affirmative action to abortion—knowing full well that the gender fissure is the result of none of those programs.

Which is the ultimate irony. To the extent that it exists, the gender gap gives the lie to the most basic feminist beliefs about the differences between men and women being the result of the oppression of women. As women have been accorded more equal opportunity and have achieved a more equal status in American society, they have become increasingly different from men politically. The first year pollsters noticed a substantial gap, 1980, was in fact the first year in the nation's history that more than half of American women worked outside the home.

That's because the gender gap exists for decidedly antifeminist reasons. Even *Ms.* magazine acknowledged that in reporting a 1992 survey in which readers were asked to rank the issues that most concerned them: Balancing work and family was number one; abortion finished at the bottom of the list, the preoccupation of only 2 percent of those polled. No matter how NOW or the Feminist Majority spins it, the gender gap has nothing to do with women's support for feminism, or even for most feminist policies. The only "women's issues" that are relevant to the gender gap are traditional family values, about the social welfare state and about women's perception that Dole was from Mars and Clinton from Venus—hardly the center of feminist thinking. Look at what Bill Clinton had to become in order to attract women voters: not the great feminist, but a neo–Pat Buchananite prattling about family values. The only nonfamily issue that seems to move women more than men is the environment, not equal rights legislation or domestic violence programs.

Thus the celebration of the gender gap in feminist circles seems almost absurd. When 110 women's organizations launched "Women's Vote '96" to get out the female vote, the troops seemed to assume that that vote could catapult feminists and their principles into every nook and cranny of the federal government. The National Organization for Women sponsored a women's mobilization drive in states like California, calling it a "Fight the Right" campaign, as if women's votes were antithetical to the conservative agenda. But while mobilizing women might have helped elect Bill Clinton, it did so only once the president began supporting welfare reform, tax credits for working parents and a dozen other conservative demands—only once he moved far enough to the right to satisfy the very women NOW was organizing.

The bitter truth is that the leaders of NOW and "Women's Vote '96" don't particularly like, and have never been very supportive of, the very women they are exploiting to make political hay out of the gender gap. Dozens of polls indicate that while those women line up behind a few liberal proposals—national health care and gun control, in particular—they also support such decidedly unliberal proposals as lengthy jail sentences for criminals, the banning of books whose values they dislike, curfews for teenagers and the ban on partial birth abortion.

The gender gap has become such a morass of self-interest and misinformation that it has reduced women to paper doll caricatures that are as degrading and demeaning as any prefeminist stereotype. Does any self-respecting person of the female persuasion really want to think of herself as a soccer mom, to be thought of as what she does with a tiny fraction of her week, when she might spend the rest of it as the CEO of her own company, the director of her church choir or the mother of five other children who hate soccer? Do the rest of American women want to be represented by that caricature? Is it really to our advantage, either individually or collectively, to be thought of as an enormous mass of breasts with a single mind? That is what feminist cheerleading about the gender gap has accomplished in the quest for power and political advantage.

So it's worthwhile to pause, for a moment, and give shading and color to the diversity of faces that have been lumped together under the heading "woman voter," to look at the differences among women rather than comparing them endlessly to men (which, after all, reeks of holding males up as the "norm") and to answer the question: Which woman voter? One caveat: This will not be a discussion of presidential elections, since there's no evidence that one's choice about who will occupy the White House says very much about political thinking and ideology. Remember that in 1960, Richard Nixon—not John Kennedy—won the female vote, and in 1976, Carter had more male support than female. Get my point?

The profoundest differences among women parallel those among men: race and class. But the most interesting, and ignored, disparity is age. Despite their self-image as conservative, older women—women living on fixed incomes and dependent on social security and Medicare—are fervently loyal to the Democratic Party, and they are the women most likely to vote. Theoretically their votes could be balanced by those of white women under the age of 35, who seem to be drawn by the Republican message on the economy and personal responsibility. However, the younger women tend not to vote in great numbers, so, at least for the moment, the Democrats are at an advantage. But the implications for the future should not be ignored.

Poor women and female members of union households are die-hard Democrats. No surprise. But the women who seem the most logical members of the core constituency of groups like NOW—professional women—are split right down the middle between the two parties, both individually and as a group. They are secular and pro-choice. They like the Democratic positions on education and the environment and worry about the influence of religious conservatives. But they prefer Republican initiatives on taxes, the budget and welfare, and agree with their messages on values and personal responsibility. Neither party can count on them at this point because they don't fit comfortably into either camp.

The most stalwart Republican women are what the crowd pollsters call married moms, which has some overlap with soccer moms, who are the supermoms of earlier years. The only issue that pushes them toward the Democrats is education. But that inclination is far outweighed by their conviction that in what they see as uncertain economic times, the Republicans are more likely to provide them and theirs with security. They are not, however, as important a force as the group Celinda Lake calls the "waitress moms"—blue-collar working mothers without college educations—who are twice as numerous as the soccer fanatics. Longtime Democratic supporters, they have followed their angry white husbands and ex-husbands partway in their drift away from the Democrats. But the women have stopped short of definitive desertion. They gave Clinton the presidency in 1992 but stayed home in 1994, which left the men free to elect a Republican Congress. Like soccer moms, they are stuck in the middle: skeptical about the shape of the economy and very influenced by appeals to traditional family values, but worried about the Republican record on health care and education. If the Democrats regain their loyalty, they will reemerge as the majority party. If the Republicans manage to wrest them out of the center, the GOP will gain control of both elected branches of government.

There is, of course, another real possibility: that soccer moms, waitress moms and supermoms will become irrelevant, because in the end, the gender gap can cut both ways. If men continue moving to the right, unless women rush out of the middle in droves to compensate for the shift, the margin women give liberal politicians won't make up for male defections. So far, there's no sign that women move to counterbalance men—that they think, "Hey, Joe, Tom and Harry are all voting Republican, so I better vote for the Democrats, just in case." But there's plenty of evidence that the more men think of the Democrats as the Mommy Party, the more they flee to the GOP.

So the gender gap may well turn out to be a case of "Daddies unite, and soccer moms be damned."

The Outlaws

Kay Sheil's modest brick ranch house sits nestled in a solid middle-class subdivision in Kansas City, Missouri, built just long enough ago that the trees are now dense and tall, the kind of neighborhood where Donna Reed might have lived if she had been more than a figment of television's imagination. Chintz curtains frame the windows of an immaculate living room. The couch is comfortable, tufted leather, and a well-worn book on French Impressionist painting is perched on the edge of a glass-topped coffee table.

Kay isn't elegant enough to swoop into a room; her demeanor verges on diffidence, twinged with a light dose of no-nonsense. Her hair is cut short, in a sensible do. At age 54, she is beyond striving for beauty queen plaudits. She has a tendency to pinch in her cheeks and purse her lips when she speaks with disapproval, in a gesture that defines moral outrage for women of a certain age and certain circumstance. That gesture dominates her face as Kay serves tea and talks about politics and the state of the nation.

"I'm frustrated," she says in a voice worn into huskiness by years of smoking. "There are too many issues out there, so it's too easy to forget that there is one issue that is really important, and that's civil liberties. I'm discouraged because conservatives seem to want to use the same tactics as liberals. They talk about mandatory school prayer and requiring the press to print all sides of a story. That's not right; it's dangerous. It just swings everything the other way."

Liberals aren't any better in Kay's book. They talk a good game, but in the crunch, they just aren't around. Just a week before our interview, she and a group of like-minded friends had driven out to Lone Tree, Missouri, to protest a "Good Ol' Boys" picnic sponsored by the Ku Klux Klan and the

Aryan Nation. The year before, Kay and her friends had caused a minor national stink when they and political allies in Alabama released a videotape showing FBI and BATF agents at a Good Ol' Boys Roundup along the Ocoee River in Tennessee, where the entrance was emblazoned with a banner reading "Nigger Check Point" and the most popular item on sale was a T-shirt depicting Martin Luther King Jr. in the crosshairs of a gun. This time they'd set their sights on racists closer at hand, and Kay had asked area churches and the major civil rights organizations—the American Civil Liberties Union, the National Association for the Advancement of Colored People and the National Organization for Women—to join the planned demonstration. "Obviously racism is a political issue in the United States," she said. "They have the right to have a racist picnic, but we have a responsibility to protest it." But when she and her friends showed up wielding signs reading HOPE WE RUINED YOUR PICNIC and THE BILL OF RIGHTS IS COLORBLIND, Kay and company were alone. The civil rights groups hadn't bothered to send anyone to join them.

"I don't get it," Kay says, leaning back and looking out the window. She could see the flag waving at the top of the flagpole in her front yard, white letters on a black background: DON'T TREAD ON ME. Kay does "get it," at least on a literal level. She knows that no self-respecting liberal leader would join a demonstration organized by Lieutenant Colonel Kay Sheil, executive officer of the 51st Missouri Militia, numbered in honor of the victims of the Waco conflagration, who endured a fifty-one-day siege by federal agents. She just doesn't have any tolerance for their narrow-mindedness and stupidity. "I resent the assumption that militia members are all racist pigs. We are people who have more faith in society than in the government to solve problems. The government is a bully, and always has been. Democracy only works on a local level. We would never harm our fellow citizens. Militias are not offensive groups. We are fighting to preserve our communities and we have to depend on our communities to support us in that fight."

That rhetoric sounds like a nineties version of something from the Black Panther handbook, circa 1968, which is close to the mark from which Kay began her political odyssey. The daughter of classic labor-union Democrats, she cut her political teeth in the civil rights movement and, almost inevitably for that era, wound up protesting the war in Vietnam. Like so many of her peers, Kay refused to settle for the liberal view that racism and imperialism were somehow either accidents or vestiges of old ways of thinking. A young radical, she was clear, even then, that America's troubles ran deeper. "There was no need for the Civil Rights Act, for the Fourteenth Amendment or the Equal Rights Amendment," she says. "People already had those rights by virtue of the Constitution. The problem was that the government was refusing to protect them.

"The question is, Why has the American government betrayed the people over and over again? I lost three friends in Vietnam. Why? Why were our young men sent over there to fight for someone else's freedom? It's the same thing today. Look at Iraq. It's awful to shoot missiles indiscriminately. I don't think it wins friends and influences people. It's easy to stop terrorism: Just keep your nose out of everybody's business."

For Kay, the road from sixties radical to nineties militiawoman was a straight shot. In her mind, the issues have barely changed; nor have the solutions. "You don't elect a solution," she says. "Voting for a president is about as meaningful as voting for prom queen. What kind of democracy is it that says whoever gets the most votes rules, and can do pretty much whatever they want? That's not good enough. We're told that the duty of citizens is to vote. I think the duty of citizens is to watch their government and make sure it's doing what it's supposed to do, and that the only real duty of the government—its moral obligation—is to protect the rights of its citizens. Period."

Kay's self-defined job as second in command of her militia unit is to preach to the unconverted rather than to spend her time running around in a field training for Armageddon. "I don't want to crawl thorough the woods and get covered with ticks and break my nails," she says. "I've worked very hard on our community image." Kay lectures to church and community groups whenever they will have her, and pounds the streets trying to create alliances. In 1995, she sought out the local leadership of NOW after a joint law enforcement team from the state highway patrol, the local sheriff's department and the Bureau of Alcohol, Tobacco and Firearms raided the home of Laura Kuriatnyk and held her and her four children at gunpoint while they searched the house for dynamite. As her 6-year-old wailed, Laura tried to explain that she had no dynamite, that any tip they had received was probably from her neighbor, who had been feuding with her for years. They paid her no heed. Finally, finding no dynamite, they charged Laura with brandishing a gun at them—although the gun she allegedly brandished had a lock on the trigger and was a legal weapon. Kay asked the local NOW activists to join her in protesting Laura's treatment. They demurred; they were too busy picketing a store advertising Miracle Bras.

In an effort to rectify the image of militia members, Kay turned up at the Eggs and Issues forum at Missouri Western University in a crisp coral suit, chosen to contrast with the dark suits she knew the other panelists—representatives of the FBI and the U.S. Attorney's Office—would be wearing. She spoke about the Constitution and the way the federal government trounces on the rights of citizens. A rabbi in the audience refused to address those issues. No matter what she said, he insisted she must be a member of Christian Identity, a semireligious group whose members espouse openly racist and anti-Semitic theories of history, not the least of which is that the lost tribes of Israel fled to Britain, which would mean that white Anglo-Saxon Protestants are really God's chosen people. "The government violates peoples' rights regularly," she continued. "Why? The fault is not entirely with the President, Congress, the Courts, or law enforcement agencies, but the American people who, seeking to feel 'safe and secure' agree to give up small amounts of freedom. Pretty soon these small amounts of lost freedom begin to add up. . . . Ask yourselves where does this loss of freedom stop." The audience members asked when militia members planned to start shooting. Kay didn't know whether to giggle or weep at the utter ignorance.

Although Kay walks and talks softly, she does carry a big stick—well, not so much a stick as an AK-47 assault weapon and a 9-millimeter Glock handgun, both of which she knows how to use. Actually, she is required to have a rifle, as are all members of the 51st "not otherwise opposed for conscience sake." For Kay, the right to carry a concealed weapon is as fundamental as the right to free speech. It is not only a form of protection from the violence of modern society ("and it is easier to train yourself to protect yourself with a gun than with martial arts," she quickly points out). It is a principled stand: Forget the Constitution and give up your gun now. Then, what other right will you be expected to give up next? she asks.

WHEN I went in search of militiawomen, I expected to find Bubba tramping through the woods, his wife in tow. Or some semiliterate wackos spouting off about black helicopters sent by the United Nations to impose the New World Order, while their girlfriends brought them cold beers. But for every woman I found flashing a militia membership card because she believed her husband, who insisted that rich New York bankers were trying to shove a One World religion on her family, I found a dozen Kay Sheils, and scores of women terrified about what their children were learning in school and about the crime rate in their neighborhoods, confused because they no longer understood who was deciding that their water bills would be raised or why Vicki Weaver was murdered by federal agents, furious because politicians seem more concerned about lining their pockets than representing their constituents, fed up with the arrogance of government bureaucrats who forget that they are employees of the citizenry.

Wendy Dalton wound up in the United States Militia Association based in Blackfoot, Idaho, because she became convinced that increasing taxes and government regulation would make it impossible for her 11-year-old son Jacob to build much of a future. "My biggest worry is that my son will not have the freedom to pursue what he wants the way we did," Wendy, 43, told the *Washington Post.* "The government has grown too large; it does not realize that it is a servant and not a master."

Darlene Donaldson started down that same road to the so-called patriot movement when she and her son Rick tried to get the state of Texas to certify the fruit they were growing as "organic." The nightmare of regulation and paperwork wasn't worth it; they opted to advertise their produce as "naturally grown" instead. But the experience convinced Darlene—a classic June Cleaver–type mom who was a Sunday school teacher and a Cub Scout den mother—that politicians, lawyers, federal agents and bureaucrats have gone too far in telling Americans how to live, when to work, where to live and what to think. "I'm not anti-anything, I don't think," Donaldson said. "I am not doing anything except trying to mind my own business and make ends meet."

Kay, Wendy and Darlene aren't as far out of the mainstream of America as they might appear. When Gallup asked a random sampling of Americans if they thought the federal government posed "an immediate threat to the rights and freedoms of ordinary Americans," 39 percent answered yes. What are the threats? The whimsical tyranny of the Internal Revenue Service, says one militiawoman, a certified public accountant. The Federal Reserve Board, suggests Annamarie Miller, a schoolteacher with her own weekly television program on a public access channel in northern California. "Why has it never been audited? How do we know it hasn't already bankrupted the country?" Education, responds thousands of women anxious about what their children are learning in public schools.

Few of the militiawomen prepare for battle against those threats by running around the woods in fatigues toting automatic weapons. Kristina Sanchez of Phoenix—who uses an alias when talking about her militia activities—spends what time she has left over after home schooling her five children preparing a monthly newsletter, *American Phoenix,* which keeps Arizona patriots up to date on what's going on in the state legislature, while her husband and his buddies in the First Mounted Rangers are off training with their latest weapons.

Clara Pilchak drives from one end of Michigan to the other organizing: against sex education in the schools, against social workers who think they know better than parents, against abortion, gun control, U.S. troops fighting overseas under the command of the United Nations, outcomes-based education and nuns like Mother Teresa who worry more about feeding people than about saving their souls. She shows up at PTA meetings to hand out literature on home schooling. She's been known to whip out her Michigan Militia membership card in the grocery store if she overhears a conversation that needs correcting. When she's not organizing in person, she's on the telephone or sending faxes, keeping in touch with the hundreds of other women she's met who are convinced that America will go to hell in a handbasket if they don't do something quick.

One day she drives into Detroit—saying the rosary en route—to block an abortion clinic, although she's cooled on the Right to Life movement. ("They've become greedy," she explains. "And they are too anxious to back a winner.") The next day she's on the phone with a neighbor whose son fidgets in school; the teacher wants her to put the boy on Ritalin. "I want to drive around with a sign, 'Schools Are Putting Your Kids on Drugs,' " she says. "All kids fidget and pick their noses, and some even eat boogers. Ritalin isn't going to change that." A beautician in town does her hair for free and neighboring farmers give her eggs and meat. She's the mama bear of the community, the self-anointed protector of all the local cubs.

Drinking coffee at the Sunrise Cafe in suburban Detroit and wearing turquoise polyester slacks, rosy-cheeked Clara—mother of eight and grandmother of twenty-five—doesn't look much like the kind of woman who would be the target of intense FBI scrutiny. But after the Oklahoma bombing, agents appeared at her farm. She's dangerous, after all. Not simply because her husband is a local militia commander and she knows how to use a gun. "It's my mouth," she insists. "My biggest weapon is my mouth," she says, laughing. Clara laughs easily, freely, which is why the local kids seem to spend more time at her house than at their own. "I'm a mean mother," she adds, talking more about her politics than her relationship with her children.

Clara (who was insistent that I not call her Ms. Pilchak, explaining, "After thirty-three years of marriage, I've earned my Mrs.") also works on the men in the militia movement—talking to them, nagging them, writing articles for their newsletter, trying to convince them that "they can win the war, but if the other side has our kids, so what? Men don't get it. They're too egotistical. Someone told me they spend an average of thirty years longer than women in purgatory. Our kids are held hostage six hours a day, nine months a year, and men don't want to see it. Children in government schools learn death and despair. They've misused the public trust so bad. People think they are doing geography, reading, writing and arithmetic.

"People think I'm a radical when I talk like this," she says, interrupting herself, as she does often. "I am. I have no choice because I have knowledge. Without knowledge I could be a happy liberal."

But many of the younger women refuse to be consigned to the "ladies' auxiliary," and most militias accommodate what might seem like their in-house feminists. The Idaho militia association held a special three-day conference for thirty of its members, where they mixed discussions about gun control and women's liberation with weapons training. The female members of the Ohio Unorganized Militia train alongside their men, learning how to track, shoot and survive in the wilderness. Women in Texas, Oklahoma and New Hampshire think about the murder of Vicki Weaver, and learn to protect themselves.

No one knows how many women have joined the militia movement, which is hardly surprising since no one knows how many men are involved either. The United States Militia Association says that a third of their fifteen hundred members nationwide are female, but paranoia makes it impossible to check these figures. The antimilitia types put the figure at 10 to 20 percent throughout the dozens of militias that have cropped up in every state. Again, the figure is impossible to verify.

Among the hundreds of X-ray technicians and housewives, real estate agents, teachers, clerks and radio talk show hosts who have cast their lot with the new patriots, not everyone is as reasonable as Kay Sheil. There are plenty of the wackos who've blackened the movement's reputation. "Some of this is strictly off-the-wall," Darlene Donaldson told *U.S. News & World Report*, as she listened to a speaker denouncing the federal government for forcing food additives down the throats of citizens. "When there is paranoia, I just let it roll off my back."

Linda Thompson, the macho mama of Militia World, gives new meaning to the word "paranoia." I admit that I don't know this firsthand, since she refused to speak with me after I told her I was writing for Scribner, which she insisted was a CIA front. Then again, she refused an interview with *Time* magazine for the same reason, though she granted one to *Esquire*, since it is owned by Hearst, which was okay because Hearst is owned by the Mob, she said. A reporter for the *Washington Post* never learned who owned his paper since Linda refused to open her door when he showed up for their scheduled interview. "I know what you're trying to do!" she screamed into the phone when he called. "You're trying to get the militias! You're out to get us!" Minutes later, a man in an olive green T-shirt burst through the door of Linda's building and began photographing the reporter's car.

When a CBS producer named Amanda Pike wrote asking Linda for her assistance in preparing a balanced report on the militia movement, Linda replied thusly: "First of all, you aren't a 'journalist,' and likely don't even know what the word means. Secondly, I don't talk to media whores. I've been told this line of baloney time and again, Just want to air your side. Everyone is nicey-nicey until they get what they came for . . . I'm suing media whores as we speak and I'm not stopping until every one of you lowlifes has been made accountable for your lies."

Linda—a stout 44-year-old who always packs a pistol—insists that the American people are on the verge of enslavement to a power-hungry centralized government, but will be saved by the 70 million Americans who have woken up to the dangers and taken up arms through the militia movement. Linda land is a reality so alternate that its creator claims that Timothy McVeigh, the convicted Oklahoma bomber, had a microchip in his buttocks, probably implanted by the government; that Hillary Clinton is part of a Marxist terrorist organization; that a train repair depot near her home in Indianapolis is really a concentration camp, built to accommodate protesters, who will soon be rounded up by leaders of the New World Order; that U.S. Army forces are being used in "Operation Garden Plot" to conscript peaceful, law-abiding citizens for slave labor; that black helicopters follow her everywhere she goes and that a laser-type beam is focused on her office windows and occasionally zaps people off their feet and scrambles her electronic equipment; and that the Clintons are behind scores of assassinations.

Linda, who runs her American Justice Federation office out of a suite in a suburban Indianapolis strip mall, knows that most people find it hard to believe anything she says. The self-styled "Abbie Hoffman of the right" says she used to find the notion of, say, an international banking conspiracy to be off-the-wall. "I put it in the category of Elvis and aliens down by the trailer!" Which is all another way of saying that if you knew what Linda knew, you'd be paranoid too. She started out, she explains, as a relatively normal person with pretty grounded liberal credentials. In Atlanta, where she worked before moving to Indianapolis, she had a reputation as a tough feminist civil rights attorney. She sued the mayor and the police chief of Chamblee, Georgia, for failing to protect a women's clinic from antiabortion protesters. When she moved to Indiana, she sued the state police on behalf of a local marijuana grower. She took on the antiabortionists, claiming that a group of pro-life physicians directed by Joseph Scheidler, head of the Pro-Life Action League, was conspiring to prevent abortions by withholding pregnancy test results from women whose tests showed fetal genetic abnormalities.

But when agents of the Bureau of Alcohol, Tobacco and Firearms threw up a cordon around the Branch Davidian complex in Waco, something just snapped, and Linda flew to their rescue. Rather than quietly offer legal advice or assist in the negotiations between David Koresh and federal authorities, Linda proclaimed an "unorganized militia," and faxed out a call to arms. "JOIN US!" it proclaimed. "The Unorganized Militia of the United States of America will assemble, with long arms, vehicles (including tracked and armored), aircraft, and any available gear for inspection for fitness and use in a well-regulated militia, at 9:00 a.m. on Saturday, April 3, 1993, on Northcrest Drive, off I-35." A photograph of her at that first assembly, in camouflage twirling an AR-15 rifle over her head—a sort of nineties version of Vanessa Redgrave with the Palestinians—is a treasured memento proudly displayed in her office. "I call it my Cochise picture!" she bragged to one reporter, giggling with delight.

If Waco was to the patriot movement what Tiananmen Square was to the Chinese democratic movement, it was Linda's coming-out party, and she's ridden the Waco train ever since with her video version of the event, *Waco, The Big Lie,* and *Waco, The Big Lie Continues,* which have earned her in excess of $300,000. That version bears little relationship to the story of Waco as written even by other right-wing conspiracy-plagued pundits, for Linda preaches that the fire that killed one hundred men, women and children in April 1993 was not a simple, evil government plot against gun ownership and religious freedom, but a cover-up for the well-planned execution of four BATF agents who had been Clinton bodyguards and knew entirely too much about his past.

Linda doesn't just uncover conspiracies, she does everything in her quite limited power to provoke the authorities to actions to which she can then point and say, "See what vicious tyrants they are." In July 1994, she maneuvered her car across Indianapolis traffic to block a bus carrying supporters of Clinton's health care plan. The police who arrested her found a .45 caliber pistol, a derringer and an assault rifle with 295 rounds of ammunition in her car.

Then she announced that the "Unorganized Militia of the United States," of which she was the self-appointed "acting adjutant general," would lead a march on Washington of armed and uniformed militia members to present Congress with an ultimatum: Repeal the Fourteenth, Sixteenth and Seventeenth Amendments to the Constitution, the Brady bill and NAFTA—or else. The sideshow, she said, would be the arrest of "Congressmen who have failed to uphold their oaths of office, who will then be tried for Treason by citizens courts."

Linda, who has a bawdy sense of humor, insists that no reasonable person could have interpreted those plans as an insurrection. "Just because you're armed and assembled doesn't mean you're crazy," she says. She wasn't advocating violence, she "just wanted to make people realize that [an armed uprising] was a viable option."

Despite her almost hysterical attempts to capture that title, Linda has not exactly emerged as the poster girl of the patriot movement. After she posted her call for the Washington march on the Internet, the John Birch Society issued an official admonition to its members to stay clear of her and her "insane" idea. "Bo" Gritz, the movement's survivalist guru, has labeled her an irresponsible and divisive force. Others suggest that she might be a government agent, planted to provoke militia actions that would give the government an excuse to crush the groups. But most patriot leaders agree, quietly or openly, with the assessment of Bob Brown, publisher of *Soldier of Fortune* magazine: "I suppose some uncharitable individual might suggest that she does what she does and more for money and public exposure, and I wouldn't argue with that."

Linda is hardly alone in her fantasies. Eva Vail, the redhead from Hayden Lake, Idaho, who issued one of the first calls for the formation of a true militia movement, believed that not only the Council on Foreign Relations and the Trilateral Commission, but eleven alien nations are involved in a conspiracy to impose the New World Order on the United States. The first female member of the John Birch Society chapter in Idaho, Eva, who died shortly after her interview with me in late 1996, was a stately woman of comfortable means whose home was decorated with plush white leather furniture. In her late sixties, she still carried herself with the flirtatiousness of a teenager, with the look of a vamp despite thinning hair that had a pinkish cast. Eva owned nursing homes and drove a Lincoln Continental to patriot meetings and seminars across the Northwest—when she was not flying off to Texas for a preparedness convention. Eva's name and opinion carried enormous weight in certain circles of the movement. A denizen of her Christian patriot bookstore—God and Country Books—she purveyed videotapes like *I Was a Sex-Slave for the CIA* and audiotapes explaining how the Oklahoma bombing was revenge by the Japanese for CIA poison gas attacks in their subway system.

"We used to believe that we were fighting communism," Eva said, reflecting back on the days when she worked with the Guardians of Freedom against fluoridation of water. "Now we know that communists were just a front for the Illuminati." Now, the Illuminati are the mysterious, secret hand that is moving all the rest of us around like marionettes. Most of the famous names in history have been Illuminati agents; they are an invisible force that has been pulling the global strings for centuries in order to quench their lust for power and wealth. They have used the public schools to alienate children from God, their parents and nature, by pushing them into homosexuality and plucking out the bright ones for recruitment. They have taken over most of the organizations in the world—from churches to corner grocery stores—and control the media, the stock market and the writing of history.

They already have 131 underground bases and prisons ready for their final assault on American freedoms. Their military equipment is warehoused at Wal-Mart stores, and they are on the brink of creating a crisis that will give Clinton—an Illuminated One, of course—an excuse to declare martial law. Then UN troops will swoop down on towns and cities across the nation. The forces of evil—since this is, in the end, the war between good and evil, between Jesus and Satan—will try to starve the populace into submission, as they did in Ukraine.

They might prevail, Eva explained in a perfectly flat tone, as if she were explaining how to use Windows 95, because American men have not fulfilled God's commandments about their responsibilities. Her tirades against the male gender would have warmed the hearts of feminist male-bashers—if they weren't motivated by her outrage that men are refusing to be competent patriarchs. "Women shouldn't have to do this," she said of the organizing work which defined her life. "Men were assigned the job of protecting our freedoms. But the spirit of our Heavenly Father has withdrawn from many men, so we are doing the job they were to do."

In Eva's ideal world, women would not work outside the home or vote. Strong men would provide for their wives and children, God would be in heaven and all would be right with the world. Ironically—or not—it was shortly after Eva began spouting these beliefs that her husband divorced her. "That's not unusual in the patriot movement," she explained. "There are a lot of divorces when one partner doesn't get it and the other does."

It's tempting to write Eva's world off as a grotesque theme park for paranoid schizophrenics. But that would be a mistake. Militiawomen aren't crazy, they're scared; and they're not scared because they believe conspiracy theories. Just the opposite. They've grabbed on to conspiracy theories because they are scared and don't understand why their husbands can't find jobs and their children are disobedient, why their taxes are rising and churches are empty. Nobody but the conspiracy theorists is offering them clear-cut explanations, and there are just enough elements of truth to the explanations offered by the conspiracy theorists to give desperate women something to hold on to. They know from *Dateline* that the Internal Revenue Service can be arbitrary in seizing personal property. They know from Peter Jennings that their right to bear arms has been restricted. They know from their own experience that their children are not learning how to read and write and figure as well as they did, and that they are learning a whole lot of other things—about sex, psychology and Thomas Jefferson's extramarital affairs—that they don't approve of. They are thus ripe for recruitment by anyone who offers them coherent explanations for—and potential solutions to—these unpleasant realities.

For every person on the fringe like Linda Thompson or Eva Vail, the movement has attracted ten mothers worried because they don't have health insurance. For every old-fashioned racist or anti-Semitic zealot on the firing range, there are a dozen women at patriot meetings whose eyes mist up when they talk about their fears that they will wind up old and alone, eating canned tuna. For every paranoid, there are scores of potential militia recruits because American women, even more than American men, live weighed down by anxiety—which is what all those endless polls before the 1996 election demonstrated with startling clarity. Almost two-thirds of women who work say that they *must* do so, and do so only to survive. A survey commissioned by Harvard University, the Kaiser Family Foundation and the *Washington Post* found that nearly a third of the citizenry is mired in pessimism and distrust of the government—and the most pessimistic of the pessimists were female.

Militiawomen are drawn from the ranks of what used to be the solid middle class, for whom the decline in real wages means not a summer without a vacation but having to go out and wait tables in order to make ends meet. Many come from farming communities and feel deceived by the government, which urged them to borrow heavily and plant intensively to fulfill the Soviet grain deals of the 1960s, and then turned around and canceled it. They are women and men who watched their parents take vacations and go out to restaurants for dinner, luxuries their grandparents could never afford, and now wonder whether their children will be able to look back as fondly at their parents' progress.

They are angry and frightened and confused and, like good Americans, they want someone to blame. Communists don't work since there aren't enough of them around anymore. On the fringe, they blame the Illuminati or Jewish bankers, but that kind of scapegoating doesn't have widespread appeal. Blacks and women are a more credible target since the empowerment of women and minorities has challenged the traditional privilege and status on which so many lives were built. But women are too close to the core of the group, and racism isn't as morally satisfying as it once seemed.

Ironically, the old and not-so-old enemies have been supplanted by the enemy that leftists have long claimed as their own: the government, which the new right considers to be indifferent, if not hostile, to their needs. Since they feel, and probably are, powerless and outnumbered, they watch government officials make regulations that destroy jobs and homes—and wonder what happened to citizen input and accountability. They see congressional representatives from New York City and Los Angeles raise their taxes, negotiate the sales of their produce, bar them from hunting where they have always found deer—and wonder who is running America.

That kind of simmering populist resentment, which is class resentment, although Americans seem remarkably uncomfortable using the word "class," is nothing new. It has fueled scores of political movements, from the Whiskey Rebellion to Huey Long. It arises from a vague sense that "they" are running things, that "they" are indifferent to our needs. For the fringe elements, "they" might be the Trilateral Commission or the Council on Foreign Relations. But for most militia members, "they" means wealthy liberals from the major cities on both coasts—writers who make fun of devout Christians, urban environmentalists who care more about trees than loggers, lawyers who get rich off devising ever more complicated ways to rip off the little guy.

For the most part, the militiawomen simply want to be left alone. They repeat the same mantra over and over: Give us control over our schools and our neighborhoods, and do whatever you want with yours—which is precisely the problem. They haven't been left alone, and they know that situation is not about to change. Think about the mothers of the fifty-nine sixth-grade girls who ran home from J. T. Lambert Intermediate School in East Stroudsburg, Pennsylvania, one afternoon crying and screaming. What happened? Some doctor had examined their "private parts." It turned out that state law required all sixth-graders to have physical examinations. Those who did not bring in forms from their private physicians were routinely examined at school. But parents were never told that those physicals would include gynecological examinations. And they never were given any reasonable explanation as to why their daughters weren't allowed to call home when they realized what was about to happen, or why nurses blocked the doors to prevent the children from fleeing.

Or consider the parents who declined chemotherapy treatments for their 3-year-old daughter, who had an incurable cancer. They weren't acting from religious conviction. They simply saw no reason to subject their child to a grueling treatment with no prospect for a cure. But a hospital social worker disagreed and found a family court judge to support her. Even before their daughter's death, the parents lost her—to foster care. Or Sharon and Waymon Earls of Toccoa, Georgia, near the South Carolina border, who found a packet of condoms in the room of their 14- and 15-year-old daughters. Where did they come from? A counselor at Stephens County Middle School had driven the girls to the local public health clinic so they could be tested for HIV and cervical cancer, receive prescriptions for birth control pills and sample packets of condoms.

The stories pour out of the women in and around the militia movement. You hear about the seventh-grader in Massachusetts who announced at supper one night that he'd learned all about how to have oral and anal sex. Infuriated, the child's father stormed into the principal's office and demanded to see the curriculum from which his son had been taught. The principal refused, despite a state law that gives parents the right to review such materials. Or about the parents in Colorado who received a call from the local library asking to speak with their 10-year-old daughter. Since she wasn't home, they offered to take a message. "Just tell her the book she asked for came in," the librarian said. "Oh, what book was that?" the father asked. "I'm sorry, sir, I can't tell you the title," the librarian responded. "That would violate her right to privacy."

Kay Sheil talks about these tales, although she feels peculiarly distant from them. "I don't fit the mold," she acknowledges. "Most women are coming into the movement because of social issues, because of education and what's happening in the schools. It isn't even correct to describe them as 'conservative women.' Most of them are liberals in the classic Jeffersonian sense. If you take a hard look at militias you will see a concern about the constitutional republic that cuts across all these lines, across race and religion and gender." She pulls out a copy of the by-laws of the 51st and turns to the mission statement: to "insure that all citizens, regardless of race, color, religion, sex, physical characteristics, or national origin shall have the right and opportunity to due process of law as established and guaranteed by the Great Document which guided this Great Nation." Kay leans back and takes a sip of tea. "People just don't get it. This is about defending the Constitution and the Declaration of Independence, and those are important issues to women. The Bill of Rights is nearly sacred to me ."

As I LISTENED to militiawomen denouncing federal agents as jackbooted Nazi "storm troopers," I heard the echoes of ten thousand demonstrators screaming, "Up against the wall, motherfuckers" at a line of uniformed police officers, batons at the ready. As I watched militiawomen with holstered guns and rifles slung over their shoulders, I saw shadows of Elaine Brown in a black beret with a rifle slung casually over her shoulder, leading members of the Black Panther Party. As I heard Eva Vail shake with anger at the murder of Vicki and Sam Weaver, I flashed to the image of four students lying dead on the lawn at Kent State.

I don't want to think of the militiawomen, especially of the right-wing wackos, as the nineties version of the Weathermen and the Black Panthers. But as I listened to the outlandish conspiracy theories of Linda Thompson and Eva Vail, it was hard to forget that twenty-five years ago most members of my crowd insisted that public schools were concentration camps in which the imperialist powers brainwashed the nation's youth, that elements within and without the government were plotting to exterminate black America or that FBI agents had been planted in radical organizations to provoke militant actions that would give the government grounds to declare a police state. When I heard Bill Clinton connect the Oklahoma bombing to the rhetoric of violence spewed out on the airwaves by Rush Limbaugh and G. Gordon Liddy, I couldn't help but remember H. Rap Brown exhorting audiences: "Do what John Brown did, pick up a gun and go out and shoot our enemy." Or SDS's J. J. Jacobs proclaiming, "We're against everything that's good and decent in honky America . . . we will loot and burn and destroy." Or Malcolm X's watchwords, "by any means necessary."

Playing revolutionary was a dangerously popular sport in the 1960s. The *Anarchist Cookbook* circulated favorite bomb recipes on every college campus. Students speculated regularly about kidnappings, seizures of property, blowing up buildings and "bringing the war home" by napalming the White House so President Johnson would know what it felt like to watch a grandchild burn. And it wasn't mere speculation.

On the night of October 8, 1969, a group of three hundred helmeted radicals stormed out of Chicago's Lincoln Park and into Drake Tower wielding sticks and pipes. Their target was the infamous Judge Julius Hoffman, who had turned the trial of the Chicago Eight, which quickly became the Chicago

Seven, into a mockery of judicial civility. They never found the judge, but they went on a four-day rampage smashing windows and cars, battling police block by block. Proclaiming that students were ready to divest themselves of their bourgeois trappings and join the revolution, members of the Weathermen broke into classrooms and harangued pupils and teachers about American imperialism. When the "Days of Rage" calmed, scores of police were nursing injuries. One was left confined permanently to a wheelchair.

The following August 24, the antiwar movement launched its first fatal attack when Karl and Dwight Armstrong, Leo Burt and David Fine packed fuel oil and fertilizer into a white van and drove to the Army Math Research Center at the University of Wisconsin at 3 A.M. Students had been protesting their university's connection to government-funded military research for months. Just days before, the campus newspaper, the *Daily Cardinal*, had suggested that violent acts might be "needed to strike fear into once fearless men and rid this campus once and for all of repressive and deadly ideas and institutions."

The Armstrongs, Burt and Fine had decided to heed that call. Violence against property didn't violate their revolutionary ethic, so they gave the police five minutes' warning before the building was supposed to blow up. However, their principles were more developed than their skill with explosives. The bomb went off before a zealous graduate student in physics trying to crack the secret of superconductivity could be warned. Bob Fassnacht, age 33, was blown to bits along with the hated edifice. He, too, had been opposed to the war in Vietnam.

The next month, on September 23, three Brandeis University students—Katherine Ann Power, Susan Saxe and Stanley Bond—and two other men carried out the first two parts of a three-part plan to funnel weapons to black revolutionaries. The first was an attack on the Newburyport National Guard Armory, which they firebombed after stealing the few weapons stored there. The second was a bank robbery in Brighton, Massachusetts, an attempt to raise money to buy explosives, which they would use to derail trains carrying weapons. During the bank robbery, however, a policeman named Walter Schroeder got in the way. He was shot and killed.

As I contemplate the murders at abortion clinics, the Oklahoma bombing, standoffs with federal officials in Montana, I think back to the Armstrongs, to Kathy Power, and Susan Saxe's attempts to resist government-perpetuated evil and to hold back the apocalypse. When I hear militiawomen who are convinced that abortion is murder praise Paul Hill, who killed Dr. David Gunn in Pensacola, Florida, I hear Bernadine Dohrn, one of the leaders of the Weathermen—SDS's most famous progeny—at a meeting in Flint, Michigan, just after the arrest of Charles Manson for the murder of Sharon Tate: "A lot of us are honkies and we're scared of fighting," she said. "We have to get into armed struggle. . . . Dig it. First they killed those pigs, then they ate dinner in the same room with them, they even shoved a fork into a victim's stomach! Wild!"

As Congress debated the antiterrorism bill hard on the heels of the Oklahoma bombing, I waited for an outcry against provisions that would have legalized emergency wiretaps with warrants and limited habeas corpus appeals—clear and blatant violations of civil liberties which imperil legitimate protest. Ironically, the loudest voices came from the radical right. President Clinton declared the militias to be "un-American" because they "despise your government." I almost choked. He sounded like a member of the House Un-American Activities Committee during the reign of Joe McCarthy. And I was haunted during the 1996 elections by the fact that only one candidate talked about the issue that has always been dear to the hearts of those of us who grew up in the new left: class. That one candidate wasn't even Ralph Nader. It was the militia members' favorite, Pat Buchanan.

I read an interview with Tom Hayden in which he explained, seemingly impatiently, why the comparison between the militias and SDS or the Black Panthers was just another example of vapid media stupidity and sixties-bashing. Hayden was one of the founders of SDS back in the days before the group became disenchanted with "participatory democracy." He went on to achieve fame by marrying Jane Fonda and using a great deal of her money to win a seat on the California legislature. Since Fonda left him and married Ted Turner, Hayden has received considerably less attention from the media.

"It's perfectly true there was violence by radicals," said Hayden, who could hardly have denied such a well-documented, and well-remembered, past. But leftist violence, he insisted, "was directed primarily at property and concentrated in the period . . . when society was most on the threshold of breakdown and many believed that most electoral means [of change] had been exhausted." Then he added, "The [leftist] activists of the '60s were against the Establishment because we saw it as a bastion of racial and economic privilege. The militias don't think it's enough of a bastion."

Hayden obviously hasn't spent much time talking to militia members, and for a person who knows firsthand how skewed media portrayals of dissidents can be, he shows a remarkable willingness to accept them willy-nilly. After all, militia members also believe that society is "on the threshold of breakdown," and most have as much faith in the electoral process as Hayden himself had in 1968. Finally, Hayden seems totally out of touch with the fact that, unlike his cohorts—with their degrees from Michigan, Columbia and Yale—today's radicals have had no contact at all with "economic privilege." They are members of the working class he once romanticized and, as such, are attacking a government they are convinced has been seized by the elite.

They are, in fact, demanding the same revolution in America that Hayden et al. enshrined in SDS's famed Port Huron statement: participatory democracy, the empowerment of the masses of citizens to control their destinies without undue interference from the state. It's difficult to understand how anyone, least of all Tom Hayden, can glorify those principles when they are espoused by upper-middle-class college students but deride them when they are proclaimed by a bunch of carpenters, grocery store clerks, loggers and veterans who listen to country and western music and wear polyester pants with the kind of flannel shirts sold at Woolworth's instead of Lands' End.

In fact, the only way to denigrate the new radicals without disavowing their new left counterparts is to belittle their complaints—to say, straight out: Come on, we were trying to save Vietnamese children from napalm and black people from the genocidal violence of police in their own communities. No matter what you think of our tactics, our motivations were pure. We were good guys fighting true evil. How can you compare our desire to make America a more just society to the desire of militia members to impose evil, retrograde measures on the nation? Even if their goals aren't evil, how can you compare the war in Vietnam and virtual apartheid to sex education and IRS overzealousness?

That argument *feels* persuasive. Taking up arms against sex education and government regulation sounds a tad *excessive,* particularly when weighed against a war that killed more than fifty-eight thousand Americans, or racial violence that exposed American ideals as a pack of lies. The problem, of course, is a matter of perception and priorities. Militiawomen believe that their kids' futures are in danger, and that their kids' futures are every bit as valuable as the lives of Vietnamese or black Americans. They are angry that the powers that be, whoever that vaguely defined group might be, are refusing to take their concerns seriously, that they are acting as if they were the only Americans wise enough to decide what issues are of national importance.

That anger brings the sixties-to-nineties argument around full circle, for that was precisely our logic thirty years ago when Americans refused to take the war in Vietnam, racial injustice, sexism and workers' rights seriously. The issues militiawomen bring to the table might sound, to outsiders, about as significant as mounting traffic regulations, but the question—raised both by their movement and by radicals in the 1960s—is, Who runs America? Who decides? Their answer is identical to that offered by radicals of an earlier era: a bourgeois elite that couldn't care less about anything but its own power and wealth. The war, now as then, is against outside forces or agencies controlling the lives of Americans, as individuals and as communities.

Tom Hayden shouldn't have to like militia members, or their goals, to identify with their analysis. As he should know, the downside of democracy is that "the people" don't always support what is right or good or true. The danger of demanding "power to the people" is that those people won't always use that power the way you might wish.

He also shouldn't have to like militia members, or their goals, to identify with their persecution. After all, survivors of the new left of the 1960s still bear the scars of a government all too inclined to agree with Bill Clinton that despising the system is "un-American," and all too willing to forget that even the "un-American" have constitutional rights. From Kent State to Waco; from Chicago, December 4, 1969, to Idaho, August 21, 1992.

Just before dawn on that cold December day in 1969, fourteen Chicago police officers burst into a four-and-a-half-room apartment on West Monroe Street and, with no warning, began firing .45 caliber Thompson submachine guns and M-1 carbines. Earlier that summer, FBI director J. Edgar Hoover had written a memo to his agents directing them to "prevent militant black nationalist groups and leaders from gaining respectability. . . . Prevent the rise of a black 'messiah' who would unify and electrify the militant black nationalist movement." That morning, with the cooperation of county state's attorney Edward V. Hanrahan, the FBI and the Chicago police fulfilled that directive. Fred Hampton, the charismatic 21-year-old leader of the Chicago chapter of the Black Panthers, who was asleep in his bed when the storm troopers burst in, was hit by forty-two shots. When the shooting ended, one policeman cautiously entered Hampton's bedroom. "Is he dead?" another called from outside the door. Two shots were fired. "He's good and dead now."

Hampton was not the only casualty. When the police began cleaning up the battleground, they found the corpse of Mark Clark and four other wounded Panthers. At a press conference declaring victory over the forces of anarchy and violence, Hanrahan insisted that the Panthers had initiated the firefight. The remaining Panthers opened the apartment to public view to allow the media and citizenry to judge what had happened for themselves.

All but one shot had been fired by the police. Nonetheless, a federal grand jury ruled the deaths "justifiable homicide." Only in 1983, after a protracted civil suit, did the government award the survivors of the raid and the families of Hampton and Clark $1.85 million, and a judge rule that the government had conspired to deny the Panthers their civil rights.

SITTING AT Mike's on Main Street in Noxon, Montana, just after the fourth anniversary of the murders at Ruby Ridge, Idaho, Carolyn Trochman chokes up when she begins talking about Friday, August 21, 1992, the day that Sammy was shot. Sammy Weaver wasn't just another random 14-year-old boy who'd been killed somewhere in America. He was the son of her friend Vicki, the brother of Sara, her son's girlfriend.

Carolyn had just come home from the Kmart that Friday morning when she heard the news that there had been shooting on Ruby Ridge. She was not surprised. Federal marshals had been stalking Randy Weaver and his family for more than a year, since he had failed to show up for his trial on charges of selling illegal weapons—two sawed-off shotguns for $450, to be exact. Carolyn believed that Randy had been set up by the Bureau of Alcohol, Tobacco and Firearms, and she probably wasn't far off the mark. Six years earlier, during one of Randy Weaver's three visits to gatherings of the Aryan Nation, he'd met a BATF informant posing as a weapons dealer catering to bikers. When the two men met again at a 1989 gathering, Randy invited him to his home, a primitive two-story cabin on twenty acres he and his wife had built when they moved from Iowa to Idaho in 1983.

The Weavers had decided to live off the grid—to withdraw from a world filled with moral rot. Vicki, a former executive secretary, wanted to home school her children to protect them from being polluted by "secular humanism," but her home state of Iowa wouldn't allow it. Idaho, especially the densely forested Selkirk Mountains of northern Idaho, seemed like a paradise where she and Randy could keep their kids at home, find neighbors who shared their values, and await Armageddon. Those values were based in the Christian Identity movement, which holds that white people are God's chosen people, that blacks are subhuman and Jews are satanic scum. The movement doesn't preach violence against inferiors. It preaches separatism, which is precisely how the Weavers intended to live.

Randy, a tractor mechanic, ex–Green Beret and former Amway salesman, bought some plywood, scrounged ends of boards from local sawmills and hand cut lumber off his property to build the family a home. They had no phone or plumbing. But with an outhouse, a generator, an ample vegetable garden and woods teeming with wildlife, they were comfortable. The children studied the Bible and the Constitution. Vicki enforced Old Testament injunctions against eating "unclean" foods such as pork. When she and her oldest daughter Sara menstruated, they moved into a small wooden shed to protect the males from their "uncleanliness."

Neighbors knew the Weavers as another family of survivalist quacks. In 1988, Randy ran in the Republican primary for sheriff, promising to enforce only those laws the local folks agreed with. He even handed out "Get Out of Jail Free" cards, pledging to honor them if elected. His 102 votes, out of a total of 486 votes cast, didn't catapult him into office, so he worked as a logger, prayed with his family and pretty much left everyone alone.

Randy's new acquaintance, the BATF agent, had been instructed to keep his ears open for information on leading figures in groups like Christian Identity, and finally heard a piece of gossip that interested him when Randy mentioned that he had met Carolyn's husband, John Trochman—"a very Christian man," to Randy; a dangerous antigovernment nut, to the BATF. Instructed to pursue his friendship with Weaver, the BATF agent met with him again on October 11, 1989, and talked, once more, about his lucrative gun business. Randy took the bait and, explaining that he needed to keep feeding his kids, asked if his new friend might be interested in his services. The agent talked about the demand for sawed-off shotguns, and Randy agreed to make him two. When he handed over the merchandise thirteen days later, he did not know that the BATF was taping the transaction.

He didn't learn that for eight months—until June 1990, when a different BATF agent, this one identifying himself, confronted Randy at a local resort and offered him a deal: Inform for us or we'll nail you on federal firearms charges that carry a mandatory prison sentence. Randy Weaver refused to be a snitch, so six months later he was indicted for the illegal sale of two sawed-off shotguns. Although Randy had no criminal record, the BATF decided that he was too dangerous to arrest the normal way, by knocking on his front door. So agents posed as motorists stranded in an old pickup truck in the middle of the bridge on a snowy road near his cabin. When Vicki and Randy stopped to help the man leaning over the engine of the truck, the man pulled out a pistol and held it to Randy's head. Held overnight in jail in Coeur d'Alene, he was arraigned the following day and released after putting up his property as security that he would appear for trial on February 19, 1991.

Furious over the incident, Vicki lashed out at the state attorney general, addressing a letter to "Servant of the Queen of Babylon." "The stink of your lawless government has reached Heaven, the abode of Yahweh our Yashua," she wrote. "Whether we live or whether we die, we will not bow to your evil commandments." This family might be trouble, the attorney general concluded, and forwarded the letter to the FBI for assessment. Real trouble, the FBI agreed. They think the end of the world is coming and they might see Randy's arrest as part of the final battle.

So when Randy didn't show up for his trial, Idaho law enforcement officials were worried, even though neighbors told them that Randy believed that his court date was March 20, the date a clerk in the courthouse had erroneously typed on his summons. Nonetheless, on March 14, the assistant U.S. attorney had Randy indicted and asked the U.S. Marshals Service to bring him in. The Idaho marshals wanted no part of the case and turned it over to the Special Operations Group, a unit trained to deal with dangerous fugitives. They, in turn, hired a Texas psychologist, who suggested they try to capture Randy alone and away from his family. Otherwise, he said, he and Vicki might resist an assault, to the death.

Carolyn Trochman didn't know about the behind-the-scenes machinations within the Marshals Service. She just knew that Randy and Vicki had holed themselves up inside their cabin after they decided to resist what they saw as illegal government encroachment into their affairs. She and other friends and neighbors would occasionally drive past the painted plywood sign reading "Every knee shall bow to Yashua Messiah" and up the steep dirt road to the cabin to bring them supplies, especially vanilla ice cream for the children.

Even Carolyn would not have believed how complicated the Marshals Service was making the arrest of a man who had never been convicted of any crime, who had no history of violence and who was accused of nothing more serious than selling two sawed-off shotguns. They launched "Operation Northern Exposure" as if they were tracking a well-armed band of experienced soldiers. They mounted elaborate surveillance of the Weaver property with solar-powered video cameras. They talked about using rubber bullets to attack the cabin, or charting Sara's menstrual cycle so they could kidnap her from the shed. In June, on the basis of no information whatsoever, they began worrying that Randy might have booby-trapped his property with grenades and explosives.

The surveillance continued throughout the summer of 1991, and in October, the Weavers, by then totally entrenched in paranoia, asked neighbors to deliver the marshals a letter. "Your lawless One World Beast courts are doomed," it read. On March 27 of the following year, when a BATF agent tried again to arrange for Weaver's surrender, he received a curt reply: "Stay off my mountain."

When spring came, the agents set up an actual base at a condominium resort twenty-five miles from the Weaver homestead. Their new plan was to have two marshals pose as husband and wife, buy property adjoining the Weavers' and befriend the couple. Five two-man teams would accompany the agents on each visit to the Weavers' home, hiding in the woods hoping to catch Randy alone.

By August, the marshals had conducted about two dozen surveillance missions and compiled hundreds of hours of videotape. One more reconnaissance mission and they'd be ready to put their plan in action. On Friday, August 21, six marshals donned military camouflage and black boots at two-thirty in the morning, packed cameras, film, medical equipment, a sniper rifle, a .223 caliber M-16, a shotgun and a 9-millimeter submachine gun with a silencer into their car, and left their resort headquarters. They were under orders to complete one more surveillance mission "under cover of darkness" and to provoke no confrontation.

Inexplicably, they were still in the woods near the cabin at 10:45 A.M. when the Weavers' three dogs picked up their scent. Alerted by the barking, Sammy Weaver and a family friend named Kevin Harris, 24, left the cabin with Sammy's yellow lab, Striker, leading the parade. Sammy, a tiny boy not yet five feet tall and weighing less than eighty pounds, was carrying a .233 rifle. Rachel, 10, ran behind her brother, skipping along. Kevin had a 30.06 semiautomatic slung over his shoulder. Everyone was hoping the dogs had smelled a deer, and the thought of roasted venison brought the whole family out that hot afternoon.

But Striker had smelled the marshals, not deer, and as he approached them, one agent panicked and fired. Seeing his dog bleeding on the ground and an armed man in camouflage on the edge of the woods, Sammy started screaming and fired at one of the marshals, who turned his submachine gun on the boy, almost severing his elbow. Kevin saw Sammy fall and took aim at the marshal who had fired the shot. Urging Sammy to run, Kevin headed for the cabin. Hearing another shot fired, he turned and saw Sammy fall, blood pumping out of his back.

"Sammy's dead," Kevin told Vicki, Sara and Randy when he reached the cabin. Wailing and sobbing, they ran down the road and found his body. They carried it to the shed where Vicki stayed during menstruation and where she had birthed her children. She and Randy washed Sammy's body and covered it with a sheet in the traditional Old Testament fashion. They prayed and cried, then crouched with their rifles on the rocks, waiting for the marshals to come for the rest of the family.

Carolyn Trochman didn't learn about Sammy's death until hours after the news of the shoot-out had spread throughout eastern Idaho and western Montana. As soon as her husband John had heard—while Carolyn was still at Kmart—he and the other men in her family had taken their sleeping bags and left for Ruby Ridge. Carolyn sat in Noxon, helpless, until he called. "You've got to let me bring food, John," she said. She and the women of the family began cooking spaghetti sauce, grating cabbage for coleslaw and baking cakes. By the time John called back to give them the go-ahead to make the trip, the car was almost packed.

Carolyn had just stopped at a fruit stand to pick up a donation when she heard the news report of Sammy's death. She began to weep. No time, she told herself. This is no time to grieve. The announcer added that a U.S. marshal had also been killed, presumably by Randy Weaver. When he mentioned the type of weapon used, Carolyn knew the government had already begun to lie. Randy had no such weapon in the house.

By the time Carolyn arrived in Ruby Ridge, the U.S. Marshals Service, the FBI and the Department of Justice in Washington had begun to mobilize for the battle of Ruby Ridge. Word was out that agents were pinned down on a mountaintop, and the FBI hostage rescue team was called up. Within hours, they had loaded their equipment onto a private FBI Sabreliner jet. By dusk, they were en route to Idaho.

As they mobilized all-terrain vehicles, armored personnel carriers, tanks and scores of troops from the FBI, the Marshals Service, the National Guard and local law enforcement agencies, no one seemed to stop and ask, What are we doing? This is one guy, his wife and a couple of kids. They had convinced themselves that Randy had booby-trapped his mountain and that their comrades were pinned down by hostile fire. They had built Randy Weaver up into a one-man army happy to die in a conflagration with federal agents, and Vicki Weaver into a religious zealot who'd kill her own children rather than surrender.

No one stopped to ask what evidence they had for all their elaborate presuppositions. No one stopped to tell the leaders of the troops that Randy Weaver's son and his dog had been murdered. There was too much testosterone flowing for such reasoning to occur. Instead, the leaders of the FBI forces rewrote their ordinary rules of engagement and ordered their men to shoot if they saw any armed adult.

Saturday, August 22, was cold and overcast. Carolyn had gone home the night before to take care of the kids, but she was back early to cook eggs and French toast over a fifty-five-gallon drum. Her group—friends and neighbors and rowdy skinheads—was camped out three miles from the cabin. At the roadblock to the Weaver property, one man stood with a handmade sign, "REMEMBER: KENT STATE, RED SQUARE, TIEMINAM SQUARE, MY LAI, RUBY CREEK." Another strung up a piece of cardboard with a different message: "THE WEAVERS TODAY! OUR FAMILIES TOMORROW." As the troops rumbled by their encampment, Carolyn shouted, "Which one of you is going to shoot the baby?" She was haunted by the fact that Vicki's parents were due to arrive that day to see their new grandchild.

The FBI snipers listened to the Weavers mourning and praying. They watched Sara and Randy shut in the chickens, feed the dogs and fill plastic milk jugs from the spring. Just before 6 P.M., the dogs started barking again. Sara ran out of the house, then signaled to Kevin and her father that the coast seemed to be clear. Randy emerged and, with a heavy step, walked with Sara and Kevin toward the shed where Sammy's body lay. As he reached for the handle, a shot rang out through the silence and a bullet pierced his upper arm.

"Run, to the house, to the house!" Sara shouted. Clutching her infant, Elisheba, Vicki opened the heavy door of the house and walked onto the porch to see what was happening. "Bastards! Murderers!" she shrieked at the agents in the woods, as Randy, Sara and Kevin raced to the door for cover. Another shot rang out. FBI agent Lon Horiuchi, famous for being able to hit a quarter-inch target at two hundred yards—the distance he stood from the house—had trained his scope on the window in the Weavers' front door. His bullet hit Vicki Weaver in the face, severed her carotid artery, then lodged itself in Kevin's upper arm. His chest and arm were pockmarked with bits of bullet and bones from Vicki's face. Randy and Sara pried Elisheba out of her mother's arms, pulled the corpse inside the cabin and drew the checked curtains.

Only then did the FBI broadcast a surrender announcement to the residents of the cabin. By then, it was far too late.

Carolyn heard the shots, but it was days until she learned that her friend Vicki was dead. Word filtered out after federal agents planted listening devices on the floor of the cabin, which was raised on red fir stilts. Meanwhile, hearing the noise beneath their feet, the small Weaver clan became convinced the agents were planting explosives. On Monday, the FBI tried burning the Weavers out of their home. This is Carolyn's story; the agency denies it. In the morning they dumped fuel on the house, but the rain washed it away before agents could light it, she says. By then, her husband John was worried and led a cameraman up the mountain so that he could look down on the scene. Witnesses, he thought. Please God, at least let there be witnesses. In the afternoon, as the agents readied their fuel cans for a second attempt, Carolyn says, they caught a glint on the hilltop above them, saw the cameraman and quickly withdrew.

For ten days, Carolyn cooked and collected money and shopped and drove back and forth between Noxon and Ruby Ridge, dreading the news, unable to resist listening to it. She knew that the aroma of her elk steaks and turkey dinners was reaching the agents at their camp, which they had dubbed "Camp Vicki," and she invited them to share the food. They declined. As she and about three hundred others held an alternately angry and grief-stricken vigil by Ruby Creek Bridge, helicopters flew overhead, and all-terrain vehicles moved up and down the trails, running over Striker's corpse. Crews demolished the outhouse and moved on to the birthing shed. Fortunately, they checked inside before crushing the fragile structure. That's when they found Sammy's body.

Negotiators, who had been locked out of the war to that point, tried desperately to make contact with Randy Weaver. They sent a 750-pound robot containing a loudspeaker and a telephone to the cabin and begged Randy to call them. He was not that foolish: a 12-gauge shotgun was visibly mounted on top of the strange metal beast. The psychological-warfare types took over and targeted the cabin with floodlights and loudspeakers blaring recorded messages, directed mostly, eerily, at Vicki, whose bloody corpse, covered with a blanket, lay in a pool of blood under the kitchen table. "Good morning, Vicki. How'd you sleep? We're having pancakes for breakfast? What are you having?"

Carolyn kept trying to imagine the scene inside the cabin. She knew that boxes of canning jars were sitting on the back porch, ready for Vicki to fill with the harvest from the garden she'd tended all summer. No one would be sitting on the rocking chair next to the playpen on the front porch, looking out at the Kootenai River Valley below. In fact, inside the cabin, Elisheba was wailing constantly. Her sisters fed her syrup from canned peaches. Rachel played babysitter while Sara treated the wound on her father's arm with herbs and cayenne pepper and tried to help Kevin, who was coughing up blood. Mostly, the family hugged the wooden floor and read from Scriptures.

Finally, the following Sunday, August 30, Randy Weaver allowed Bo Gritz to enter the cabin. Gritz is a hero among the Armageddon crowd and had flown to Idaho to offer his services as a negotiator. He didn't know Randy

Weaver, but he assumed his name would have cachet. Gritz persuaded Randy to let him take Kevin out of the cabin. A helicopter flew the young man to a hospital in Spokane, where he was promptly arrested for the murder of the federal marshal.

Randy also agreed to let Bo remove Vicki's body from the cabin. The two men removed the 9-millimeter pistol still packed in her holster and placed the corpse in a bag. Bo solemnly carried it down the back stairway. Jackie Brown, a friend of Vicki's, was allowed into the cabin with buckets of water. She scrubbed the blood and body tissue from the floor.

But Randy, Rachel and Sara would not budge. Bo begged and pleaded that the feds were about to storm the house and take them by force. Finally, the small family stood in a circle and prayed. Then they packed a few things into small cloth bags. Rachel unstrapped her 9-millimeter gun and placed it on the table. Sara followed suit. They changed Elisheba's diaper and stepped toward the door. Randy emerged carrying his now motherless infant, his daughters trailing behind. As they were driven down the mountain, they passed a sign that once read DEAD END. It had been changed and now read DEAD MOTHER AND CHILD.

Randy Weaver and Kevin Harris were indicted in October 1992, and charged with murdering a federal marshal, maintaining a mountain stronghold for the purpose of "causing a violent confrontation with law enforcement officers" and organizing a group "unified in their opposition to the United States government with the terms 'Z.O.G.' " (Zionist Occupation Government). Their trial began in Boise, Idaho, in May 1993, and after two months, Kevin was acquitted on all charges and Randy was acquitted on all but the original weapons charge and the charge of failing to appear in court. He was sentenced to eighteen months, most of which he had already served. "You've suffered probably far beyond what the court could do," the judge said when passing sentence.

In 1995, the Justice Department paid Randy Weaver and his daughters $3.1 million in compensation for the wrongful deaths of Vicki and Sam, although they refused to admit any responsibility. Several FBI agents involved in the debacle were reprimanded, but the U.S. marshals involved were given awards for valor.

"People think that *we're* nuts," says Carolyn, sitting in the luncheonette in Noxon sipping herbal tea. The decor is early deer head and elk horn. Everyone who comes in greets her warmly. A few folks stop by the table to ask her advice. "We're not nuts. Awards for valor for shooting innocent people—that's nuts!"

Carolyn is a shy, sweet-looking woman with very long blond hair and very blue eyes. She talks admiringly about what she calls sturdy women, which is precisely how she could be described. No makeup, no fancy clothes, no nonsense. Her family motto is "If you can't eat it, shoot it or feed it, do you really need it?"

Carolyn is the mom of MOM, the Militia of Montana, a family-run operation which is the nerve center of the militia movement in the United States. Her husband John does the speaking and organizing, her nephew Randy runs the home office and the newsletter, and his father, David, takes care of their mail order operation. MOM was born in the anger of Ruby Ridge in October 1992, when John and 174 other activists gathered at a closed-door meeting to form a Weaver support group, the United Citizens for Justice. The Trochman family quickly became disaffected with what they saw as the explicitly racist nonsense of their fellow UCJ leaders and, in January 1994 held a family meeting and opened their own shop. During their first months in existence, MOM's founders toured Montana and neighboring Idaho preaching the evils of the federal government. They struck a chord with their neighbors, who had dismissed the notion of the government as evil enemy as claptrap until the murders at Ruby Ridge. They tapped into fears that federal environmental regulations would ruin the logging industry entirely, that the environmentalists would destroy their children's prospects for building a future near home. They pulled in the tax resisters and the "allodial land rights" folks, who believe that landowners should be able to become sovereign nations. They attracted the terrified and confused with warnings about impending martial law and the New World Order.

From their headquarters in Noxon—a town of 350 along the Clark River, hard up against the towering evergreens of the mountains—they spread revolution by fax, by Internet, by telephone and through an enormous mail order business. MOM's catalog offers scores of videos, audiotapes and books on everything from how to escape from a concentration camp to the latest theories on the strategy of those attempting to impose the New World Order. Whether you want to know about hand-to-hand combat, sniper training or claymore mines, you can order it from MOM. If you want to show your political edge, you can order a baseball hat that says ENOUGH IS ENOUGH, MILITIA, or a MOM T-shirt. You can purchase a dozen books and pamphlets that tell the story of Ruby Ridge.

Carolyn doesn't spend a lot of energy on theory. She's the practical member of the family. She wants to talk about action. "We're asking people to get educated, to question authority," she says. "Become an investigator in your own town. Remind government officials that they are responsible to you as taxpayers. Demand an audit of the community books. Look at whose land is being taken for taxes, and then look at which lawyers and bankers are buying it for pennies. Whatever is going on in your community, research it. Start snooping. When you get answers, take an ad out in your local paper."

Carolyn speaks from a lifetime of experience. MOM might be in its infancy, but she has been fighting on local issues for twenty years. "We had a drug problem around here and I went to the police about drug deliveries from Mexico," she recalls. "But every time they arrested someone, the judge would put them back on the streets." She finally went to the judge and called him a "worthless piece of shit." He didn't change, but she felt better.

Carolyn terrorized the local school system for almost a decade, demanding that officials keep parents informed of what was going on with their children and with their education. "I kept telling them I wanted to be notified if my children were getting into fights in school, if they were having problems, and they wouldn't take me seriously. They thought I was an overprotective mother. But if my kid was wetting the bed and hating school, I needed to know why. So I'd storm into school and I was constantly finding teachers who hated kids. So I needed to tell them, 'If you don't like children, get the hell out.'"

At one point her local school authorities discovered special education money. "They realized that the more special ed children they had, the more money they'd receive. The next thing we know, three-quarters of the kids are in special ed. But they made a mistake. They forgot to get parental signatures, so suddenly they sent home these forms and asked us all to sign them. Well, I organized the parents not to sign them. If they want to put children into special ed, they need to show us the tests and the results and explain why."

Then Carolyn got custody of her brother Donald from her parents. She asked to see his school file; the principal refused. She went to the county attorney and threatened to file a lawsuit. Almost every day, disgruntled with something, Carolyn would drive right to the school from the woods where she was working as a logger. When she finally pulled the kids out and brought them home to educate them herself, the school officials were so relieved that they ignored the fact that she refused to file any of the required paperwork.

"Women think home schooling is hard, but they need to take the time to ask themselves whether they are feeling incompetent or whether they are just worried about being tied down. You can't get discouraged thinking you don't have enough education. You taught them to talk, you taught them to walk, you taught them to brush their teeth. Why do you think you can't teach them to read, write or do arithmetic?

"I needed to make sure that every one of my kids knew how to think for himself," she says, laughing. Clearly she can't imagine her children—who were reading Phyllis Schlafly's *Child Abuse in the Classroom* before they entered high school—not questioning authority.

Like most militiawomen, Carolyn is a dyed-in-the-wool anarchist, although she'd never use the word. There's not an institution in society that meets with her approval. "Christianity is a scam," she says. "It causes more division among people than politics does. I don't like to use the word 'Christian.' It does damage because there are so many different denominations that all think they are right. It just turns into evil backbiting. I know who my Heavenly Father is."

The militia movement meets her high standards only because it is too amorphous to even be called a movement. "The word 'militia' has given people something to take a hold of, a way to think about taking back responsibility. It puts some bite behind investigating work. But there's nothing to join. If you're concerned with defending your own backyard, you are a member of a militia."

Feminism, predictably, does not meet Carolyn's standards and, ironically, she rejects the very notion of women's liberation—although her life might well be a paradigm of what Americans would consider "liberated" behavior. To Carolyn, it's just the way her daddy taught her to behave. She loves to tell the story about the day she came home from school and complained to him that the little boys were bothering her, lifting her dress up to look underneath. He marched over to the school board, but got no relief. "Boys will be boys," they told him. So her father, who had already taught her to cook (her mother taught her to shoot), showed her how to use her fists and her feet and where to direct them. The next day, a group of boys went home with bruises and black eyes. The school board called her father in for a meeting. "This has to stop," they told him. "I can't do anything," her father replied. "Girls will be girls."

Carolyn drifts naturally from that story into the tale of her first marriage, which sounds as if it is going to be more traditional: she met him at Bible camp, they married and produced three children. Then, however, Carolyn continues, she realized that he was never going to be a working partner, so she kicked him out. "If you run into a man who wants no part of working together, if he is not supportive of you or you are worried about the safety of your children, send his ass down the road. And vice versa."

After the divorce, Carolyn had three children to raise—Caleb, Joshua and Letitia—and no money to feed them. She worked in the woods as a logger and a skidder. Then she'd rush home to bake bread and cookies before dashing off to a meeting to raise money for a local ambulance. Finally, she met John Trochman when he stopped in Montana to visit his brother. They never dated, since John promptly went back home to Minnesota. But they courted on the telephone for more than two years. When John asked for her hand, Carolyn presented him with a checklist of demands. He had to agree not to smoke, drink or go to all-male Bible study, to show full interest in her three kids, to help out with home schooling and to learn how to square dance. "He wasn't taken aback," she says, chuckling. "He had a list of his own—but it was shorter."

When Carolyn flew to Minnesota for the wedding, she carried an ivory wedding dress with a hoop, a hat with silk flowers, a boutonniere and a bottle of champagne with her onto the plane. Shortly before landing, she gathered her things together to deck herself out. The stewardesses were so taken with her plan that they moved her to first class and appointed male passengers to help move her belongings. When Carolyn disembarked from the aircraft, John was standing in front of a chair in a departure lounge. He took one look at her and collapsed in hysteria, then kissed his bride-to-be for the first time.

Carolyn's philosophy is an eclectic mixture of ultratraditional and dyed-in-the-wool feminist. "I don't agree that women should have had the right to vote," she says. "I think it's a violation of family values. A woman's top priority should be her family. When her children are grown, she should be at liberty to walk side by side with her husband." She always wears a skirt, explaining, "God made me a woman, I intend to look like one—although I may not always talk like one." In the winter, she wears bloomers underneath to keep her legs warm.

Then, in the same breath, she breaks rank with what would seem to be traditional thinking. "Too many women allow fear to manipulate or control them. They need to work on their self-esteem. I don't need anybody or anything to tell me who I am, what I am, what I am capable of doing. I don't feel that anybody needs to boost my ego or pump me up. I've been a feisty, spunky woman for years. I don't see what I do as being liberated. I see it as standing up against injustice. You don't have to be liberated unless you fall into the category of being entrapped."

As Carolyn weaves through her personal history, her frustration with American politics and her hopes for social change, she returns, again and again, to the murders of Vicki and Sam Weaver. They haunt her—but less as a nightmare than as a responsibility.

"I'll never let them make me scared," she says, her voice falling in pitch and volume as she becomes even more serious. "All they've done is intensify my determination to expose the wrongs that are being done. I don't have time to be scared. America doesn't have time for me to be scared. I've gone way past fear. I'm just mad as hell."

A Digression into Cooking Up Trouble

By 1995, Chey Simonton was fed up with the militia movement. It wasn't that she disagreed with them, at least not entirely. But their research was terrible and their tactics were downright silly. A bunch of guys running around in the woods playing revolutionary was hardly going to reroute a country traveling straight to hell. So one afternoon, after a long conversation with a friend in Maine got her juices flowing, Chey went on the offensive with her own declaration of arms.

"I have been following the media-hyped concerns over the various growing militia movements across the nation," she wrote in a letter to her local newspaper that was also posted on the Internet. "I must say that the media is once again in the Johnny-Come Lately mode in accurately covering this movement. The REAL STORY is not about the men's patriot movement where a few GI-Joe-Style gun totin' guys get together once in awhile; the REAL STORY is the Kitchen Militia that has been called to arms around this nation since George Bush first acted upon his announcement to become 'The Education President'

"We are thousands of mothers and grandmothers-cum-researchers located in every state of this country. We have micro-researched every facet of the so-called 'restructuring' and in the process have become experts on the United Nations, the US-Soviet Education, Technology and Cultural Exchange Agreements, federal and state legislation (past and present), philosophy, sociology, psychology, and pedagogy. In short, if there is any program or agenda we perceive as a threat to our families, somewhere there is a Kitchen Militia mother who tracks it down and gets the word out on the grapevine radio call-in shows, fax networks, audio cassette, video tape or any other jungle drum available.

"We're not armed with guns. Guns are so messy . . . we have Congressional Records, legislation and official documents We have documentation to prove whatever we say and hoard quotes from air-head politicians like a miser hoards his gold.

"The media dismisses us as the Christian right; although Christians, Jews, Buddhists and atheists are all involved in this relentless research and dissemination. Our numbers include people in government agencies and local school districts.

"We are the most dangerous threat to the 'restructuring" of this nation. Remember the old slogan, 'The hand that rocks the cradle rules the world.' This is fair warning. The fastest growing militant group in this country is the Kitchen Militia. Our numbers swell every day, every time some new piece of socialist garbage is introduced that threatens our families."

The media paid no attention. The FBI did not turn up at Chey's door. Militiamen . . . well, they kept running around in the woods. But the women, that was a different story, Chey explains with a note of playful satisfaction in her voice. Her phone started ringing day and night, and her phone bill—already topping $500 most months—skyrocketed. A woman in Maryland called looking for information on the new superintendent of schools in her county. Chey just happened to have his Ph.D. dissertation on hand, and it was embarrassingly contradictory to every statement he'd made in his interviews. Female clerks inside the Beast—in state and federal offices—called shyly, offering to serve as Deep Throat. And Canadian women rang up to announce that they'd formed their own kitchen militia.

Chey had struck her chord. Thousands of women across the country—traditional women, established activists, homemakers worried for the futures of their children—were already reading and researching and pestering their state legislators. Chey had given them a name, an identity. But nothing else. No formal structure. No national spokesperson. No leader. No single issue.

"Anarchy," Chey brags to me. "That's what makes us so dangerous.

"We're the next step beyond feminism. In the 1970s, we all got that assertiveness training brought on by feminism. Now we're just as assertive as we were trained to be."

The ladies of the kitchen militia are the invisible revolutionaries of the new right. From their kitchens and their living rooms—between vacuuming, canning and outings with their kids—they comb through the resumes of employees of the Department of Education searching for bureaucrats with suspiciously liberal credentials. While their home-schooled children sit at their desks studying the Constitution, their mothers wait for the latest gatherings from their Freedom of Information Act requests. Their fax lines ring constantly with new discoveries forwarded by compatriots. Determined to uncover every seedy deal, every corrupt official, every striking paragraph of doublespeak, they are the most cynical and suspicious rebels in contemporary America. "We can't afford to be very trusting, very liberal," says Chey, the mother of two, who works for a roofing contractor in Washington State. "No one is liberal when it comes to protecting their family."

While they work, the women keep their shortwave radios tuned to Norm Resnick's broadcasts on the American Patriot Network, sent out by Worldwide Christian Radio. Norm is their Peter Jennings, the only member of the American media to have discovered this phenomenon. Norm—that's Dr. Norman Resnick—is a phenomenon in his own right, a retired college professor and religious Jew who hosts the most fanatical of the patriot radio shows. Hassled by the left (since he is an acute embarrassment to liberal Jews) and the most crazed segments of the right (who despise him because he routinely hangs up on any caller who expresses racist, anti-Semitic or sexist sentiments), Norm runs his wing of the revolution from a chaotic studio—a jumble of books and pamphlets and notes and aging equipment that looks like an underground radio studio at Berkeley in 1967. From that space in an abandoned farm implement store on the only corner in Johnstown, Colorado, that has a traffic light, he anoints the kitchen militia the high priestesses of the movement.

"These women are fabulous," he says, sitting outside the studio in blue jeans, looking like an aging hippie. "I'd rather face King Kong in a closet than tangle with them."

Norm's revolutionary goddesses are less popular in other quarters of the far right because they refuse to toe any party's line. They hate the Democratic and Republican Parties with equal venom. They deride the boys in the militia movement. They are social and political traditionalists in a world dominated by libertarians and Christian militants. And as fundamentalist about the Constitution and the Bill of Rights as Phyllis Schlafly and Beverly LaHaye, the female leaders of the religious right, are about the Bible, they are as likely to wage war on any of their so-called allies who dares evince a trace of disrespect for a literal interpretation of those documents as they are to storm the bastions of liberalism.

That means that they take a variety of positions that seem entirely surprising for allegedly conservative women. Chey, for example, is violently opposed to prayer—or even a moment of silence—in public schools. "Haven't you read the Constitution?" she asks, clearly rhetorically. "Do they really want to give the government control over religion?" Her friend Kelly Nelson, a Tennessee baker who is another four-star general in the movement, is leading a battle against privatization, whether of schools or tax collection. "You can't take services out from under the control of elected officials and turn them over to private, for-profit capitalist organizations," she explains. "It isn't okay to privatize things the government is constitutionally charged with providing. This is just a handout to Wall Street."

Their fellow kitchen militiawoman Anita Hoge is in Pennsylvania mobilizing the troops to battle tuition vouchers, another sacred cow in conservative circles. "It will just give the state more control over private and parochial schools," she says. "That's ridiculous. They already have too much control over public schools."

All three women are steadfast opponents of Pat Robertson, believing that half of his platform proposals would violate the Constitution. And despite the bill's popularity in conservative circles, they are working actively against the Parental Rights and Responsibilities Act on similar grounds. "Whenever the state begins to delineate your rights and responsibilities, you've lost some rights," Kelly explains.

They even break ranks with most of the right on the issue of abortion—not because they deny that it is murder, but because they worry, actively and regularly, about anything that will give the government even more control over the lives of the citizens. Chey, for example, is entirely cynical about the right's interest in abortion. "It has given them a tremendous amount of clout and brought them all too much money. I doubt they really want to win. It's the best thing they've got going."

In fact, the kitchen militiawomen aren't entirely convinced that the conservative movement—in either its religious or secular incarnations—is much more than a play for power by a few crazed individuals. "Everyone blames the liberals," says Betty Mills, one of the godmothers of the movement. "Sure they're a problem, but the bigger problem are the so-called Christian conservative organizations, people like Phyllis Schlafly, Beverly LaHaye and Paul Weyrich. They pulled in people who saw this nation going down the tubes if they didn't do something, then they misinformed, under-informed and noninformed them. Once people got in there, they were walking in La-la Land."

What's wrong with these leaders and their groups? "Think for five minutes," Mills says, impatiently. "If you do, you'll realize that these people have taken in hundreds of millions of dollars and hundreds of millions of hours of volunteer time. What have they accomplished? Nothing. Everybody knows that with that kind of money and determination, if—and it's a big IF—the leaders were sincere, this nation would not be in the shape it's in.

"Some of them are just greedy. Some egotists. And some aren't true Americans, but internationalists," she says, pronouncing the final word syllable by syllable to emphasize its evil connotations.

Chey, who describes herself as "pretty much of a conservative Christian," wholeheartedly supports Mills's position, but worries as much about the allegedly secular wing of the conservative movement as about its religious side. These days her personal research focus is on think tanks. "The American people need to understand that think tanks have been virtual shadow governments," she explains. "Politicians don't think for themselves anymore. As soon as they decide to run, they find a think tank that will think for them. They become the puppets of groups like the Heritage Foundation or the Progress and Freedom Foundation, on the right, and the Institute for Policy Studies or the Economic Policy Institute on the left. Who are these people? We didn't elect them. And if we didn't elect them, they're not supposed to have any power over our lives."

The kitchen militia has no fixed agenda. It issues no position papers and endorses no legislation. After all, Chey says, every woman has the right to disagree. The closest thing they have to a platform is the "action program" of the Council on Domestic Relations, a group founded in November 1992 to protect the Constitution because its members believe that almost all the nation's problems can be traced to America's gradual migration away from these fundamental principles.

"Good and honest government begins at the local level, then the state level, then federal level," says Jackie Patru, a Pennsylvania housewife who runs the CDR, and is a heroine to kitchen militiawomen nationwide. "A strong and constitutional Congress could put a halt to the presidential dictatorship which has grown stronger with every administration since FDR— and that includes Ronald Reagan. Putting our hopes in one man, a president, is a pig in a poke."

Jackie's action program is based on that same firm adherence to a literal interpretation of the Constitution:

1. Opposition to regional/global government. She believes that the United States has begun to cede its powers, little by little, to the United Nations.
2. Opposition to disarmament. She argues that the armed forces are being dismantled and turned over to the United Nations' "peace-keeping" force.
3. Opposition to a constitutional convention. A plurality of state governments have joined the call for a constitutional convention. Jackie and company worry that such a convention could lead to a rewriting of the entire document and the abolition of the Bill of Rights.

4. War on corrupt officials. The Council on Domestic Relations battles "pseudo-governmental organizations," which includes everything from think tanks like the Heritage Foundation and the Rand Corporation to the Council on Foreign Relations. Members are particularly vigilant to expose public officials who are members and supporters of these organizations.

5. Opposition to the Food and Drug Administration. "The FDA has become the totalitarian dictator over American health care to the point where they are threatening our freedom to obtain vitamin supplements and alternative treatments," the CDR says.

6. Opposition to NAFTA and GATT. The CDR challenges the constitutionality of these treaties, arguing that in them, the federal government has given up some of its constitutional authority to regulate foreign trade.

7. Demand for an investigation of vote tallies, which the CDR calls "VoteScam." They believe that elections have been tampered with and computerized tallying has made it impossible for ordinary citizens to verify election results.

8. Support for property rights. The CDR opposes federal seizure or control over private property for any reason, whether failure to pay taxes or for environmental protection.

9. Opposition to outcomes-based education (OBE). These educational reforms would shift the emphasis of education from the teaching of facts to the attainment of character traits and specific skills.

The last item is the major rallying point of kitchen militiawomen across the country, the issue that has mobilized scores of women to run for their school boards, to organize members of the PTA, get out the vote to replace politicians who don't endorse "back-to-the-basics" and pressure the "educrats" and the members of the NEA, which they call the "National Extortion Association." Educational reform is more a crusade than political action. "Rise up now! Rise up now before it's too late! . . . They're your children! . . . Your tax dollars!" orated Vanessa Thrasher, when she ran for the Southfield Board of Education in suburban Detroit in 1993. Thrasher was catapulted onto the campaign trail when Michigan educators tried to phase in OBE by doing away with nonpassing grades, dunce caps, the appointment of valedictorians and other traditions that allegedly promote competition; by encouraging cooperative learning and "self-esteem" education; and by abolishing curriculum outlines, leaving teachers free to map out their own plans for helping students achieve the required skills.

"This isn't education," explains Bettye Lewis, a leader of the antireform movement. "This is some kind of 'feel-good' program. Self-esteem is earned, not learned. We'll solve many of our social problems if we just give kids the academic skills they need to function in society. . . . A false sense of pride is more damaging than a low self-image. When our kids get out into the world, they're going to realize they're not as good as they thought they were." Marion Dalton, 67, a member of Grandparents for Independent Association, another Michigan group against school reform, was even more pointed. "This . . . is just one step toward communism."

The Michigan women came to the fight late compared to their counterparts in Pennsylvania, but then Michigan didn't have Anita Hoge to contend with. Hoge is a kitchen militia classic from a tiny town of 250 people in western Pennsylvania. The mother of three, she owned a day care center and an antique store, and served on the town planning commission. Pretty bland stuff. Then, one afternoon in 1981, her son, an eighth-grader, came home and told her about a strange test he'd been given in school, a test filled with questions about his social attitudes, his values, his religious beliefs.

What business do they have asking about his attitudes? Anita wondered. So she did the unusual: she asked. She didn't get any answers beyond the fact that the test, the Educational Quality Assessment Test, was standardized. So she kept asking, writing state officials daily, calling and pushing. Still no response. So Anita became her own investigator and, discovering that the schools were creeping into areas she believed to be private, filed a complaint with the federal Department of Education, charging that the exam was a psychological test that violated students' privacy and intruded on family matters.

Anita won, but her victory was pyrrhic. The state agreed to seek parental permission before giving the test, although they had already stopped using it—coincidentally, officials insisted. But the struggle prepared Anita for the larger battle that was just heating up, against outcomes-based education.

In 1989, Pennsylvania lawmakers and education bureaucrats began discussing how to reform the state's education regulations. For two years, they held meetings with business leaders, lobbyists and members of boards of education, congratulating themselves on their "grassroots" process, which they called a real "bottom up" approach. But when they decided to throw away all the regulations requiring seventh-graders to learn about George Washington and the Constitution and high school seniors to study advanced algebra, they never seemed to consider consulting parents. They never conceived of the possibility that someone might oppose a system that would focus on "outcomes" rather than a set curriculum, even though most of the outcomes were about attitudes and values rather than things like multiplication tables.

In January 1992, state education bureaucrats discovered just how drastically they had miscalculated. Anita Hoge and Peg Luksik, an antiabortion activist and president of the Pennsylvania Parents Commission, called together players from thirty groups around the state—taxpayers groups, Christian organizations, school choice advocates—and proposed that they unite behind a single overarching goal, stopping OBE. Peg defined the problem clearly and succinctly: Educators seem to feel parents aren't capable of teaching children values. "Frankly," she said, "the schools are not doing a very good job teaching reading and math. Let them clean up their house before they move into mine."

The new coalition members didn't disagree with all of the outcomes on the list of 575 mandated by the state. But they couldn't imagine why educators should require students to prove themselves able to "make environmental decisions in their personal and civic lives" in order to receive a high school diploma. Or demand that children demonstrate their appreciation and understanding of others by relating "in writing, speech or other media, the history and nature of various forms of prejudice to current problems facing communities and nations, including the United States," in order to graduate. And the notion of measuring citizenship with 405 questions—345 attitudinal and behavioral, 30 mathematical and 30 testing verbal analogies—seemed to them emblematic of an educational establishment gone mad.

Anita's coalition divided Pennsylvania into four regions, prepared an organizational flow chart and honed a series of pointed attacks which they would repeat at every opportunity: OBE doesn't work. OBE is too expensive. OBE is overly concerned with values. OBE will eliminate local control over education. The educational establishment, which had initially dismissed these rhetorical attacks as the rantings of a bunch of stupid and uninformed zealots, was unprepared for the reaction of parents throughout the state, who began demanding explanations of the new program. The bureaucrats had little ammunition. The program was, in fact, woefully ill defined. More importantly, no research existed to support the merits of the reforms they had decreed.

By the time Anita and Peg finished with the state education gurus, the number of outcomes had been whittled down to 55, with most of the values-related ones eliminated. Furthermore, the legislature explicitly mandated that the achievement of the outcomes "does not require students to hold or express particular attitudes, values or beliefs," which pretty much pulled the rug out from underneath everything liberal educators had hoped to accomplish in the first place.

Anita has continued writing and researching, her latest target being Goals 2000 and other educational reforms she is convinced increase the power of the federal government over the private citizen, and she has an army of kitchen militiawomen in every state feeding her documents, statistics and horror stories. "Let the men go play with their guns. While they do, we're playing with the real weapons: fax machines and the Internet. We're armed with real power; we're armed with information."

That is the credo of the kitchen militia. This is its prayer:

"Heavenly Father, grant us strength, direction, and guidance so that we might protect our children, our families, and our beloved country, America.

"Give us wisdom to awaken and activate our fellow slumbering citizens, so that we might remain a free people; a free nation. Open our eyes and enlighten us to the oppression and tyranny of Big Government.

"You are our Master, Lord—not government—We bow only to Thee, not Caesar!

"Grant us wisdom and courage to guard against all attempts to subvert, violate, or alter our Constitution and the Bill of Rights. Deliver us from compromise, pragmatism, and those politicians who would sell their birthright of freedom for expediency, power and control, and earthly riches.

"Grant us discernment enabling us to expose and defeat the dismantling of our American sovereignty as a nation. Instill in us a yearning for a return to our heritage, our identity, and a true understanding of our historical traditions that have made our country so richly blessed.

"Grant us mercy for obedience, not to deceivers and traitors in our midst, but to a Just and Merciful God we surrender and ask forgiveness.

"Create in us a will that tolerates no surrender to the Enemies of Freedom.

"We reclaim America in the name of our Lord and Savior, Jesus Christ.

"Amen!"

The Apostates

Pat Millette doesn't want to be a conservative, but these days she just doesn't have enough energy to be a liberal. Most weekends, she juggles two or three weddings and a few private parties whose hostesses have an annoying habit of changing the menu at the last minute. The guy who owns the rental company is notorious for shorting her on linens. And just when she's about to pack up the last truck with the day's deliveries, an inspector from the health department or the Environmental Protection Agency is bound to show up with some complaint about an exhaust fan or a sheaf of forms she needs to fill out to comply with some new federal regulation.

Liberalism was fine when Pat was young. It led her to sneak out of the house and head for the Democratic National Convention in Chicago in 1968, where the violence on the streets was her first concrete lesson in political tolerance. It motivated her to choose VISTA over the University of Rhode Island when she graduated high school that same summer. It brought women the right to abortion despite the opposition of people who think it's just fine to "kill the big ones but not the little ones—the abortion doctors but not the fetuses," she says.

Liberalism made sense to Pat when the economy seemed to be expanding infinitely, so everybody had plenty of money to waste on meaningless and wasteful bureaucracies and programs. It made sense when it still held out the promise of solving the problems that have always troubled her—grinding poverty and racism. So, like her father and mother before her, Pat voted a straight Democratic ticket, believing that she was supporting the good guys against the party of big business and indifference to the little guy. She even joined Women in Construction, a local group formed to expand women's opportunities in construction trades.

But no more. Call it treason, but Pat Millette has gradually, and grudgingly, moved dramatically to the right, along with several million other women who own their own businesses. Pat runs Gallimaufry Good Foods out of a cramped office trailer next to the overcrowded kitchen and shop where the business began in 1992. A small-boned woman with a frame that seems too fragile to contain her energy, Pat is virtually obscured by a mountain of invoices, proposals, recipes and messages stacked before her on her desk.

"I can't afford to be a liberal Democrat anymore," she says as she simultaneously converses, answers phone calls and handles questions from her staff. "I can't afford to support illegitimate babies, women who have five abortions and poor people who don't want to work. I can't afford incompetent saints like Carter. Right-wingers scare me. I'm afraid of the Bible-thumpers; they would put us back to where we were two hundred years ago. But I'm also afraid of left-wingers. It feels like everything has gotten out of hand."

Pat's desertion from liberalism began when she and her husband, Paul, used their $1,000 savings as the down payment on a small catering business in Providence, Rhode Island. Pat had spent years working in construction as an estimator and a painting contractor, Paul as a mechanical engineer. Suddenly they had to write their own paychecks and pay their own social security and health insurance. The mortgage payment on their house was due on the first of the month, but their clients—especially their government clients—habitually paid late. The price of food kept rising. The paperwork to prove that they were complying with city, state and federal labor rules, environmental guidelines and health regulations was so staggering that Pat wound up spending weekends in the narrow trailer that serves as her office while Paul managed the growing traffic in the kitchen. Then Paul developed a neurological disorder that caused lapses in his memory. Some days he'd be driving down the freeway and suddenly have no idea where he was headed. Other days, he'd be fine, but they could never predict when he might black out. Their health insurance was woefully inadequate. By the time they could convince the Social Security Administration that Paul's losing the ability to add a simple column of numbers constituted a disability, they owed $25,000 in taxes.

Pat suddenly looked around and realized that America wasn't in much better shape than she was. "Maybe I was just naive," she says, "but I had never realized how strongly the burden of righteous freethinkers like me fell on the middle class. When I was younger, I never realized that all that money that was being pissed away belonged to ordinary little people like me who couldn't afford to finance a bunch of programs that were more about building little kingdoms for bureaucrats than about solving social problems. It never occurred to me that each dollar spent to solve social ills or drop bombs was coming out of the pockets of every small business owner struggling to stay afloat. And it feels as if it's gotten much worse. That's when I decided that politicians were so busy being left or right that they were ignoring the business of the country."

For Pat, America's problems aren't simply the predictable litany of taxes, overregulation and an unbalanced budget. They are Americans' attitudes toward themselves and each other—simpering, whimpering self-pity and a frightening level of self-indulgence. She has no patience with whining and moaning about discrimination and lack of opportunity. She's bashed down enough doors in her own life to know how easily they can give.

Pat had little choice since, as a young woman, she was stuck with a husband not making much money, two sons and a set of career possibilities that didn't extend much beyond pink-collar misery. She knew that she could paint and draw, however, so she walked into the office of a local contractor and said, "Show me a picture and I can paint it." Nothing much threatening about that, and she began to make good money painting murals. Pat quickly discovered that the mural business, while lucrative, was pretty limited, so she decided to branch out. She learned to read blueprints and to estimate the cost of commercial painting jobs. She still lacked a dozen skills, but she had "a willingness to work for dirt" that got her onto job sites and into contractors' plan rooms.

The guys on those sites were less than thrilled at her presence. They complained that her perfume was a distraction; she countered that their tight pants had the same impact on her. The older Italian men who dominated the construction trades in Rhode Island thought she was kind of cute, but she never yelled, set up a soapbox to demand her rights or outside help. "It never occurred to me that I couldn't get what I wanted just because I was a woman," she says. "And I was turned off by women who were overly confrontational, and I still am. Lots of women have hurt the cause by running equality up their asses. That just puts up walls. There's a way of getting what you want without beating men over the head."

Pat won the men over by playing little sister to them until she began working on bigger and bigger projects—the painting of companies like

Pfizer, a tea bag factory where she and her crew had to work above functioning machinery without mucking it up, even a windmill on Block Island, which the crew painted while hanging in harnesses buffeted by the wind. She made plenty of progress, but her boss still wouldn't pay her what she was worth. "You don't need it," he insisted. "You're not a breadwinner."

That didn't last long. At home, Pat was doing all the homemaking and caring, along with cutting the wood and fixing the roof. She knew couples where the women did "women things" and weren't allowed to think about "men things." That just seemed stupid to her—illogical, which is the worst crime in Pat's book. But she also thought it was illogical for her husband to refuse to do "women things" while she was doing "men things." When he refused, she kicked him out and marched into her boss's office. "Okay, I'm bringing in as much work as you do and now I'm a single parent, a breadwinner," she told her boss. "Where's my raise?"

Nowhere, he responded. Pat walked out and wound up working for an American company on a construction project in Israel, where she met and married her present husband, Paul. When they moved back to the United States, she tried to play the game again. She fought the bureaucrats and the bullshit until she simply couldn't stand it anymore, and went out on her own. "It was never a conscious decision," she says. "It just happened. They ground me down. It was just like getting numb; you don't notice it until you can't feel your legs anymore."

Pat never even considered the possibility of sticking around and fighting it out with equal rights laws and affirmative action. Although she supported the idea of affirmative action, she'd seen too many of its abuses. "In construction, everybody knows women who are the owners of plumbing companies or electrical contracting firms who don't know a nipple from a pipe wrench or a circuit breaker from a circuit tester," she says. "The new hawk in me says, like in Vietnam, if you're going to do it, do it right. And you can't do it right if you don't monitor it." Anyway, she isn't the type to complicate her life when there are easier ways to solve the problem, and she despised the thought of becoming somebody's "token" woman. So, with no capital and no experience in the food business, Pat decided to open her own business.

While feminist leaders were busy complaining and litigating about hiring discrimination, glass ceilings and flextime, millions of practical, no-nonsense American women like Pat went out and dealt with these problems on their own, virtually unnoticed. They took the skills they'd picked up on the job, talked banks into lending them money or maxed out their credit cards, and became their own bosses. Almost 8 million of the nation's 22 million small businesses are now owned by women, and their number is growing twice as fast as that of male-owned small businesses. Today, women-owned businesses are the fastest-growing sector of the nation's economy, with an annual revenue of $2.28 trillion and 35 percent more employees than the Fortune 500 companies together employ worldwide.

These are not the small-potatoes, low-rent operations that women have historically run to keep themselves and their kids going when their husbands die or disappear. Today's female small businesswoman has an education, training and experience, and parlays that background into independence, a higher income and control over her life. For men, researchers say, opening their own shop is a business strategy. For women, it's a life strategy, a refusal to be held back by any glass ceiling, to be subject to the whims of downsizers or to be forced to choose between a successful career and time at home with their children.

Like Pat, these women might be caterers or store owners, but they are just as likely to venture into engineering, computers or some other traditionally male-dominated field. The top growth industries for women-owned businesses are no longer in retailing or service, but in construction, wholesale trade, transportation, communications, agribusiness and manufacturing. And they are succeeding despite the massive risks of opening a small business. Women-owned businesses now employ one out of every four U.S. company workers, and employment in women-owned firms with a hundred or more employees has expanded six times faster than in the rest of the economy. Their gross sales and market share are identical to those of male entrepreneurs, and their businesses are considerably less likely to fail than those owned by men. They are largely responsible for the fact that 41 percent of Americans with gross assets above $500,000 are female. At the current rate of growth, they and women like them will own half of all U.S. businesses by the new millennium.

Their role models are women like Nanci Mackenzie, who began to work outside the home as a saleswoman for a fuel-oil broker after her divorce. Antsy working for somebody else, she saved her money and bought half the business that employed her. A dozen years later she founded her own company, which buys gas from producers and rents space in pipelines to transport it to cities and utility companies throughout the Midwest and West. U.S. Gas Transportation had $131 million in revenues in 1995, making it one of the fifty most successful female-owned businesses in the country. What was Mackenzie's trick? "My role models were always women who worked," she told *Working Woman* magazine—especially her mother, who ran the movie theater in Texarkana, Arkansas, and gave Nanci her first job, taking tickets and selling popcorn when she was only 5 years old.

Then there's Linda Alvarado, founder of Denver's Alvarado Construction Co. and one of seven owners of the Colorado Rockies baseball team. Among the nation's wealthiest Hispanics, Linda began working part-time for a commercial development company while a student at Pomona College in California in the early 1970s. By 1973 she realized that there was no way she could climb the corporate ladder in her firm, or in any other construction outfit. "A man started in as a laborer, then became a cement mason, foreman and superintendent and eventually started his own business," she told *Women Incorporated*. As a woman, she knew she wouldn't have the chance to climb the first rung on that career ladder, so she decided she'd just have to skip the middle steps and go directly to ownership. "It was a radical idea for a woman, particularly a Hispanic woman," she acknowledged, and it seemed even more radical to the banks and other lenders she approached for start-up capital. Finally, her parents mortgaged their home to give her the money she needed.

But architects, owners and developers were just as skeptical as banks about a young, female, Hispanic construction manager. "I'm not the figurehead they expect to see," she said. "They are looking for someone who is six foot three." One day a developer actually leaned across his desk and asked her, in all seriousness, "Does your mother know you're doing this?"

Today Linda can afford to laugh when she goes to a meeting and a client assumes she is the secretary. Hers was one of two companies that built the Colorado Convention Center (an $85 million project), the High Energy Research Lab at Kirkland Air Force Base ($13 million) and the largest naval training facility in the country ($10 million). She and her husband, who has his own fast-food empire, have an estimated net worth of $35 million.

Female would-be entrepreneurs have read all these stories in *Women Incorporated, Working Woman* and dozens of other publications thriving because of them. They know that things have improved dramatically for women in business, both because of government pressure and because businesses have finally realized that equity is in their interest. At Barnett Banks, Florida's largest bank, a third of the senior and executive vice presidents are female. They have on-site child care and are reimbursed for child care costs incurred due to business travel and unexpected overtime. At Amoco, the controller, the treasurer and the group vice president for natural gas exploration are all female. At Blue Cross/Blue Shield of Massachusetts, 44 percent of the senior and executive vice presidents are women, along with 52 percent of officials and managers.

But a growing number of women just don't want to play the game, no matter how much fairer the rules have become. Why should they, when they know about Marilyn Marks, who as a 34-year-old accountant led a leveraged buyout of a trailer company with annual sales of $160 million? Or Ninfa Laurenzo, who started with a single restaurant of ten tables and built it into a fifty-one-restaurant food empire, parlaying $10,000 she raised from mortgaging her house, a $3,000 loan from a family friend, her ability to cook and five children skilled at taking orders, waiting tables and washing dishes into $75 million in annual revenues.

While the explosion in woman-owned businesses has caused a revolution in the American economy, it has provoked an even greater revolution in the lives and perspectives of these female entrepreneurs. Women who have always believed that big government is essential to providing a social safety net wind up furious at the government for interfering in the economy. Women who once trusted that the government would help them pursue the American Dream have come to believe that the American Dream would be accessible if not for the feds. Women who thought that Republican grousing about overregulation was mere posturing have suddenly discovered the costs of those regulations, and that many simply make no sense.

If they do business with the government, they are expected to file papers detailing their employees' race, sex and national origin, although they are forbidden to ask potential employees about any of these matters. They are required to lower curbs to accommodate people in wheelchairs, but quickly discover that those same lowered curbs wreak havoc on the navigation of their blind customers.

Judy Hooper, a baker in Evanston, Illinois, learned about government regulation the hard way—by becoming a target. In 1994, inspectors from the Occupational Safety and Health Administration showed up to inspect her premises after a disgruntled employee complained about excessive heat. The inspectors didn't discover any excessive heat, but they did find that Judy had not issued warning sheets about hazardous chemicals to her thirty-three employees. Judy argued that the only chemicals used at the bakery were ordinary household bleach and pink dishwashing liquid. Irrelevant, OSHA ruled, and fined her $2,500.

They also found that Judy had no written plan for emergencies such as fires and hit her with another $2,500 fine—although her first-floor shop has four clearly marked exits that had passed muster with her local fire department. And the inspectors wanted another $500 because Judy also had not maintained a daily accident log mounted on the wall, despite the fact that in the five years she'd owned the bakery the worst accident anyone suffered had been a cut finger.

For Karla Hauks, the nightmare wasn't OSHA but the Department of Justice, which filed suit against her and her husband, who owned a Days Inn franchise in South Dakota, for discrimination against the disabled. Karla thought they had complied with the Americans with Disabilities Act when they designed several rooms of their new motel to be accessible to people in wheelchairs. But they didn't read the fine print when they added a whirlpool in the basement. Suddenly, their two-story motel became a three-story facility and required an elevator—at $100,000. Okay, Karla said, we'll remove the whirlpool. Forget it, the Justice Department responded; we've already declared the basement occupiable space, so an elevator is still mandatory.

Anita Cragg's complaints are about another government agency, the U.S. Fish and Wildlife Service. In 1992, her company bought a subdivision in Country Cove, Florida, planning to build new homes on the site. She received the dozens of required permits, found buyers for the houses and was about to start building when several Fish and Wildlife Service employees declared that they had seen two scrub jays—foot-long blue-and-gray-crested birds—fly across the property. Scrub jays are endangered, so Cragg's sites were declared hazardous to the birds, and construction was halted.

The problem was that neither the Fish and Wildlife Service nor an independent contractor hired by Cragg herself ever found any scrub jay nests on the property. Cragg fought for eighteen months to have the construction ban lifted. Finally the Fish and Wildlife Service offered her a deal: Buy four nearby acres for every acre you develop to compensate for the potential loss of a scrub jay habitat on which no one could find any scrub jays. Price tag: $100,000.

Federal regulations are only the tip of the iceberg of the dilemmas the government creates for small businesswomen. One of the most vexing is the Internal Revenue Service's rules about independent contractors, which bedevil both business owners and the independent contractors themselves. The IRS has a twenty-point litmus test for deciding who is an independent contractor, which means a person who pays his or her own state, federal and social security taxes, and who is an employee.

The distinction might seem theoretical—until you open your own business. Arlene Kaplan, for example, classified the nurses who used to work for her at Heart to Home, Inc., a company that provides nurses for home health care, as independent contractors. The seventy nurses who worked through her agency were happy with the arrangement, since it provided them maximum flexibility to determine their own schedules. But the IRS declared the nurses to be employees, and demanded that Kaplan ante over $250,000 in back taxes and fines for misrepresenting her workers to the IRS. In the past seven years, the IRS has reclassified half a million employees and received $750 million in fines from their employers. At the 1995 White House Conference on Small Business, this problem was the foremost issue for the eighteen hundred delegates, who insisted that the IRS regulations were impossible to understand, inconsistent and unevenly applied.

For the 3.5 million women who own businesses based in their homes, the nightmare is IRS regulations about home office deductions. For business owners who would like to farm out jobs as piecework to women at home, the stumbling block is the Labor Department, which bars women from doing this kind of work. For women in every kind of business, from retail to manufacturing, the problem is the overwhelming amount of red tape that forces them to obtain, on average, fifteen to twenty licenses just to get off the ground, and to keep an accountant and lawyer close by to make sure they don't unwittingly violate yet another new rule.

"I never used to think about government rules and regulations and licenses and those kinds of things," says Pat Millette. "Now I have no choice. They run my life, and I'm sick of it." Pat is specifically sick of having to charge sales tax to customers who buy half a loaf of bread when she doesn't have to charge any to customers who buy whole loaves. She's sick of paying a yearly city littering tax when Providence does not provide garbage pickup for businesses. And she's especially sick of thinking about the $5,000 grease trap she was forced to install when she doesn't cook with grease. These experiences have pushed the lifelong Democrat into the arms of the very Republicans she has always despised. "It feels weird to be voting for a Republican," she says, "but I don't know what else to do. I just want the liberals out of the White House."

PAT MILLETTE is hardly alone in that dramatic political turnaround. Almost half of the women business owners surveyed by the United States Title Company in 1995 said that the government was making things worse for their business. More than 90 percent felt threatened by the required paperwork. Unlike women who don't own their businesses, they no longer see the government as beneficent, or even benign. How could they? Between 1989 and

1992, the number of government regulations they had to worry about increased by 34 percent, and their costs had risen by $130 billion.

The 1993 tax hike—touted as a "soak-the-rich" scheme—was a disaster for small businesses, which represented almost three-quarters of those who were expected to send extra money to Uncle Sam. Not surprisingly, 69 percent of small business owners say they took some political action in response. The Clintons' health care plan infuriated them, especially Hillary Clinton's indifference to the devastation that it might cause small business owners. Her insistence that she could not be held responsible for "every undercapitalized entrepreneur in America" cost her husband tens of thousands of votes. And the administration's veto of recommendations from the White House Council on Small Business—changes in small business expensing, a reduction in capital gains tax, estate tax reform and health care reform to create tax equity—was the last straw.

Small businesswomen have not limited the changes in their attitudes to the federal government. They are rethinking their positions on a wide range of issues, from welfare to abortion, as they are forced to consider bottom lines that seem to keep rising every day. "I absolutely, positively am pro-choice," Pat Millette says, "but if the discussion is about federal funds, I have mixed emotions. I'm definitely willing to pay for abortions for victims of rape or women with problem pregnancies. But should I be expected to pay for six abortions for a woman who is too lazy or stupid to use birth control? I think not."

Perhaps the most dramatic change is in these women's attitudes toward feminism, the very movement which encouraged them to think independently and self-confidently enough to open their own businesses in the first place. "So where are they?" Pat asks. "If there are 8 million of us who could use some help from loudmouth women, why aren't they screaming about the issues that hold us back? Sometimes I think they don't want us to succeed, so they can keep people feeling sorry for us. Well, that doesn't do me any good, and I don't know anyone it does."

If the Democrats have largely ignored these new female entrepreneurs and if feminists have likewise turned their collective backs on them, the Republicans have read the numbers and understood the potential. By the time the 1994 election results had been analyzed, pollster Kellyanne Fitzpatrick had declared small businesswomen ripe for Republican recruitment. "They have neither the time nor the desire to entertain Democratic allegations that the GOP is anti-woman," she explained. "They are busy advocating regulatory relief, fighting for tax reform and resisting compulsory health care coverage. They have found support for these stances in the Republican Party, which has proven itself to be the best friend of small business."

So Bob Dole dragged Susan Molinari along on a special series of campaign stops geared to demonstrate his concern for small businesswomen. The Republican National Committee blitzed the women's business community with a series of reminders that they, not the Democrats, were the party committed to cutting taxes, untangling federal regulations and getting the government off their backs. And their female congressional candidates—Helen Chenoweth, Sue Kelly, Barbara Cubin, Sue Wittig—most of whom had been small businesswomen themselves, hit the stump with a clear message: The future of the American economy is in the hands of the small entrepreneurs, and the Democrats don't give a damn about you.

FOR THE first time in her life, Carol O'Dowd listened, albeit tentatively, to that Republican message—which was not an easy transition for a former socialist and practicing Buddhist who still thought of herself as a kind of Saul Alinsky type struggling to give power to the people. Carol had started working for the Democratic Party well before she was eligible to vote, campaigning for Hubert Humphrey and rising to become the first female president of the Young Democrats at Florida State University. She had been raised to be a public servant, and the public she had in mind were the ordinary people—clerks and shopkeepers, farmers, retirees, factory workers and all the other assorted Americans who seemed never to have made it onto the Republican agenda. Carol's vision of serving those people was clear and, in the 1960s, clearly liberal: Wrest control over the country away from the monied interests so that free citizens could regain control over their own lives and communities.

That view of the challenge to America didn't change, even after Carol got her first job as a town manager and swore off partisan politics, figuring the job required her to be neutral. If anything, running Morrison, Snowmass and finally Aspen, Colorado, reinforced Carol's antipathy to allowing outside forces to push around decent and honest Americans. She remained suspicious of the wealthy, antagonistic to the powerful and committed to building communities. But when she opened her own consulting business in 1995 and felt free to reenter party politics, Carol did not head right over to Democratic Party headquarters. Her politics might not have changed, but she wasn't sure that the same thing could be said about the Democrats'. "We have an enormous layer of government employees spending their time deciding how people should live," she said, "when people should be making that decision for themselves. For the Democrats, the total solution seems to be government, more and more government. I'm not sure that's really empowering the people as much as it is empowering a bunch of bureaucrats in Washington."

Carol's suspicion had grown from years of coping with the massive amount of unnecessary federal regulation she'd seen as a town manager, and from her abiding belief that communities and neighborhoods could be more effective in developing their own solutions to whatever problems they had. She kept thinking back to an old woman in Snowmass who had not paid her water bill. The town was about to take legal action against her when Carol intervened. "It was crazy," she said, "punishing that old lady for not paying a water bill she couldn't afford to pay." The woman was too proud to accept a waiver of her bill, so Carol worked out a reduced payment plan with her. "That's the kind of thing you can do at the local level. At the local level fairness can be part of the equation. I don't think the Republican Party has the answers, but at least it is open to the possibility that government might not be the answer. They are willing to put on the table a serious discussion of what the role of government should be and to look at the issue of self-sufficiency in communities."

So in March 1996, Carol showed up at the Seat at the Table Conference that Evelyn McPhail, cochair of the Republican National Committee, sponsored in Denver as part of her attempt to encourage Republican women to become leaders, and women leaders to become Republicans. Carol was dragged there, in fact, by her friend Elaine Demery, president of the largest woman-owned business in Colorado. I'll just listen, Carol thought. Check them out and hear what they have to say.

"We are putting women in positions of power," McPhail told the 150 women sitting alongside Carol and Elaine in a conference room at the Holiday Inn. McPhail proudly recited the long list of women the Republicans had appointed to positions of leadership in the party and the Congress. "We are listening to women," she continued, citing Republican efforts to nail deadbeat dads, to fund child care and to change tax laws to make health care more affordable for self-employed women. "We have to send the message to young women, to seniors, to minority women, that the American dream is fast getting away from us. You need to be the messengers in your churches and at home, in your schools, at the grocery store, the country club and the Lions. It is the Republican Party that places women in positions of power."

Carol applauded politely. Placing women in positions of power was not high on her priority list. It wasn't that she didn't care about women's issues.

It was that Carol was still a radical—the kind of anarchist radical who seems to have disappeared with most memory of the 1960s—and thus remained skeptical about changes at the top, cosmetic or not, female or male. Hers was the tradition of communes and communitarianism. Old socialist that she was, she still believed that the problems in America were structural, and she was checking out the Republicans because, despite their reputation as blue-bloods, they had begun speaking her language. She chuckled at the irony that she might have become a Republican by default, without changing any of her political thinking.

Her friend Elaine, on the other hand, a lifelong Republican, applauded McPhail until her hands threatened to swell. Although she began her political activism as a Goldwater girl, Elaine cared deeply about women's power, which was beginning to make her feel like a poor stepsister in her own party. "I was born a Republican," she says, "and I stayed a Republican because I was always taught that that meant less government, less regulation, lower taxes. Logically that should mean fewer impositions on my body, but that's not what has happened. My party changed on me. The pro-life movement is so strident that they invite confrontation. They ostracize middle-of-the-roaders like me." *Also pro-choice feminist!*

Elaine decided to stay and fight to take the party back rather than to bolt, and she has become a virtual Republican missionary among Denver's small businesswomen, preaching the gospel that at least one party understands the importance of entrepreneurs, hoping that her recruitment efforts will swing the GOP balance of power back in her direction. Elaine had no small measure of influence in those circles. She has served as the president of the Women's Chamber of Commerce and the chair of the Women's Leadership Coalition, and is almost fanatically excited about all the networking and mentoring going on among women in the state. She is thoroughly enmeshed in the organizational frenzy that the explosion of female entrepreneurship has sparked, and every pore of her body radiates women's pride and feminism. "Absolutely I'm a feminist," she says quickly, leaning back in her chair, adjusting the fashionable hat she's wearing. Then, just as quickly, she backpedals just a step. "That doesn't mean I'm going to burn any bras. I'm not an extremist."

Elaine is a classic moderate Republican woman, an admirer of Christine Todd Whitman and Nancy Kassebaum. Ironically, that brand of Republicanism holds little appeal for her friend. Carol doesn't care all that much about the party's position on abortion. "I don't think it should be dealt with in the arena of government," she says, "but I also don't think it should define feminism." She cares about women's issues for the same reason that she cares about smashing the power of the federal government: because she believes that ordinary people in ordinary communities need to control their own destinies.

Carol was drawn to the Republican Party by its new face, not its old. While other women were rejecting the party because of their antipathy for Newt Gingrich, Carol was pulled in because Gingrich seemed to share her vision of reshaping government and decision making. "Participatory democracy is becoming a reality in this country," she says. "People are more educated and have more access to information. But elected officials are still twenty years behind. They still think, I'm elected, now go away, as if they instantly became more intelligent the minute they won their election. Well, that's the old role of elected official, the elected official as power broker and decision maker. We don't need that anymore. Elected officials should be information brokers who gather and disburse information and create networks. Newt understands that."

By the end of the daylong workshop, Carol was sounding more like a Republican than Elaine, but six months later, on the eve of the presidential election, she still hadn't crossed the party line. "I'm impressed with a lot of things about the Republican Party. They understand that they have to help communities to define what they think their problems are and find their own ways of developing solutions. That's important because it brings more people into the process. They used to think that the solution was big business; now they seem to understand that small businesses and communities are a major part of the solution.

"But Dole's era is a hard one for liberal women to relate to because it was such a rough era for women. The Republicans put women out there, but the message was not received, or received as a great show. They talked a good game, but it won't work with women like me until they give power to a new generation. Clinton may be an asshole womanizer, but he grew up knowing women are tough. The Democrats aren't doing anything that would motivate me to become active again, but the Republicans still haven't shown me enough to pull me in."

In the end, grudgingly, Carol voted for Clinton, but that vote was offset by Pat Millette, who, just as grudgingly, voted for Dole. They symbolize the tension rampant among small businesswoman caught between their own liberal pasts and their skeptical presents, between their fear of being branded as selfish and their conviction that deserting liberalism is not merely self-interest. Both women long for a viable third party; neither expects to see one emerge. "Nobody is speaking for us," Pat says. "In this country of 250 million people, nobody is speaking for women like me, women who own small businesses, women who are fed up that the business of the country is going down the tubes. Not the Republicans, not the Democrats, not the feminists. The new hawk in me says that it's all going to have to fall apart. . . ."

A Digression into a Posse of Pistol-Packing Mamas

Ishwari Silberman and her friends are plagued by dilemmas most American women can scarcely imagine. Should they jam their guns into the backs of their snug jeans and risk having them snag on their waistbands when they try to draw? Could they don shoulder holsters under tailored suits without ruining the line of their jackets? Would they be better off with bra holsters, or with those new designer-colored fanny packs specially equipped for guns?

Purses are out. You can't go digging through the tangle of keys, lipsticks, papers, checkbooks and Danielle Steel novels at the bottom of your purse when someone has a knife at your throat. What if a cigarette lighter or a lipliner gets caught in the trigger guard of your revolver?

And what kind of gun does the nineties woman carry, anyway? Gun salesmen insist that autoloaders just aren't made for dainty hands, even the new models designed for women. Women still can't rack the slides, they say, and they might chip their nails. But the feminist furies at *Women & Guns*, the holy bible of armed females, disagree: Women can rack a slide with the best of them.

What about the kids? How do you keep the little ones away from your weapons? Combination and key locks are as passé as storing ammunition in a locked safe. A woman can't be expected to fumble with a lock at 2 A.M. when she hears footsteps downstairs, and what would she do if the bullets were in the safe in the hall, and the rapist in her bedroom? American capitalism, ever inventive, has met the demand in the form of the Magna-Trigger, which renders a gun useless to anyone not wearing a special magnetic ring. Wear it around the house. Wear it to the store. Wear it to bed. Johnny and Mary can play with your Ruger all day without danger if it has a Magna-Trigger—and an assailant can't turn a weapon back on its owner.

Finally, who should you tell, and how, or should you just remain in the gun closet? Should women counsel their parents not to worry that they're living alone, because they have their old Smith & Wesson to keep them company? What about men? Do female gun owners announce that they are packing on the first date, or should they wait until they know the men better? After all, so many men still can't get over the myth that nice girls don't carry.

Ishwari knows that the gun control types aren't overly sympathetic to these or any of her more serious problems. The divide between women who are armed and those who find the notion of arming themselves as unacceptable as, say, ritual torture, or at least wearing a striped blouse with a checked skirt, is something akin to a cosmic light-year. It is as if we were members of two different species, speaking two different languages. Neither side can fathom why the other doesn't "get it." Neither side wants to find any common ground. As much as the abortion wars, guns divide women into mutually incomprehensible camps.

I found Ishwari sitting behind a Second Amendment rights booth at the Libertarian Party convention in Washington, D.C., over the 1996 Fourth of July weekend. The chairperson of the women's issues and information committee, and the director of the right to self-protection task force of the New Jersey Rifle and Pistol Clubs, she wore a bright purple dress under an oversized pink jacket. A striking-looking woman even at 47, her natural flair was capped off by a pair of trendy-looking, multicolored glasses, which turned out to be made for children by Fisher-Price.

Ishwari had started shooting for sport in 1969, when she began dating a man who loved guns. Now she's one of the rising number of women who are dedicated gun activists. As a shooting safety instructor, she promotes guns as self-defense for women. As a citizen, she works to protect Americans' rights to bear whatever arms they wish, in whatever circumstances they wish, as long as they are not convicted felons.

Liberal support for gun control so unnerves Ishwari that she can barely utter a coherent sentence that includes the name Bill Clinton. She becomes positively glib, however, at the mention of the National Organization for Women. "Why would I want to befriend an organization that says, out of one side of its mouth, that it supports women's options, then out of the other, limits those options to ones they approve of? NOW has become a group of independently wealthy dames who eat bean sprouts and shun a huge percentage of women in America and the world. They say that it's okay to be a woman as long as I'm on their side of the agenda. If not, suddenly I'm not a woman anymore. What am I then?"

Ishwari makes no sense to most women liberals. On this issue, gender isn't relevant: Gun ownership is unacceptable, period—no matter the sex of the person wanting to strap on the revolver. In liberal and feminist circles, guns are the problem, not the solution. They escalate the violence that has already turned the nation's cities into zones of mutually assured destruction. They endanger children. They don't offer women protection; they offer women increased danger. Listen to their spokeswomen: "The truth of the matter is that guns do not make you safer but will triple the likelihood of murder in the home," says Susan Whitmore, spokeswoman for the group Handgun Control. "Guns are not the answer. They make people less likely to take commonsense safety measures. It gives you a false sense of security. For every story of a woman using a gun to defend herself, there are many more tragedies."

Columnist Ellen Goodman puts it more succinctly: "If we want to live in a fully armed country, try Somalia. . . . It's more powerful to flex our muscle collectively than to buy one more .38 caliber piece of 'personal protection.'"

To which the gun crowd—which includes a healthy number of women who would like to think of themselves as liberals and feminists, if not for both movements' rejection of their stands on weapons—responds with a collective: Phooey!! In an Op-Ed piece published in the *Wall Street Journal* in the spring of 1996, Laura Ingraham, a conservative Washington lawyer and pundit who is the darling of the new right, applauded the fact that women are the fastest-growing segment of the gun-owning public. Mocking feminists who hold workshops "about how rape is really about dominance not sex," Ingraham suggested that bullets are far more effective than workshops. "If feminists are serious about ending what they see as the subjugation of women," she wrote, "they will shelve their political agendas long enough to recognize that women who choose to become responsible gun owners are, in their own way, feminist trailblazers."

Janis Cortise, a California physicist, threw down the gauntlet on her Web page, challenging women like Goodman to a duel over which side in the debate has the right to claim the word "feminist" for their position. "Those victim feminists don't own a copyright on the word 'feminist.' After years of hard fighting to break out of the manacles placed on women through patriarchal oppression, I'm not going to step right back into them now that a woman has flounced them up and put a new coat of paint on them. . . . Feminists . . . seem to think that women are at our most effective as Dead Exalted Martyrs instead of as action-oriented movers and shakers."

While the breadth of the chasm between the two sides is clear, the depth of the loyalists each side can field is more murky. The matter of women and guns is so contentious that the opposing groups can't even agree on the most basic statistics: how many American women own guns. Gun control supporters peg the figure at about 12 percent of the adult female population, with a third of that number owning rifles rather than handguns. Their sisters at the National Rifle Association—which has become a virtual women's club—suggest that the number is closer to 17 or 20 percent. But others believe the NRA is pessimistic. EDK Associates, a survey company that specializes in research about women, says its October 1993 polls showed that one-third of America's women owned at least one gun. The Roper Organizations begs to disagree. The results of their survey that same month gave them the figure of 43 percent.

If the raw numbers are subject to debate, the trend is not: women are buying guns at a record clip, and the gun industry is wooing them with a vengeance. Smith & Wesson launched a female gun line in 1989, followed by New England Firearms, which offers its own Lady Ultra, a .32 H&R Magnum, "sized to fit a woman's hand." Lorcin offers its Lady Lorcin in a pearly pink and chrome finish, advertised atop a copy of *Vogue* with the slogan "Not just another fashion statement, but an above average means of self-protection." And Taurus recently hired a company to survey women about the features they most desired in a weapon designed especially for ladies. In Massachusetts, twenty thousand women signed up for handgun instruction from the Gun Owners Action League in 1993, and twice that number applied for licenses. A new retail industry has sprung up, stores with names like Lady B Safe and Bang Bang Boutique, catering to the gals with guns. Shooting ranges and gun shops are flooded with women, and training schools have designed special all-female instruction weekends. In the early 1990s, fewer than 5 percent of the students at the NRA's introductory personal protection course were female; today that number is well above 50 percent. In 1992, sales of Smith & Wesson's Ladysmith guns, which are lighter than most handguns and have smaller grips, doubled. Today, female buyers purchase one out of every ten handguns sold by that company, with the average woman sporting a Ladysmith a relatively affluent suburbanite between the ages of 25 and 34.

When their loud insistence that all these statistics were hype—that women were *not* buying guns in record numbers—became a futile attempt at damage control, the anti-gun crowd changed tactics and began blaming the National Rifle Association and the gun manufacturers for preying on the fears of women for their own profits and power. "There are ironies everywhere when men whose professional lives have been devoted to eroticizing violence so that they can sell ever more killing machines suddenly find themselves trying to sell those machines to women," wrote Bob Herbert, a *New York Times* columnist. "It's odd, for example, to hear these worshipers of unlimited firepower mangling the language of feminism as they talk about 'empowering women' by giving them the 'freedom to choose' among the latest and deadliest assault weapons."

Herbert was summarily slapped down as a sexist swine by the executive editor of *Women & Guns*. "Were this not so insulting, it would be laughable— unsuspecting women dragged against their wills into gun shops on the basis of advertising claims which, almost exclusively, can be found only in firearms publications," wrote Peggy Tartaro in a letter to the editor of the *Times*. "The dangers with which most women feel uncomfortably familiar these days need to be addressed with more than paternalistic rhetoric."

Female members of the House of Representatives cast more blame on the National Rifle Association than on the gun manufacturers. They had said nothing in the 1980s when the lobbying group began looking seriously for female members, or in 1990, when they set up an office on women's issues. But in October 1993 the NRA crossed the liberal tolerance line with the launching of a massive public relations campaign called "Refuse to Be a Victim." Built around a three-hour course in self-defense that the NRA was offering for $20, the campaign was advertised in *Cosmopolitan, People, Family Circle* and *Redbook* as a public service to women, who were pointedly reminded that three-quarters of them would become the victims of crime, a third of whom would be assaulted, raped or robbed at least once in their lives.

When the campaign began, Representative Nita Lowey of New York and five colleagues staged a protest at NRA headquarters in Washington. "They are preying upon the legitimate concerns of women," Lowey said. "They are cynically veiling their safety pitch to get women to buy more guns and join their effort."

The NRA insisted that the campaign was not a membership drive, and pointed to the contents of the seminar, which stressed home and phone security, alarms sprays and stun guns. But the pamphlet promoting the program pictured actress Susan Howard on the cover saying, "Like you, I've felt the fear of being female in a society where violence against women has become commonplace. That's why I have refused to be a victim, and why I'm active in the NRA."

Ishwari dismisses the complaints of both Herbert and Lowey as idiotic. In her experience, women don't need either gun manufacturers or the NRA to convert them to gun ownership—and they certainly don't need women like Lowey, whom she dismisses as a typical liberal contemptuous of anyone who dares to disagree with the liberal mantra. "If the NRA is going after women members, it's because there are a lot of women out there who are interested. And manufacturers didn't need to go after women to buy guns. They saw an increase in the number of women buying them, and began marketing for their newest consumers. Guess what? I'm glad. I'm glad the NRA has enough

women members that people are forced to confront the fact that gun owners aren't all a bunch of macho types. And I'm glad that they are making
guns smaller and lighter. They're safer that way. Or do those people not want
our guns to be safe?"

Ishwari's and Susan Howard's are the modern faces of the NRA, what was
once thought of as the ultimate, and unbreachable, old boys' club. The
NRA's president, Marion Hammer, is female, as is the executive director of
the Institute for Legislative Action, the NRA's second most powerful officer.
In 1996, the top two spots in the election to the NRA board of directors were
captured by a woman physician from Colorado and a female lawyer from
Ohio. Hammer is old-style NRA, a woman who owns guns because her
mother and her grandmother did before her. The tiny, gun-toting grandmother drilled a rifle bullet through an apple when she was 5-years old, and
she expects her grandchildren to follow suit. "We're a family organization,"
she says of the NRA, "with family activities and family competitions. We
believe the family that shoots together stays together."

Her second in command, Tanya Metaska, is more the modern, tough,
postfeminist woman. Asked for the spelling of her name, the Smith College
graduate responds, "AK as in AK-47, SA as in semiautomatic." As the NRA's
chief lobbyist, she was responsible for the letter provoked by the Waco
killings that called federal agents "jackbooted government thugs," the letter
that led George Bush to resign his lifetime membership in the organization.
She opposes any kind of gun control whatsoever, even something so seemingly innocuous as a recent Virginia law that limited gun purchases to one
new weapon per month. "If I see two handguns I like, I now have to make a
choice between one and the other," she says. "Why?"

Women aren't just activists and lobbyists in the American gun wars.
They are entrepreneurs at every level of the multimillion-dollar industry
that is gun ownership. Sylvia Daniel, the first lady of firearms, is the co-
owner of S. W. Daniel, which manufactures everything from pistols to $5
adapters that transformed plastic soda bottles into silencers—at least until
the government declared them illegal. Sylvia offers no romantic or political
rationale for her product. "The bottom line is money," she told *Rolling Stone*.
"I'm just a businesswoman who happens to be in the gun business. I make
an honest living."

The armed female entrepreneur of the nineties is a paralegal from Ben-
salem, Pennsylvania, who carved out her own niche in the burgeoning
firearms subculture. Linda Mutchnick founded a line of custom garments
for the armed woman called PistolERA, "to signify this really is the era of the

woman-and-the-pistol, of course." Linda's pistol is never out of reach, even when she's in the bathtub. The stylish grandmother has fire-engine-red fingernails that she maintains carefully, despite the time she spends on the shooting range. Her clothing line features jackets and vests that are roomy enough to allow a woman to hide up to three guns inside them. The waistbands on her slacks and skirts are reinforced to support a gun and can be adjusted so that even a pregnant woman could wear them, at least for the first few months.

But the typical face of the armed female is not an entrepreneur reaping profits from guns, or an NRA professional for whom weaponry is a job. Most are women who have been scared and made the pragmatic decision that if they can't beat 'em—if they can't get all weapons banned—they'll join 'em. "It's no longer a question for philosophical debate," writes Paxton Quigley, the guru of this crowd. "The question is one of survival in an increasingly violent society. We cannot depend on anyone to protect us. We must do it ourselves. The only way is to acquire the firepower it takes to dissuade violent criminals."

Quigley is a deserter from the antigun brigades. In the late 1960s, she lobbied actively for passage of the Handgun Control Act, the nation's first antihandgun law. Then, late one night in 1986, her phone rang. A close friend was in the hospital, bruised and shaken, having been raped by a stranger in her Beverly Hills home. "Do you think if you had a gun you could have stopped the attacker?" Quigley asked her the following morning. When her friend answered yes, Quigley's politics took a turn to the right. The next day, she signed up for a firearms class. Now she owns Personal Protection Strategies in Beverly Hills, which offers firearm and self-defense training to women, and is the author of a best-selling book, *Armed & Female: Twelve Million American Women Own Guns, Should You?*

The women who are answering yes to that question are being pushed, inexorably, to the right by the refusal of both feminism and liberalism to embrace, or at least tolerate, their perspective. Now, as young female professionals network at the shooting club, they trade horror stories about the latest Democratic proposal for gun control. When they hang out in the locker room after club competitions, they share their frustrations over feminism's refusal to allow women to defend themselves. As they emerge from the closet in which female gun owners have lived for decades, they wear an air of proud liberation, with a concomitant edge of mischievous attitude. They know that liberals think they are buying into machismo, that they are using guns as penis substitutes. So, like black people in the 1960s who grew their hair into Afros, or gay men who parade down Broadway in drag, they flaunt their great equalizers, reminding everyone, with their bumper stickers, that "A Lady with a Gun Has More Fun."

In so doing, after a lifetime of identifying with other educated, urban women, they are traveling a road that links them with Lee Ann Callear, of Orofino, Idaho. "I've never understood why the NOW women love Mr. Sexual Harasser Bill Clinton and won't defend a woman's right to carry a weapon," she tells me, sitting in the bleachers of the local stadium, the mountains towering above her. "I mean, don't they care about what's good for women? It's clear that sexual harassment isn't and being able to defend yourself is. You shouldn't need to be some professional to understand that. Guns are the last frontier of feminism."

 PART II

The Old Faithful

The Holy

It was so hot when I drove onto the farm in an isolated corner of central Illinois that the air seemed too thick to breathe. The sun was so intense on the flat fields in early July that even in dark sunglasses I had to squint to follow the dusty track. I rolled past a motley array of tents and trucks and campers, following a steady stream of teenagers trudging up the hill to a natural amphitheater, and as I crested the rise, I looked down on thousands of young people sitting on the lawn in shorts and tank tops. Multicolored mohawks dotted the crowd, clashing with bright tie-dyed T-shirts. Young men steamed under their dreadlocks.

The night before, the lights on the stage below had swirled and blinked as the sounds of Crashdogs fractured the tranquillity of the rural night; the mosh pit just below the band had been crammed with sweaty bodies. That morning, however, the crowd was hushed. As I looked down on the scene, hundreds of hands raised toward the heavens and seven thousand voices became a single chant.

"Praise God from whom all blessings flow. Praise him above and here below. Praise him above ye heavenly host. Praise Father, Son and Holy Ghost."

Not everyone was packed into the amphitheater. Ten teenagers sat huddled together reading the Bible in the shadow of a VW van that looked almost familiar—as if I'd seen it at a dozen Grateful Dead concerts, as if I'd driven it to a dozen antiwar demonstrations. But the message scrawled into the mud and dust on the side of this one read, "If Jesus were coming, he'd be wearing Doc Martens." Dozens more gathered to pray with their parents or ministers. Scores of individuals wearing T-shirts with sentiments like WHY BE

POLITICALLY CORRECT IF YOU CAN BE RIGHT wandered quietly alone, Bibles in hand. A small group encircled three young men playing on drums. Their bodies brightly painted, they twirled and flailed as if high on LSD and marijuana. They were chanting, "Jesus is Lord of the Earth." No one seemed any the worse for wear even after four days of rock and roll. But that was four days of rock and roll without drugs or alcohol.

I'd gone to Cornerstone, the nation's largest Christian rock festival, to try to make sense out of what April Lassiter had told me about the spiritual hunger of younger Americans, out of a survey in *Swing* magazine that reported that almost half of young people attend church at least once or twice a month, out of the images I had of thousands of women at Christian Coalition conventions. I'd read the surveys. I'd studied the reports. I'd seen the pictures. I still wasn't prepared for Cornerstone.

"Do you have any interest in politics in general, or in feminism?" I asked one young woman. I'd headed right for her when I noticed that her hair was a riveting shade of blood red and that she had twelve earrings on each earlobe, a pierced nose and a pierced belly button, which was visible beneath her halter top and above a tiny leather miniskirt. She looked puzzled at the question. For a moment, I thought she might be too stoned to respond. Then I caught myself.

"Politics?" she asked in a tone that suggested I had queried her about an alien universe. "Feminism? Why would I need either when I have the Lord."

THE LORD. Until I got to Cornerstone, I'd never heard anyone talk so easily, so matter-of-factly, about the Lord. My parents were Jews of a post–World War II mind-set for whom Judaism was a history, an identity and a set of ethical principles more than a religious faith. And my friends and neighbors on the Main Line of Philadelphia, a community dominated by the ethic of understatement that pervades the American upper class, were equally divorced from any religious passion. Which hardly made them unique. While in comparison with Europeans, for example, Americans appear a religious people, in the suburban social circles that have generated the zeitgeist of liberalism, religious belief and spiritual longing are private matters. One simply doesn't discuss the Lord in public. It just isn't done.

When religion has surfaced in public life, in my view, it is inevitably formulaic: an invocation at a college graduation, a passing thanks to God at the Oscars, an actor praying as a device for clubbing the tragedy in some disease Movie of the Week. Nightly television dramas might focus, briefly, on extraordinary faith, but that faith is inevitably presented as a confounding phenomenon that some rational, sympathetic actor tries—usually without much success—to unravel. The only situation comedy to acknowledge the existence of religion seems to have been *The Beverly Hillbillies,* and Hollywood turns to Christianity either to mine it for triumphant hypocrisy (as in *True Confessions* and *Priest*) or as a springboard for broad comedy (as in *Leap of Faith*). In the creative communities that produce our entertainment, after all, the Jews and gay men who set the tone of the industry's culture are unlikely to be sympathetic to Christian complaint, convinced that if the roles were reversed, so too would be the disrespect.

Women of faith, then—of the kind of faith that structures one's life, that is not ashamed to be spoken—seemed almost exotic to me. After a lifetime of living and working in urban centers and on college campuses, I was more comfortable chatting about anal intercourse than about my beliefs concerning the afterlife. I could be almost blasé regarding the former; the latter seemed too intimate to discuss with strangers. And as a Jew, I experienced those few public discussions of religion I overhead, discussions that were inevitably Christian in content, as anti-Semitic, a witting or unwitting marginalization of those not much interested in Jesus Christ. Like most American Jews, I never questioned the disappearance of any sort of religious demonstration from public life. Why would I? It only made *my* life more comfortable.

A stereotype of Christian women was engraved in my mind, of course: narrow-minded, backward, uneducated. Christian women lived in small towns in the South or Midwest, wore shirtwaist dresses and were subservient to their husbands. They didn't think. They didn't question. They were Stepford wives in the name of Jesus. My impression of Orthodox Jewish or Muslim women wasn't much different, except that they lived in Brooklyn or some other urban center, and actually kept themselves covered, summer and winter.

So I was hardly prepared for Cornerstone. I could never have imagined teenagers going to a rock festival with their parents, or a rock festival where skinheads would party half the night but wake up early for prayer meetings. I would never have anticipated that young Christians would be so thoroughly imbued with feminist assumptions that they have become part of their everyday gospel. Those visions violated every preconception I've ever had about youth and parents and people of faith.

My first morning at Cornerstone I rushed distractedly past signs advertising new bands ("Move your bootie—a sound more powerful than Bill Clinton . . . faster than Carl Lewis . . . able to leap from a stage in a single bound") and missionary work in Latin America, past the Prayer and Ministry Tent en route to the Imaginarium for a lecture on Foucault, Adorno and relativism entitled "Postmodernism and Pop Culture." I dropped my notebook and a young woman in a T-shirt reading LAZARUS GENERATION COME FORTH and a young man with long hair, wearing a black leather jacket, a falcon glove with spikes and a heavy metal cross, ran after me to return it. I could tell that they, too, had been distracted. "What are you up to?" I asked. She pointed to a Bible. "We're centering ourselves for the day."

The Cornerstone kids could talk knowledgeably about music (their favorite bands were Jars of Clay and D.C. Talk, Christian bands that have crossed over into the mainstream market), the coolest sites on the Web (Sound Theology for music buyers, Pneumatic Launchpad for a regular chat or, for singles looking for mates, Equally Yoked) and the phatest (coolest, for readers over the age of 30) verses in the Bible (Timothy 5:2 and Corinthians 13). But they had nothing to say about politics or feminism or the momentous topics of America today, except for abortion, which they universally condemn as murder. No one could explain the difference between Republicans and Democrats (which, at first, convinced me that they were extremely well-informed). The only distinctions they made between liberals and conservatives were based on modes of biblical interpretation. And their eyes simply glazed over at the mention of the word "feminism."

So I was startled when I found Joyce at the Crashdogs booth. Crashdogs is a band, an important force in Heavenly Metal, and Joyce, who was dressed like a biker moll, is a groupie. She is also a tax accountant for a major corporation in Chicago. "Feminist women are really antifeminists because they want to take on the attributes of men," she said bluntly. "That's a contradiction." She rolled on with no hesitation, responding to my questions. She was different from most of the twelve thousand people at Cornerstone in July 1996; she was 49 years old. "There are wrongs that need to be righted, but affirmative action is the wrong way. If someone doesn't know better, affirmative action isn't going to change that. He only knows what he's taught. He has to do it in the Lord."

Something in the glazed eyes and pat answers she offered disconcerted me. When I asked Joyce about welfare, she responded, "Welfare keeps people locked in bad situations. Jesus is the answer." When I pressed her on abortion, she said, simply, "Abortion is not a God-given option." It wasn't just Joyce. Everyone I met was well mannered and polite, all smiles, cheery dispositions and pat responses. What's with these people? I wondered. Jesus as Valium?

If I'd ever articulated my position on teenagers, I'm sure I would have said all the predictable things about wanting them to be careful and thoughtful about exploring their sexuality, wanting them to think, to care about things outside themselves, to be polite and sensitive to each other, to avoid living in fogs of alcohol or drugs. But still to be young, to explore their identity in their hair and clothes, to sing and dance and gather in herds. Yet when I was confronted with those very teenagers, I was instantly skeptical. They sound brainwashed, I thought, forgetting that liberal responses to political questions can sound equally pat and practiced. I was almost scared at so much wholesomeness. Some of my reaction was pure, middle-aged cynicism, mixed in with confusion provoked by the dissonance of so many skinhead Pat Buchanan supporters. More importantly, this was the heart of evangelical Protestantism, and none of the assumptions I'd lived with all my life applied. It seemed like some alternate universe, as if I were trapped in a time warp and had returned to a different time line of America.

Then I realized that I *was* in an alternate universe. My framework didn't make a lot of sense because it was based on assumptions that simply did not apply. It was easy to be fooled by the kids' dress, by their earnest discussions of homelessness and hunger. They didn't seem very different from the children of my friends. Then one afternoon I sat discussing abortion with Jill, a junior at the University of Nebraska. She, of course, was immovably opposed. I began telling her the story of a pro-choice friend of mine, a married woman, who was then grappling with an unplanned pregnancy. She'd considered abortion, I explained, but finally concluded that she simply couldn't go through with it. Jill was mystified. "But you said she's pro-choice," she puzzled. I didn't quite know what to say. "Have you ever met a liberal feminist or a pro-choice activist?"

"I don't think so," she responded hesitantly. "I guess we just don't run in the same circles."

Which is the point of events like Cornerstone: to keep young Christians—especially young Christian women, for whom the consequences seem higher—in safe circles, far from dangerous influences. The organizers of the festival are the new wave of Christian activists, women and men who understand that the old fundamentalist approach to protecting their young from the evils and temptations of secular society is radically out of synch with modern America. Parents and ministers can no longer simply exhort young people to turn their backs on a secular culture; for better or worse, that culture is part of their lives. These kids live in the heart of the beast, so to speak. They shop at the mall, watch television, go to the movies, attend public schools.

Jesus People USA, the Chicago-based Christian commune which sponsors Cornerstone, provides Christian kids an alternative setting and an alternative approach to being young and devout. They never get hung up on hip clothes and language. They never try to convert them to the kind of studied etiquette that their home churches attempt to impose. Instead, they teach these young people that a repackaged version of the fundamentals of feminism—self-respect, pride and equality in the sight of God—is part of the core doctrines of their faith. They help them sort through the complexities of sex and drugs and God's will so they will have the tools to resist the temptations of the materialism of modern America, which they would call "fending off Satan."

"Part of us wants to blend in and not be different," Wendy Kaiser tells a group of teens and twentysomethings assembled on Saturday morning. "I understand that, but you don't have to live two lives, one Christian and one secular. You can't." She reminds them of the number of "broken people" in American society—people broken by sexually transmitted diseases and abortions, multiple pregnancies out of wedlock and divorce. "We're told that this is freedom. There can be no freedom without the acceptance of responsibility for our actions. You got to play by the rules. God wrote the book."

Wendy Kaiser is the Janis Joplin of Christian rock and roll, a member of Resurrection Band (fondly called REZ band), the wife of the band's lead guitarist, Glenn Kaiser, the Jerry Garcia of the movement, and a founder of Jesus People USA. She is not a lonely female star; Christian rock is even less a boys' club than its secular counterpart. She is one of dozens of women performing that week—Ashley Cleveland, Sarah Mason, Leigh Nash of Sixpence None the Richer. On stage, with her disheveled and wild red hair, Wendy looks as if she could comfortably trade places with Melissa Etheridge or Joan Osborne. It is highly unlikely. Wendy, 43 and the mother of three kids, defines her singing as ministry.

"You don't have to deny that you are a sexual being," she tells the group of seventy-five young people crowded into the tent during the time set aside for seminars. "But you don't have to glorify your sexual feelings either." Wendy, wearing oversized red sunglasses and bermuda shorts, is talking about sex, but she never strays far from the topics of equality, responsibility, dignity and self-respect. Without ever mentioning the words, she is preaching feminism as an integral part of Christian life. Her audience is an eclectic mélange of skinheads, white breads and hippies, and they hang on Wendy's every word, taking notes and following along in her study guide. Couples trade gazes and glances and comments as Wendy speaks, clearly anxious for a blueprint that is both Christian and modern.

"Sex without commitment is very dull," she continues. "It lasts for five seconds or so." Wendy's advice is clear and concise: Don't date anyone who isn't a Christian. Figure out in advance how to control your passion by avoiding temptation and by setting limits on physical affection so that you'll know what to do if someone knocks your socks off. Take an abstinence pledge; write it down, sign it, date it and ask someone you respect to witness it.

Wendy serves herself up as a living testimonial to the dangers of the world outside the narrow confines of Christian America. "Before I became a Christian, I was very promiscuous," she tells them. "I led an immoral, self-destructive lifestyle. I was desperately looking for love. I sold myself very cheaply. Even when I began to accept Jesus, I'd be sitting in a prayer meeting and I would be praying about sexual fantasies and masturbation. Satan kept telling me that I was damaged goods. I believed him."

The young people can hardly imagine Wendy's tale. They have never known a teen like Wendy, "the teen from hell," as she describes herself. By the time she reached high school, Wendy was drinking, popping uppers and downers and stopping by bars to pick up anyone, male or female, who would make her feel loved. "I wanted to be brash and bold," she told me later. "I smoked a cigar. I wanted to show them, 'I can outdrink you, I can outfuck you.' I knew I was lost. I didn't know how to go back."

Then one night, in a Christian coffeehouse in Wisconsin, a fat old hippie with red hair and a beard turned to Wendy and said, "No matter what you've done, no matter what has been done to you, you can be clean, like a child." Wendy ran to the bathroom and began to cry. She made a one-year commitment to trying it "God's way." She flailed and rebelled even then, showing up at Bible study in hot pants and coming on to every man in the room.

Then she met Glenn Kaiser, who was hardly her romantic fantasy. He was wearing polyester jeans that were too short, white socks and a bowling shirt, carrying a Bible and singing Ricky Nelson and Bobby Darin songs. Man, this guy is too weird, she thought. But Glenn, who'd also clawed his way back from drug and alcohol abuse, had a vision of ministry that would reach out to the young people he and Wendy had been. He shared Wendy's vision of a Christian community. He was "a feminist in the sense that he never thought he was better than I was. He never lusted or condescended. He wasn't a wimp but he was never coarse or disrespectful."

On the first night of their honeymoon, before going to bed, Glenn got down on his knees and asked God to make him and Wendy one sexually. Twenty-five years later, he still says that prayer.

As Wendy takes time out from the frenzied rhythms of the festival to tell me her story, we're interrupted constantly by a stream of young people with questions and problems. Finally, one young man comes into the trailer that serves as the Cornerstone office, clearly shaken. He's just heard that birth control pills are being used to induce abortions. He doesn't know what to do. "We've lost our soul," Wendy says, wearily. She's been singing and praying and holding hands with others for five days. She is so hoarse that she sounds sultry, even talking about abortion. "If you can abort a child at eight months, why not abuse a child at three years? Life has been devalued." She prays with the boy and guides him to the Rock for Life booth on the festival grounds.

Wendy and Glenn straddle two worlds. They are still Jesus Freaks, living collectively in Chicago—feeding the poor, sheltering the battered and ministering on the streets. But they've also battled their way to some level of acceptance in mainstream churches by insisting, quietly, "Okay, so we have long hair and you don't like our music, but we love the Lord." Cornerstone is their dream, a place where they can reach out to teens in their own vernacular. "These kids don't know right from wrong," Wendy says. "No one has ever given them any rules. Everyone just tells them to work it out for themselves. Even if they're part of a church, they get the message that they have to find their own way. Somebody has to talk to them. That's what Cornerstone is about."

Although Wendy lives in a remarkably self-contained world, she's entirely up to speed on the standard texts of feminism, from Susan Brownmiller to Germaine Greer. She knows what she's supposed to think about women's roles and has found her own way to incorporate feminism into her belief system, a clear—if unacknowledged—example of how the women's movement has insinuated itself even into a world that has allegedly rejected it.

On the one hand, Wendy says: "Feminism doesn't speak to Christian women because we know we are equal where it counts, in the eyes of the Lord." On the other, she adds: "This is a terrific time to be a Christian woman because we are a more respected voice than ever. Women are now collaborators, not just housewives who go to prayer meetings on Wednesdays. Women can be involved in everything. There is still a problem in some of the older churches, but if a woman is having a problem, she should just go to a different church.

"But the problems women face today aren't in the churches, and they're not problems feminists are doing a very good job addressing. The problem is that half have to make it on their own while raising their children. There are only twenty-four hours in a day and women have to be breadwinners, spiritual leaders and parents. They are endangered economically and less respected than women used to be. Men don't walk outdoors and look around to see if anyone is about to rape them. It's dangerous out there for women."

ELIZABETH HOLSCHER has never heard the name Wendy Kaiser. In fact, she's never heard rock music, and she knows nothing about the dangers of the outside world that worry Wendy so deeply. Her home sits right on the road in Hobart, New York, but it's the kind of road that seems heavily trafficked if four cars pass in an hour—and the town is six miles away. There's a television set in the living room, but it's only turned on when her parents have a new video they want her, her brother and three sisters to watch. Behind the house there's a small chapel, where her father holds services on Sunday mornings, but it's a rare Sunday that more than two dozen people show up. Her schoolhouse is the kitchen table, the living room, the barn and the pond. Her schoolmates are her brothers and sisters. Her teacher is her mother, the Christian female role model to which Wendy Kaiser is a dramatic alternative.

When Elizabeth was born her parents, Linda and Dave, checked out the public school. They visited the Christian school. Then they looked at each other and decided that God was calling them in a different direction. "We wanted to have her in the best possible environment morally and spiritually," Linda says. "Home schooling was the best option. Only later did we realize that it was also the best option educationally."

Linda and I relax at the kitchen table, which looks out over what I think of as a quiet view, a view of gently rolling hills and old stone walls. Their spaniel, Emma, races in and out of the kitchen. Linda is always a tad distracted, keeping one ear tuned to the upstairs, where the baby is sleeping. Her older children have just finished work on a unit about animal reproduction and care, and the younger ones have made themselves cups of tea and are playing under a blanket they've made into a tent. Elizabeth and her sister Claire don't budge from the table. They never do, always eager to be included in the conversation. "Their grandparents were concerned about socialization," Linda continues. "That's just not a problem. Socialization is about training children to get along with other people, about being kind and cooperative. You don't accomplish that by putting a large number of little children together in a room for six hours a day where they meet other kids who are mean, or intolerant, or talk bad. We have the privilege of having a big family, so they learn from each other not to be selfish, to cooperate, to talk kindly to other people.

"When we send the children out, it's to the right environment with the right children. We pick the situation and we pick their companions."

Wendy Kaiser does damage control, almost full-time, trying to protect children who live in cities where they hear people cursing on the streets and where they see women dressed in slinkily seductive outfits. Ultimately, of course, they cannot be protected; the best Wendy can do is to provide them with some armor. Linda and Dave, on the other hand, have created a permanent "safe space." Their children might have some vague concept of the world that lies beyond the borders of their farm, but it is as distant from them as the reign of terror in Bosnia or starvation in Zaire. It has no power over them. Which is precisely the point.

Both Linda and Dave grew up in Christian families, but they studied in public schools in New England and the University of Connecticut, and bear scars from the experience. Dave suffered from being a religious outcast in a secular society where Jesus wasn't cool. Linda was seduced by that world, running with the wrong crowd in high school, a crowd that was into drugs and alcohol and that, in her mind, led her astray. By college, however, both were committed to following the path of the Lord, and for the first few years after they graduated and married, they worked full-time for Campus Crusade for Christ. Then they began working with a church called the Kingdom, and were sent to rural New York. "We don't want to shut out the rest of the world, but our lives are given to the Lord to be where he wants us to be. It doesn't always make sense to us. But we have to trust that this is where God wants us to be."

Linda and Dave are my closest neighbors, residents of a farm marked with a sign announcing the Chapel of the Good Shepherd. Twelve-year-old Elizabeth calls when they have extra eggs, offering to leave them in my mailbox. If the family stops by to visit, they always bring homemade bread. The children never interrupt when adults are having a conversation, but when there's a lull, they are always ready with a question or comment—usually a question. They're intensely curious, and, to them, I'm extremely exotic. But when I drive down the road to town in the summer, I see them swinging on a rope across the pond or chasing the dog. They are extremely polite and respectful Christian children. But they still are kids.

Linda has not had a free day in more than twelve years. "When they were younger, it was overwhelming," she says, laughing at the memory. "The diapers would be piling up, I was teaching Elizabeth to read and the house was a mess. I said to Dave, 'Do you think I can do this?' " Dave found a high school girl from their church to help out once a week with the cleaning. He took over the grocery shopping himself. Now that the children are older, Linda says, her life feels easy. "Easy" means giving lessons in science or history to the four older children, working with each one individually on grammar or math, taking care of two babies, doing the laundry, washing the dishes and baking the bread. Yet she is obviously puzzled when I ask her about the sacrifices she is making to raise her children well. For me, a secular Jew, sacrifice is a negative. The concept of sacrifice was the basis for much of modern feminism, a rebellion against everything women were blithely expected to give up. Linda has a different take on the word. She is proud of her sacrifices because, in her value system, they are ennobling.

"Motherhood does have its sacrifices," she says. "Putting your family first always does. The baby cries in the middle of the night and you have to get up when you'd rather sleep. When you care for people, it's always a sacrifice. But as Christians we understand that our life is a sacrifice, a sacrifice unto God. You think about what the Lord has done for you, and you realize that no sacrifice is so great as the sacrifice he made for you."

Linda knows the basics of feminism, which would have been hard to avoid at a large public university in the middle of Connecticut. "It was out there, in the air," she explains. "And I learned about it in class, depending on the professor. With some professors you got all kinds of junk. I call it junk, as opposed to the truth." But it made absolutely no impact on her. She doesn't condemn the movement. She doesn't discuss the positives and negatives of its impact on American society. She simply doesn't think about it. She understood full well that feminism, and the world it implies, was an option open to her. She just rejected it as irrelevant. "Feminists think they can make their own rules," she says. "I know I can't. I didn't write the book." The only comment she makes about feminists themselves is, "I feel bad for them. They're missing out on something special God has for them."

Dave misses the lively action of campus life and missionary work, but Linda is happy with the isolation for her children's sake. "I'm glad we're living in a situation like this where the children aren't exposed to all the decadence. They don't see people dressed, uh, illy, or hear them swear. I'm filling them up with the right things now so that they will be firmly planted when they go out into the world."

*　　　*　　　*

FOR MOST of the nation's history, America was a comfortable place for women like Linda, for fundamentalist and evangelical Christians. John Winthrop's declaration that the new land would be God's land, his "City on the Hill," marked America with such a strong sense of its own destiny that for generations the nation remained unembarrassed by its collective belief in a national higher calling. That higher calling allowed Christian conservatives to maintain the illusion that even in their involvement in civic affairs, they were not being distracted from their service to God, since the glory of America was the glory of the Lord and his work.

Dissident voices and ungodly realities, from prostitution to alcohol, blemished the holy horizon, but Satan seemed comfortably at bay until 1920, when he landed in Tennessee in the form of Clarence Darrow, and banished truth from the public schools at the Scopes trial. The introduction of Charles Darwin and his theories of evolution was proof that America was turning its back on the first book of the only constitution that counted, on Genesis and the Bible. The nation's fundamentalist community retreated into isolation, rededicating itself to its higher purpose. Yet despite their complaints about persecution (and who in America hasn't lodged such complaints?) and the godlessness of the nation, their children prayed and learned Old Testament values in public schools. Communities celebrated Christmas together in public, and those who chose to reject Christian teachings were cowed into shutting up and allowing America to be a Christian nation.

By the 1970s, however, the shoe was decidedly on the other foot. It was conservative Christians who were expected to shut up and allow America to be a secular nation. Most did, and they withdrew into a parallel universe of educational, economic and political institutions that would bolster their worldview in a nation that was increasingly disrespectful of, if not downright hostile, to them. So while most Americans sit and watch the latest hit sitcom in the evening, conservative Christians turn to the Family Channel, to Pat Robertson's Christian Broadcasting Network, to *Faith & Values* or to the programming of one of the nation's 163 religious television stations—or, like Linda, watch nothing at all. When secular Americans are troubled, they turn to their therapists or to hundreds of self-help guides that crowd the shelves of the bookstores in their local malls. Christians—an estimated 5 million weekly—tune in to *Focus on the Family* for advice and guidance from Christian psychologist James Dobson, or simply pray for divine guidance. For news on culture and politics, they read *Christianity Today* while their neighbors read *Time* and *Newsweek*. Their children subscribe to *Teen Power* instead of *Seventeen*. And the computer-savvy log on to dozens of Web sites, from Christianity Online to the home pages of hundreds of individual churches.

This world is virtually invisible to most Americans, who still think of conservative Christians as uneducated rubes. Few have wandered through any of the seven thousand Christian bookstores in the nation—with annual sales of about $3 billion. Fewer still know how popular Christian books are, because sales by Christian bookstores aren't counted when the *New York Times,* for example, compiles its best-seller list. Yet an author like Frank Peretti, who writes on spiritual warfare, has sold more than 5 million copies of a single book, which would put him at the top of those charts. The music scene of Cornerstone is part of a contemporary Christian music industry worth about $750 million a year, and it has begun to produce crossover stars like Amy Grant and Jars of Clay. Entrepreneurs have tapped this market with Christian aerobic workout tapes and Christian clothing catalogs, born-again advertising guides and travel agencies.

But secession had a downside: It weakened Christian influence over America culture and politics still further, at the very time that secular influence became harder and harder to avoid, and the sense that something had gone terribly wrong in America became harder and harder to deny. Children couldn't keep Bibles on their desks in schools, high school clinics were handing out condoms, homosexuals were paraded before the public as normal, television was teaching children disrespect for authority and women's nude bodies were being displayed even on small-town movie screens. As violence, drugs and sexual freedom began threatening their communities, a potential army of fundamentalists fulminated, but they were paralyzed—politically disorganized and culturally marginalized. "They couldn't fight back," explains Thomas Fleming, editor of *Chronicles.* "Jerkwater America didn't have the education, the wealth, or the power to do battle with the great cultural institutions."

Fundamentalist rebellion did erupt from time to time, but in isolated pockets of the country, and without much organization. When the Supreme Court outlawed prayer in public schools in 1962, Christian parents felt assaulted and threw their weight, helter-skelter, behind Barry Goldwater and his vision of recapturing American greatness. In the 1970s, parents in West Virginia stormed local school boards demanding the burning of ungodly textbooks. But without a plan, an overarching vision of how to take back the nation, Christian conservatives had little choice but to retreat, to isolate themselves even further into an almost underground society.

Then, men like Jerry Falwell declared that there was no higher calling

than regaining America for God and Jesus, and seized the moment to organize an army of the faithful to battle against Mammon. They organized ministers, community leaders and Christians convinced they were struggling
against the Antichrist for their rightful place of influence in the secular
world. At first, Christian women were loath to turn their backs on tradition
and family to enter the sordid world of politics. But they were emboldened
by a proud history of activism that had catapulted women like them to the
forefront of earlier struggles, and they were ignited by what they saw as a
direct assault on women's turf, on the very families for which God had given
them moral responsibility. Once slavery and drink had symbolized the decay
of the City on the Hill. Now, abortion and the Equal Rights Amendment
replaced them as signs of the Apocalypse.

The woman who sounded the battle cry was the wife of a California pastor who was inspired when she turned on her television set one evening in
1979 and listened to Barbara Walters interview Betty Friedan. When she heard
Friedan hold herself up as the spokeswoman for American women, Beverly
LaHaye found a new mission—countering feminists who purported to speak
for American women—or so the story goes according to movement
mythology. Beverly spread the word that she was calling a meeting of American women like her to discuss abortion, the Equal Rights Amendment and
other family issues. She would match Friedan follower for follower, and the
National Organization for Women member for member. More than one
thousand women showed up at that first rally, and out of their collective
outrage, the Concerned Women of America was born.

The women went virtually unnoticed for years, even while CWA chapters sprang up in every state. Members of Congress were polite to the properly dressed and always courteous CWA lobbyists, but saw no reason to curry
the favor of a bunch of Christian housewives. The media was so focused
on the rise of televangelism that they were blinded to the grassroots movement behind it. When journalists deigned to acknowledge the army of followers, they cast them as hayseeds duped by clever manipulators. Only
gradually did the truth emerge: Those unsophisticated dupes were at the
forefront of one of the most powerful and politically savvy grassroots movements in the history of the nation.

Today, CWA operates with a $10 million budget out of posh offices in
Washington, D.C. Its six hundred thousand members are organized into
more than twelve hundred prayer/action chapters that can be mobilized in
an instant to lobby against abortion, the ERA, sex education that includes
any message but abstinence and legislation that might be seen as placing a

stamp of approval on homosexuality. When TV network executives began to consider opening advertising to condoms, CWA flooded their offices with 1.9 million postcards opposing the change. In 1992, CWA responded to feminist support for the Freedom of Choice Act by sending its volunteer lobbyists into the office of every member of Congress and dumping petitions containing a quarter of a million signatures all over Capitol Hill.

In 1996, LaHaye and her followers launched a campaign to strip the Sexuality Information and Education Council of the United States (SIECUS) of its federal funding. Word filtered out through the network of prayer chapters that SIECUS was promoting incest and pedophilia, and thirty thousand petitions arrived in Washington. When a Texas congressman introduced legislation to turn CWA's demand into reality, five hundred thousand letters flooded the offices of congressmen. The pressure was so strong that two hundred separate congressional inquiries were made into SIECUS's activities and funding.

In recent years, CWA has gone well beyond a narrowly defined "Christian" agenda. "We support any legislation which helps the family," says legislative director Laura Hyskill. "I laugh when people say an organization like ours wants to set up a theocracy. We're just trying to help families." To Laura, that means fighting federal funding for child care that limits benefits to working mothers, since such benefits create an incentive for women not to be with their children. It means supporting school choice to give parents more control over their children's education, demanding tax relief for families in order to provide incentives for Americans to live "model" (meaning two parents, with one staying home with the kids) family lives, abolishing the federal Department of Education, limiting welfare and sending out clear signals about right and wrong. "We believe in values," she says. "If we don't believe in some absolutes we're going to lose everything. Everything in life is not relative."

Laura, 27, grew up in Connecticut convinced that the sky was her only limit. Chemistry taught her otherwise, keeping her out of premed programs, so she wound up studying traditional liberal arts at Washington and Lee College in Virginia. Like so many other conservative women, she was electrified by the optimism of Ronald Reagan. Now she speaks with passion and conviction about the CWA agenda. "The elites have seceded from everything traditional," she says, walking through CWA's handsome—and decidedly feminine—offices in Washington, D.C. The armchairs are pink. A color photograph of Beverly LaHaye dominates the waiting room, creating the sense that the "president for life" is the fundamentalist equivalent of guru

Marianne Williamson. "It's happened in education, the media, entertainment. We went from the *Sound of Music* to *Showgirls.* It took a couple of decades for people of faith to realize that this was happening and that it was going to impact on them. They didn't really get involved until things got really bad."

Once things did, CWA was able to tap into the anger of women who have felt mocked and marginalized ever since Betty Friedan declared housewifery mindless drudgery, and to channel the abject terror of women confronted with stories about sexual abuse, alcoholism, AIDS and the other inevitable by-products of the American concept of freedom into a frenzy of political action. In precisely the same way in which feminism built a movement by teaching women to be proud, CWA became a formidable political force by teaching Christian women to reach into their hearts, and their Bibles, for inspiration, thus prying them out of their homes and their reticence about civic involvement.

"I look back and I can see that many of the lessons I learned as a minister's wife with a growing family and as a lecturer on family living were stepping-stones to what I'm doing with Concerned Women for America," says LaHaye, a small woman in sensible flats who speaks with a soft midwestern accent. "In our family seminars we taught people how to insulate their homes and families against outside forces; that helped me sort out my beliefs and develop the strong convictions I have today.

"Because of my past experiences I'm probably able to reach women who otherwise might sit back in their pews and be a bit apathetic. Because they know I'm a pastor's wife and perhaps have read my books, they're willing to trust me when I say there are issues we must be concerned about.

"I believe women are being raised up for such a time as this. When you're talking about family issues, women can be very strong, very tough . . . and I mean that in the good sense of the word. The average American woman has endurance and is willing to give of herself for what she believes is right. I think God is going to use us to turn the tide from becoming a humanist nation."

LaHaye mobilized those women with a groundbreaking organizing pamphlet entitled "How to Lobby from Your Kitchen Table." She broadcasts that same message live on her own radio program to some 350,000 listeners daily, keeping them abreast of the major issues in Congress, never forgetting to give them phone numbers for the Capitol switchboard and Western Union so that they can pick up the phone and take action. Her staff keeps nonlisteners up-to-date with educational packages and newsletters filled with the Christian view (that is, LaHaye's view) of pending legislation, along with clear instructions on how to write, fax and call their elected representatives. Members are invited to Washington to train for the "535 Program," which assigns volunteer lobbyists to monitor each member of Congress. "Politicians who don't use the Bible to guide their public and private lives do not belong in office," LaHaye preaches. Her volunteer lobbyists are there to make sure that they do, or to spread the word if they happen to stray.

And chapter by chapter, prayer group by prayer group, CWA members and thousands of women sympathetic to their cause are both trained and encouraged to be watchdogs in their own communities—to study the textbooks their children read, to prepare moral report cards on members of their city councils, to organize, organize, organize in such numbers that their voices cannot be ignored. They know that a conservative Christian might never reach the presidency, but they also know that the old saw that teaches that "all politics are local" can transform hundreds of communities, that they can elect "Godly" candidates to school boards and town councils and take back America one neighborhood at a time.

CWA is not their only source of training and encouragement, since the group is part of a tangle of Christian organizations with overlapping agendas that include Phyllis Schlafly's Eagle Forum (which CWA surpassed in clout years ago), the Family Research Council, the Christian Coalition and the Traditional Values Coalition—the forces behind the ten-point Contract with the American Family that the Christian right offered up as a supplement to Newt's Contract with America. For years they looked to Ralph Reed, their very own George Stephanopoulos, for strategy. They attend conferences like "Reclaiming America for Christ," held in Fort Lauderdale, Florida, in March 1995, to learn how to squash efforts to pass gay rights legislation and how to deal with public school issues. Women like May Ellen Miller, one of the speakers at that meeting, teach them the basics, with a heavy emphasis on the basics for homemakers. Miller's aunt was a Republican precinct captain who never had any problem getting the city to trim overgrown bushes. "Why?" Miller asked rhetorically, setting up her object lesson. "Raw, absolute power. . . . She taught me that politics is people power."

Their recruits are an eclectic mix of old-time Christian activists and the newly ignited. Fran Riedemann turned up at the 1992 CWA convention from Kansas, where she runs her own art gallery. The mother of five had never been active, until the Clarence Thomas hearings. Infuriated by Anita Hill, she turned to CWA, which she thinks of as a vehicle to empower women. Judy Smith was another Kansas delegate that year, a volunteer at a crisis pregnancy center who was trained as a pharmacist but stopped working the minute she gave birth to the first of her three children. "A woman can work if she wants," she told the *Washington Post*. "For me it wasn't right."

The army includes teachers and accountants, homemakers, grandmothers, college students and cashiers, and they are following the script—and chalking up victories. In 1990, Christian activists in southern California devised a political strategy that targeted races for the kind of low-level jobs that attract few candidates and even less media attention. They used church mailing lists to contact friendly voters, flooded church parking lots on Sunday mornings with leaflets declaring themselves "Pro-Family" candidates, and kept their heads down, to avoid the attention of liberals. Sixty of their eighty-eight candidates won their races, and took up positions in school boards, city councils and hospital boards across the county. By 1992, those officeholders were ready to move up the political ladder, and to pull other Christian conservatives in behind them.

School board after school board has fallen to their stealth organizing tactics. In Vista, California, the sole conservative on the school board, Deidre Holliday, was joined by a pastor's wife and a Christian man, who defeated solid moderates. Once in office, they attacked the English curriculum for requiring high school students to read Voltaire's *Candide.* They tried to push through a policy requiring students to have parental permission to borrow any book about which a parent had ever complained. They restructured sex education to eliminate discussions of birth control and homosexuality. In Merrimack, New Hampshire, women like them were so successful with the same organizing strategy—electing, among others, the county cochair of Pat Buchanan's primary campaign to office—that the school board actually instituted a moment of silence to begin each school day and has begun to discuss adding creationism to the science curriculum.

Liberals have been caught unprepared for the breathtakingly successful organizing campaigns that have placed Christian women in positions of power—power to change curricula and reshape the debate—all across the country. Progressives, after all, invented grassroots organizing, that often tedious process of knocking on doors, stating and restating your case, whining and wheedling and inspiring ordinary people to join labor unions, to work with advocacy groups and to help create the power of an effective political movement. By the 1970s, convinced that they had won or could win the major battles at the federal level, liberals forgot to protect their rears at the very moment that Christians were raising liberal tactics to a high art.

"Outside of a few labor unions—the United Automobile Workers, 1199, the AFL-CIO campaign—and the Midwest Academy, liberal training of youthful organizers is sporadic, at best," says Joe Graybarz, executive director of the Connecticut Civil Liberties Union. Graybarz has spent his adult life trying to get other liberals to wake up to the importance of this basic grass-roots work. "The religious right has taken our strategy and put it into a church in every town. So while we're lucky to have one training center for organizers in every state, they have one in every town.

"Part of the problem is that the Democratic Party, which liberals have relied on for the past fifty years, now has political strategy that centers more on the media, on a top-down strategy, rather than on organizing. That's why we have the president and the Republicans, who've been doing the grass-roots work, control Congress." Graybarz points to the religious right's boldest organizing vision: its plan to seize control over the Republican Party. Christian women began working at the local committee level. They worked their way up to county chairs, then gained statewide positions. "It was brilliant," Graybarz says. "They developed a plan and executed it over time nearly flawlessly." The religious right thus far has taken control of an estimated eighteen state Republican Party organizations, and established a dominant position in thirteen more.

This stunning success was not just organizational. Four million people—mostly women—donate time and money to keep the momentum of the Christian right rolling. One in five Americans is in "close" or "very close" agreement with them, according to the surveys of John Green of the Bliss Institute of Applied Politics at the University of Akron. And another 30 percent of the nation is extremely sympathetic to the Christian right's family agenda. Realizing that many of the individuals within that 30 percent are not Protestants, they have moved beyond their own natural constituency, the conservative Protestant community, reaching out to Catholics, Muslims and Orthodox Jews. In 1993, just such a coalition was launched in New York City to keep out of the schools a "Rainbow Curriculum" that the board of education was considering. Mary Cummings, a Queens Catholic, realized that the curriculum's positive handling of homosexuality was offensive to a wide array of people of faith, and she managed to pull them into the battle. Not only was the curriculum defeated, but religious conservatives won half the local school board seats to ensure their power in future struggles.

Women are at the forefront of this movement, and not simply as ventriloquists' dummies for the Pat Robertsons and Ralph Reeds, as liberal women seem determined to believe. Those partisan pundits have tried to paint Christian women activists as "the Moral Majority's ladies' club," in the words of Susan Faludi. "The women always played by their men's rules, and for that they enjoyed the blessings and esteem of their subculture." That might be true, but it's not that simple. Christian women activists play by men's rules because they also subscribe to them. Those rules aren't the pronouncements of men. To religious women, they are the dictates of God. To imply that those rules belong solely to men is to suggest, with startling condescension and contempt, that Christian women are cowed into submission rather than full-bodied, equal partners in faith.

That partnership is at the heart of Christian women's rejection of feminism. The women's movement is built around the needs and concerns of women. Christian women, unwilling to divorce their needs and concerns from those of their families, reject that concept. In so doing, they are not belittling themselves, or allowing anyone else to belittle them. Quite the opposite. They are living by their faith, a faith that teaches that no one—male or female—lives in the type of vacuum that identity politics suggests.

Kirstin Hansen walks through the halls of the Capitol brandishing a pink plastic fetus and a pair of scissors to demonstrate graphically the technique used in partial birth abortion. She is girded for the fight to outlaw the procedure. Is the spokeswoman for the Family Research Council any more a toady or an opportunist than Kate Michelman, who led the troops on the other side? Is the sincerity of her principles irrelevant in light of the feminist proclamation that banning of partial birth abortion is inimical to women?

Mary Ann Glendon chaired the twenty-member Vatican delegation to the UN Fourth World Conference on Women in Beijing in 1995. To the fury of most of the American delegation, Glendon railed against the meeting's draft document for the inclusion of long sections on women's health and no mention of the dangers that sexual permissiveness pose to it; for, in her view, denigrating marriage, family and motherhood by depicting all three primarily as dangers or impediments to women. Can Faludi et al. seriously dismiss Glendon, a professor at Harvard Law School, as a puppet of the pope or a climber who's riding high on the backs of her sisters?

How can you purport to care about and respect women without conceding to them the right to choose their own beliefs?

Feminists, of all people in America, should feel particular empathy for women of faith, since the two groups bear remarkably similar scars. Like feminists, Christian women feel constantly besieged in a hostile world. They too have had to fight to make their voices heard in a society that often seems deaf. They too are regularly demeaned, degraded and reduced to second-class citizenship—not just as women, but as women of conservative faith. And, like feminists in the 1960s, after decades of passivity, they have begun to fight back, launching their own struggle for dignity and equality. In that struggle, in their language and demeanor, Christian women activists are drawing on the proudest tradition of American women who fought back—from Sojourner Truth to Susan B. Anthony—and making their own imprint on American feminism, Christian-style.

If their Betty Friedan is Beverly LaHaye, their Gloria Steinem is a 36-year-old Californian with frosted hair, hot pink fingernails and a miniskirt. She drives around Washington, D.C., in a red Toyota Maxima with a license plate that declares her "The California Girl." But the former homecoming queen of Magnolia High School is a Washington insider with a reputation as a pit bull. "There's a fine line between being tough and being that nasty word that people like to call women," she says. Congressional staffers believe that Andrea Sheldon crosses that line at least once a week.

Andrea is the Washington voice of the Traditional Values Coalition, a conservative group representing thirty-one thousand "antiabortion, pro-family" churches founded by her father, the Reverend Louis Sheldon. Working out of TVC's Washington headquarters, a dignified nineteenth-century brick house behind the Library of Congress, she spearheads the fight to bring creationism and prayer back into schools, and keep gay teachers out of them; to outlaw abortion, reinforce parental rights and return America to "Judeo-Christian values." She spends her days working the Hill, collecting information for voting guides and tip sheets on legislative targets, and lobbying, talking, pushing and persuading members of Congress to move in the direction she believes God's will directs.

No one is surprised anymore to find Andrea talking about masturbation in the U.S. Capitol. Pointing out the evils of sex education is part of her job, after all. And it's not unusual for her to pull out an AIDS education brochure and point to a section on vaginal fisting, for example, to demonstrate how lesbians and gays are using the epidemic to promote their own "lifestyles."

"God didn't create me to be an introvert," Andrea explains, laughing, poised on a couch in the living room of the TVC townhouse. That's an understatement, from a woman hardly known for subtlety.

Andrea had a stereotypical southern California upbringing of beaches, malls, dances, cheerleading and a total indifference to politics. Then, like so many other young people, she went off to college without much direction, and found herself working a summer job wondering what it all meant. But while that summer job was in a women's clothing store, the college was Oral Roberts, and her quest for meaning led her to Washington and a series of low-level jobs before she joined TVC as its lobbyist in 1991.

A hard-nosed supporter not only of traditional values but of hard work, responsibility and the Puritan ethic, Andrea is one of those women who really believes in tough love, that ending welfare will help people on welfare "regain their dignity," and she is convinced that churches and other civic groups will pick up the slack if the federal government withdraws from the safety-net business. As a member of the board of the charismatic Church of the Apostles in Fairfax, Virginia—Ollie North's parish—she organized their volunteer homeless-assistance program. She tramps to the low-end motels where the county houses the homeless to deliver food and provide moral support. She ferries pregnant women to the hospital—the type of outreach to the homeless Christians believe to be more effective than government programs.

Andrea has been mentioned repeatedly as a possible successor to California congressman Bob Dornan. "I thought about it when God was talking about retiring," she said, referring to Dornan in what seemed a surprisingly flip manner. But Dornan didn't retire; he was defeated, and for the moment Andrea seems ensconced in Washington as the hip doyenne of the religious right. "We need women in places of power to be voices," she says. "There are very few. You have the Pat Schroeders and the Ann Lewises, who say they're speaking for women. They don't speak for me or the millions of women like me who are conservative. I represent millions of women who felt they didn't have a voice."

Few of those women are playing politics inside the Beltway, of course. Andrea's constituents are home in the heartland, raising children and trying to make ends meet. And Andrea insists that within ten years she will join them. "This is fun for now," she says, "but this isn't where I belong in the long run. I want a husband and children, and I plan to make the sacrifice and stay home and take care of them."

Maybe, I said as I left Andrea Sheldon sitting demurely on the Victorian couch, dressed in a tiger-striped blouse and a black miniskirt. In my world, it would never happen, but this is a different reality. Women in the world of Christian conservatives play by a different set of rules, God's rules, as they see them, and they don't get to change them at will.

A Digression into Faith of a Different Fabric

Mary Ann Reid wears her quiet, self-contained mien as a conservatively patterned shirt, dark pants and sensible shoes. When she walks across the campus of Fordham University, not a scintilla of her flesh is in view other than the skin on her hands and face. Even her hair is shrouded, carefully contained within a discreet black head cloth.

As she watches the other students dashing in and out of classes—smoking and drinking and flirting—she recalls the days when she too modeled herself after the female stars on MTV, flaunting her long legs in a miniskirt, tossing back her long, shiny hair as she walked provocatively through the streets of Brooklyn. Then Mary Ann shivers with pleasure at the protective armor she now wears, still reveling in the natural high she felt the first time she donned *hijab*. When men stop and stare at her on the street, she delights in the knowledge that they will never know what lies beneath her garb. "You don't put a gem out in the middle of a mall," she says matter-of-factly. "You keep it in a jewelry box. When I'm covered, I feel like a precious stone."

Mary Ann's mother, however, shows no such glee at her daughter's conservative self-protectedness, in her dogmatic adherence to chastity. She's not trying to chase her eldest into the fast lane, but 22-year-olds are supposed to be out having fun, exploring the world, making the rounds of neighborhood parties, reading fashion magazines so they can style with their girlfriends and be wooed by hungry young men. Neighbors point and gossip about her. When she interviews for jobs, employers don't seem to know what to make of the serious young woman with a head covering.

"It's hard being a religious person in this society," Mary Ann says. "Being apart from society and following God's laws feels good, but it can make you feel alone. However, I've found incredible joy in freeing myself from popular culture, from worrying about what I should put on, about what I should look like and what everyone else will think. The way women are portrayed in this society is sickening, and women have become desensitized to it. I don't want to be like a white woman parading around buck naked. Those women are missing something. They think they have freedom, but I can't express to you the freedom I feel in covering my body. I can't express to you the freedom I feel as a woman in Islam."

Mary Ann has lived in New York too long not to understand that most American women think she's crazy. The popular image of the Muslim woman is a helpless female forced into virtual seclusion by malicious misogynists, a woman so oppressed that she isn't allowed to drive a car, an exhausted, semi-enslaved mother chained to the stove while her husband dallies with his other wives. Covering your body, covering your head and practicing a religion that condones polygamy is hardly the American definition of women's liberation, after all. But for Mary Ann, who converted from Catholicism to Islam, being a Muslim woman is a statement about dignity, about female pride and female honor. "People have all these ridiculous ideas about Islam," she says. "But they forget that in Islam, women had property rights in the fourth century, when Christian women were still living in caves. I have the right to a marriage contract, to ask for a divorce, to control my own money and run my own business. What's unliberated about that? Men are instructed to respect women. Is that bad? Adultery is a capital crime. Doesn't that protect women?

"The problem for many people is that Islam teaches that men and women are different, that they have different roles, and in Western society, we think that different means unequal. But Islam teaches that all people are created equal. Islam is the fastest-growing religion in the world, and most of the converts are women. I don't think that's surprising at all."

Mary Ann's journey to Islam began when she was a student at Drexel University and wrote a paper on the religion for a philosophy course. Raised in a Catholic family—and influenced by her grandmother, who ran her own church—she wasn't drawn to the religion so much by its doctrine as by the social universe it wove: family, community, a clear definition of male and female roles. Growing up in America's secular culture, Mary Ann had always assumed she'd go to college, launch a solid career, travel and then, later in life, marry and have children. But when she studied Islamic tenets and society, she found herself longing for the stability and companionship they offered. "People put marriage off like it's not very important," she says. "But that's what men and women are made for. They are like pieces of a puzzle and are meant to fit together. I don't want to be like a man, and I think it is terrible that housewives are dismissed as women who sit around eating bonbons. Feminism pushes women out of the house and into the workforce, where they wind up fighting for their rights and equal wages while their children are at the day care center. There's something seriously wrong in that."

Like thousands of other American women converts to Islam—and tens of thousands of American women who have not converted to any religion—Mary Ann wants more from a women's movement than equal pay, which she takes for granted in any case. She wants a women's movement that battles for respect for women, that fights to guarantee women dignity, stability and security, that celebrates who women have been as much as it celebrates who women can be. She found that not in the National Organization for Women, but in her Muslim sisterhood and in SisterNet, the on-line chat group she signs on to every evening. The two hundred women who "chat" electronically are searching for more than material equality, they say, and feminism has refused to speak to their other needs and longings. So they are adapting feminism to their own lives, pulling out philosophical concepts and pragmatic gains with which they agree, and grafting them onto their own system of women's thinking, one based on Islamic principles.

"I think feminism has been a double-edged sword for women in this country," explains Kim Barghouti, 36, a Muslim convert in Hobbs, New Mexico, who chats with Mary Ann on SisterNet. "On one hand, we have been benefited by the movement. Domestic violence legislation has gotten tougher. Equal pay for equal work has made the working woman's life easier. More careers are open to women than ever before. On the downside, feminism drastically shook the sex roles in this country. Woman ceased to be someone to respect. She became the competition. More and more men feel little remorse over leaving a woman and children. She is perceived as being quite able to take care of everything herself. This trickled down to the lower classes, as well, where the women are not as well educated, not as well prepared to be the sole breadwinner for a family.

"Although it is not very 'politically correct' to say so, I largely blame the downfall of the American family on the aftermath of the women's movement. There has been great disrespect shown for the traditional roles of women. A woman who chose to stay at home with her children was looked down upon or pitied. There is a generation of mothers out there—me included—who were raised to disparage the very roles we find ourselves living every day. They did us no favors."

Unlike Mary Ann, whose neighborhood teems with the smells, colors and sights that are the hallmark of a multicultural world, Kim lives in rural New Mexico, and came to Islam from a blue-collar family active in an extremely conservative branch of the Baptist Church. Women didn't speak at services. They were excluded from all business meetings. She finds it ironic, then, and not a little infuriating, that she has had to spend years defending her conversion.

"It angers me that because I wear traditional dress and practice Islam, people think I have no mind or will," she says. "I see absolutely no contradiction between being a feminist and being a Muslim. For example, I think mine is the ultimate in feminist apparel. If you believe that people should take you on your merits, not treat you as a sex object, just judge you by who you are, then *hijab* [traditional dress] is a natural way to dress. It strikes me as odd that those screaming 'Don't treat me like a sex object' have no problem wearing a spandex dress that shows every nipple and ripple. Women who dress in a very revealing manner do not realize the forces they are dealing with. It is like smearing your body with blood and going into the shark tank at Sea World. If you do not want a man's attention, don't dress for it. Putting everything on display for any man that passes by is asking for trouble. I don't have to be always on display, dressed to the nines for whoever is looking. I own shorts and slinky clothes. They simply have a place and time. I can be *selective* in my seduction.

"And it bothers me that people think that because Islam has traditional roles for men and women that women automatically have an inferior status. They are projecting on the basis of the Western system. If I say that Japanese culture is different from Spanish culture, no one gets offended. This is because their differences have never been used to systematically discriminate against one group or another. But if I say that black people are different from white people, gays are different than heteros, Jews are different from Christians, or women are different from men, people get offended. That is because the differences in these groups have been systematically used to discriminate against them. Somewhere in American history, 'different' began to mean 'less than.' But because in Islam our differences have never been used to systematically discriminate against women, no one hesitates to acknowledge our differences. In fact, we celebrate them."

Kim remains a liberal Democrat, although "not quite as liberal as before." She opposes abortion but supports socialized medicine, animal rights, arms limitations and gun control. While she makes conservative choices for herself, she insists she is "liberal in the choices I would allow others to make for themselves. We believe that we are all 'works in progress,' improving as we grow in understanding. The Prophet Muhammad—peace be upon him—told us to seek to learn from the cradle to the grave. To hold someone to a standard they cannot begin to grasp is like asking a newborn to run a decathlon."

Even while she balances raising her three children, being a partner to her husband and pursuing a graduate degree in anthropology, Kim finds deep pleasure, and meaning, in traditional female roles, in the sense of sisterhood they provide her, sisterhood of a type that feminism has never wanted to acknowledge—the sisterhood of the future, if Kim has her way. "I have come to understand more how we fit into the millennium of generations before and after us," she says. "The universal roles of wife and mother endure when the more individualistic things about us fall away. That sounds so odd. What I'm trying to say is that when we cook dinner, nurse a baby, hang out laundry or rock a child to sleep, we are doing the same things women before us have done for thousands of years, and women after us will do. This sense of the sweet continuity of life seems more essential to our natures as human beings than bringing home a paycheck. I could never have seen that, if Islam had not shown me the innate dignity and honor in the traditional women's roles."

The Operators

The 1996 Republican National Convention was a parade of the "new" Republican Party, a virtual all-girl extravaganza choreographed to give Republicanism a kinder and gentler face. Governor Christine Todd Whitman of New Jersey, the cohost of the show, trotted out the party's female luminaries and luminaries-in-waiting to regale the crowd about the brave new world that Republicans could deliver to American women. Representative Susan Molinari of New York—in a stylish khaki suit with a skirt showing just a hint of knee—delivered her version of an impassioned keynote address about the party's commitment to restoring the American Dream while her husband sat misty-eyed in the audience cuddling their 3-month-old girl. Rush Limbaugh, back in New York, bemoaned the feminization of Republican rhetoric, but the party's spinmeisters cooed and clucked about violence against women and the plight of single mothers.

The plan was to obliterate any vestigial memory of the 1992 Houston convention, where Pat Buchanan fulminated against the devil in the form of abortion, homosexuality and a myriad of other evils. Marilyn Quayle, the 1992 female attack dog who had berated Hillary Clinton for encouraging women to "liberate themselves from their essential natures," was replaced by Elizabeth Dole, who offered a stellar performance in what seemed a perfect audition either for compassionate First Lady or a slot on *Saturday Night Live* as the un-Hillary.

Few Americans saw the complete show, of course, because the same network television executives who had no qualms about broadcasting thousands of hours of the O. J. Simpson trial mounted their ethical high horses and took a stand against being "manipulated" by the Republican Party. But it would have made little difference, since the Republicans lacked sufficient experience in television production to understand that specials make less impact on viewers than weekly sitcoms. For too many years, the female stars of the Republican dramas were Phyllis Schlafly and Marilyn Quayle. Even a five-night miniseries of soccer moms and bleeding hearts couldn't displace that image.

To make matters worse for the Republican leadership, just five months earlier, Tanya Melich had declared war on the party which had been her political home for decades. *The Republican War on Women: An Insider's Report from Behind the Lines,* was her blow-by-blow description of the hijacking of the party by religious conservatives. The battle between the old stalwarts and the interlopers for the soul of the Republican Party had been reduced to a struggle over women and their bodies, Melich argued. And despite all the female window dressing trotted out for the cameras in San Diego, that battle, and Republican sympathy for progressive women's causes, had already been lost.

So even a convention that was "Republican Lite," as Clinton campaign manager Ann Lewis dubbed it, could not erase the prevailing image of Republican women as prim and proper in their Barbara Bush dresses, as pontificating and condemning in southern fundamentalist polyester or as grim and angry in Jeane Kirkpatrick severely tailored suits. The old images were still too vivid. And there were simply too many goofy-looking dames in elephant-head hats or straw bowlers festooned with flags scattered through the audience for most outsiders to take the show seriously.

HELEN Chenoweth sat demurely in the Idaho delegation looking neither prim, angry nor goofy. Although she was a member of Congress, the party leadership had evidenced no interest in displaying her before the highly coveted moderates for whom the show was staged. Wrong image. No one had ever accused Helen of moderation. The Boise newspaper had branded her a "poster child for the militias." The environmentalists had branded her a crackpot for comparing their movement to a new religion ("a cloudy mixture of New Age mysticism, Native American folklore and primitive Earth worship" was the way she put it). And she had managed to infuriate both those environmentalists and feminists by lobbying for an end to the Endangered Species Act with the slogan "It's the Anglo-Saxon male that's endangered today."

Helen Chenoweth was a leader of the forces that had stolen the Republican Party from Tanya Melich, and she was as rigidly antichoice, and just as rabidly right-wing, as the men on whom Melich heaped the blame. Congressman Chenoweth—she refuses to answer to "Congresswoman"—was one of the seven female members in the infamous freshman class that was swept into power with Newt Gingrich in 1994. The seven sisters, whose arrival in the House was dubbed the "Invasion of the Church Ladies" by the *New Republic,* were living, breathing affronts to feminism—or to any lingering stereotype about the political inclinations of modern American females. Helen had stormed into Washington with the mien of a gunslinger from the Old West, railing against gun control, federal encroachment on private property rights and the tyranny of the Department of the Interior. She bore the stamp of approval of her local militia leaders, who praised her for "standing up and defending her young, while these other snake-oil politicians ran for the nearest dark place to hide."

All of which made her wildly popular back home in Orofino, Idaho, a logging town where the beer flows freely, the churches are packed and everyone seems to enjoy feeling a bit like an outlaw. She had landed in Orofino in the 1960s when she married a local attorney there, and quickly established herself as the kind of white-collar renegade the West seems to breed. She and her husband, Nick, wanted to build an airport on the edge of town, but two large trees were blocking the end of what they hoped would be a runway. In that part of the country, cutting down a tree can require a federal permit, which is precisely the kind of nonsense that Helen can't tolerate. Helen and Nick were denied one, so they cut the trees down anyway. Helen figures that was pretty much her constitutional right, and she doesn't brook much interference from the government where her idea of constitutional rights are concerned.

When she and Nick broke up in 1975, Helen was left with two kids, no job and the full range of upper-middle-class expectations. She couldn't meet them by managing medical offices and recruiting physicians to towns and clinics in the Northwest—her work for a decade—so when the chairmanship of the state Republican Party opened up, Helen threw her hat in the ring. In the post-Watergate era, she didn't have much competition, and her rise in Republican Party politics began. Two years later, she was appointed chief of staff for then-Congressman Steve Symms; then she bowed out of politics to work as a consultant in energy and natural resources policy.

In 1994, Helen decided to reenter the game and filed as a candidate in the Republican congressional primary. Her competitors were the former lieutenant governor and the former attorney general, "both tall, good-looking and popular men," she says, "well supported by big business interests in

Boise." Helen drew an army of supporters from the Idaho-based Focus on the Family, a national group that sits decidedly to the right of the Christian Coalition. Helen crisscrossed the district—which takes nine hours, since it runs from Nevada to Canada—while that army, which was almost all female, dropped more than three hundred thousand voting guides in a thousand churches across western Idaho. Her opponents cried foul and painted her as a fire-breathing extremist—which backfired, since Idaho fell in love with Helen's unique brand of demure extremism. Pilloried for refusing to support the Endangered Species Act, she held an endangered salmon bake. She harangued the crowds about illegal government attacks on the rights of gun and property owners, insisted that Clinton had declared war on the West—and carried all but one remote county, racking up more votes than her two major opponents combined.

"Campaigning was fun," she said, sitting in her comfortable, almost feminine office in the Longworth Building. Helen's makeup is always perfect. Her voice is soft and almost lilting. Photographs of her children and grandchildren decorate her desk. Only her reception area suggests that Helen might be more than she seems. It boasts a display of smoked fillets of sockeye salmon, the species at the top of the endangered northwestern species list, and a rifle and pistol reloading manual.

"I ran and won on the issues, so I feel a real mandate. This is a new season for women in America. Women are returning to traditional lives and women are going into public policy, and I bridge that gap because I've done both. I'm one of the women who broke the glass ceiling. I was one of the first women in Idaho to work in the business world back in the sixties and, frankly, I never found that I had any difficulty being listened to. I was one of the first women in the country to be involved in the building of hydropower plants and one of the first Republican women to serve as the executive director of a state party.

"The glass ceiling would have been lopsided if we all hadn't been pushing, and we were. Now I'm serving in Congress and I'm breaking the glass ceiling that says that women have to be what the National Organization for Women wants us to be."

The day I interviewed her, Helen had just been called on the carpet by Newt Gingrich for refusing to line up behind him in resolving the federal budget dispute. Helen knew that Congress was taking a beating because of the shutdown of the government, but she thought it was the best thing that had happened in Washington in years. "The Speaker does what he needs to do and I do what I need to do," she said, casually. Helen knew her supporters might love the Speaker of the House, but not nearly as much as they loved a woman with the balls to cross him.

Helen talked reasonably and amiably about her crusade to abolish the Internal Revenue Service, her fury at what she sees as the encroachment of federal agencies on the sovereign rights of private individuals, communities and states. Unlike many other conservative women, she speaks just as comfortably about feminism and women's rights, although she defined some of them in slightly unusual ways. "Most of the remaining issues only time can cure," she said. "The only remaining issues I think the federal government should be involved in concern single mothers, who are victimized by tax policy. The federal government does more to hold women back than to promote us.

"They said that 1992 was the year of the woman, but they got it wrong. This [1995] is the year of the woman. We've really achieved parity. They're attacking Hillary Clinton and Enid Waldholtz at the same time. I think we've made it."

Helen believes that conservative men—"the old boys' network"—and liberal women have a knack for organizing that conservative women lack. In her campaign, she bucked that trend, lining up women loggers, Christian activists and an eclectic collection of female gun owners, ranchers and business owners who identified with Helen's breed of feminine cowgirl chutzpah. Those women filled the streets of Orofino in early September 1996 when Helen returned to town during her reelection campaign for the 49th annual Loggers' Day held alongside the county fair.

The Saturday morning of the big parade, hundreds of people lined the streets of the small town sandwiched between the Clearwater River and the Bitterroot Mountains. They were what used to be called sturdy folk—men and women with callused hands and faces pinched by hard work and harder times. Older couples strolled through the crowd in front of the Rex Theater (which was playing *Independence Day*) dressed in matching embroidered cowboy shirts. A group of bikers lolled on the corner by Clearwater Realty, where a stuffed cougar was displayed in the front window. The only sign that the counterculture had reached Orofino was the Flamingo Cafe, which steamed up espresso and cappuccino—but they measured the coffee out by the shot glass.

Just after 10 A.M. in a drizzling mist, the VFW Honor Guard marched down the main street followed by their Ladies' Auxiliary. The crowd stood for hours cheering rescue squads and fire engines from a dozen towns.

Twirlers displayed their skill with hula hoops, the Barn Owls Square and Round Dance Club do-si-do'ed and marching bands kept the tempo upbeat. Trucks hauling floats and displays were still emblazoned with Helen's 1994 campaign sticker, IT'S THE SPENDING, STUPID.

The week before, Helen had campaigned in Lewiston riding a giant mule. In Orofino, she appeared in jeans and a red jacket perched eighteen feet in the air atop a stack of nine Douglas fir trees—more than four thousand two hundred board feet of lumber, a sign noted—loaded onto an enormous truck. The banner leading her contingent read, ONCE YOU'VE HUGGED A LOGGER YOU'LL NEVER GO BACK TO TREES.

That afternoon, at the annual town auction—a hodgepodge of lumber, flowers, heavy equipment and kitchen supplies sold to raise money for the town's budget—Helen sat in the bleachers looking just like the members of her female cadre, who surrounded her. Lee Ann Callear, the regional coordinator of her campaign, sat at her feet and echoed the sentiments of dozens of women who were working for Helen's reelection. "We're not the kind of people who go in for being professionals," she said, her wild hair blowing in the dusty wind. "We've all been poor. None of us live in big fancy houses. My mother worked as hard as my father. She killed chickens, fished and milked cows. I have five sisters and we've all been liberated since birth. The way I figure it, if you want to be liberated, why don't you just be liberated? Why do you have to talk about it all the time? If men are a problem, just go around them like a brick wall. You don't need to bash it down. It's not all that wide."

Lee Ann was a wild kid, a young hippie showing off at antiwar protests, involved with a heroin addict. "Then I started to figure out that logging is better than using plastic. I think women should get equal pay for equal work, but I don't think women should be more equal than white males. I think we need to cut welfare because we've enslaved poor people in poverty. But I'm a bleeding heart. I want to make sure we help the truly needy."

Lee Ann talked about her position on NAFTA (she supported it), education (she regrets not home schooling her three children), working mothers ("I don't do a lot of things I want to do because I have a responsibility to my children. Too many women in the East put their careers first and just drag their kids along") and sex education. In her principled support of the latter, she broke ranks with most of Helen's other supporters, who want to eliminate it. But Lee Ann figured that she had a keener understanding of how dangerous the world can be since she'd been around the block more than once. "It's 1996," she said. "This is a dangerous time. And children need to know what happens if you get pregnant.

"Babies are a big responsibility, even if you murder them," she added, segueing seamlessly into the topic that united her with virtually every woman in town. If there was a pro-choice voice in Orofino, it spoke in a whisper. As friends stopped by to greet Lee Ann or Helen or to check on the details of the coming weeks of the campaign, the conversation returned again and again to abortion, and to the other issue on the top of everyone's political priority list: guns. Ultimately, Lee Ann said that she'd trade abortion reform for protection of her Second Amendment rights any day. "I'm no compromiser. . . . We've compromised ourselves out of too many freedoms. But if we don't guard the Second Amendment, we can't guard ourselves against tyranny. I don't hunt. I don't carry around a gun. In fact, I'm afraid of guns, just like I'm afraid of bears. But Americans better wise up and realize that gun control imperils their liberty."

Helen smiled. Two women sitting nearby yelled out, "Right on."

LIBERTY had an entirely different face at the U.S. Grant Hotel on Wednesday morning, August 14, 1996—the third day of the GOP convention. No Helen Chenoweth. No tennis shoes or work boots. Not even Birkenstocks. And certainly none of the goofy hats that the polyester delegates were sporting. This was the convention breakfast sponsored by WISH List—Women in the Senate and House—the political home of pro-choice Republicans, one of the few moderate refuges in San Diego that week. The women mingling in the hallways were Tanya Melich's old friends, the kind of affluent and self-styled progressive Republican women who had deserted the GOP in droves after the 1992 convention. The war for control of the party was being waged over the definition of womanhood and hegemony over women's bodies. Melich's crew had declared defeat.

Those who hadn't bolted were still trying to bore from within, in Leninist terms, to take their party back, one delegate, one candidate and one dollar at a time. WISH List was their vehicle. That morning, tables had been set for two hundred. Half the seats were empty. But the real news was who was seated in the other half: Governors George Pataki of New York, Arnie Carlson of Minnesota, William Weld of Massachusetts and Christine Todd Whitman of New Jersey, Senators Olympia Snowe, Kay Bailey Hutchinson, and Nancy Kassebaum, along with more than a dozen members of the House of Representatives and a small phalanx of state and local officials.

The silk dresses and designer suits couldn't hide the sense that the women were under siege. Kay Bailey Hutchinson knew she was lucky to be at the convention at all: antiabortion forces had tried to keep her off the Texas delegation because of her pro-choice politics—despite a lifetime rating of 92 percent from the American Conservative Union. Olympia Snowe of Maine was still fuming over Bob Dole's betrayal, his refusal to meet with her before he announced his position on abortion despite his promise to do so. The group had just received news of the defeat of Gale Norton, the conservative attorney general of Colorado, in the primary race for Pat Schroeder's Senate seat. Her pro-choice politics had mobilized the state's Christian right against her. Even Christie Whitman wasn't all that convincing when she silenced a standing ovation to declare, "We have been heard, we are making a difference." Only Governor Weld got a laugh. "I know you all will believe me when I say that I'm grateful for this opportunity to speak," he quipped. The laughter was hollow. Dole's refusal to allow Weld to appear before the convention still stung.

But the weary embattlement was tinged with optimism. Almost all the women who starred in the nightly convention show were pro-choice, even if they had been warned not to mention that controversial reality. And the far right had been even more effectively shut out and silenced than their own forces. Glenda Greenwald, WISH List's chair and founder, could say, with some confidence, "We have reversed the momentum of the antichoice forces." But she also had to add, "We still need to remove the plank," referring to the abortion section of the party platform.

Greenwald is the quintessential progressive Republican activist: a longtime feminist blueblood who has been able to dabble in a series of professions—she's been an art critic, a gallery owner and a magazine publisher—because her husband has plenty of money (he is chairman of United Airlines). WISH List, the Republican counter to the liberal EMILY's List (Early Money Is Like Yeast), is the home of the ultrasuede-and-pearls crowd that both liberals and the new conservatives have long derided. To the first group, their politics are pretty good but their class status makes them suspect; to the second, both their politics and their country club affiliations stink. Candace Straight, one of the nation's top Republican contributors, was a founding member of the group; Julie Finley, another financial heavy hitter, served on the group's advisory board—even while she cochaired the finance committee of the Dole presidential campaign.

To outsiders, WISH List activists seemed poised between naivete and hypocrisy. The rest of the nation understood that the base of the Republican Party had moved from the corporate boardrooms dominated by the bicoastally arrogant to the southern churches of the evangelically intolerant. The old-line moderates had struggled for sixteen years to keep control over the party, to impose their vision of Republicanism and conservatism on newer party activists who imagined a different future. They remained in the party after the 1980 convention, when their support for the Equal Rights Amendment was shouted down, and their loyalty rewarded with dismissals from party and patronage positions. By February 1984, as they prepared for the convention in Dallas, progressive women had become so desperate that they had held a secret meeting to plot their strategy. Alas, they no longer had enough clout to plan one.

The 1984 convention was the final humiliation for many of the old-line Republican women who had spent decades as precinct captains and campaign workers. Suddenly they were forced to watch Phyllis Schlafly and her upstarts serve up a GOP fashion lunch using the wives of Republican politicians as their models. More than one thousand women cheered Schlafly, who had led the successful platform fights against endorsing the Equal Rights Amendment, against supporting equal pay for comparable work, against allowing government funding for abortions in the case of incest or rape. The moderate women could do little but complain that the convention didn't represent Republican voters. They grasped all too well the grim irony that they had lobbied for more women delegates, and that those female delegates had turned out to be Schlafly-ites.

Twelve years later, in 1996, they struggled on, insisting that with time and effort, they would prevail. "WISH List was founded because we were concerned that the moderate voice of the Republican Party was not being heard," Greenwald told the small crowd at the convention breakfast. "We were concerned that we didn't have enough women in high political office. We were concerned about thousands of long-standing Republican women acting like collective Noras and leaving the party.

"It took 150 years for women to get the vote. Please don't let it take that long for us to get represented in this party."

Greenwald, wearing one of the many YANK THE PLANK buttons in the room, was the announcer at the moderates' own political fashion show of its best and brightest: Senator Olympia Snowe, the first candidate to receive WISH List money; Representative Connie Morella of Maryland, cochair of the congressional caucus on women's issues that most of the new Republican congresswomen had refused to join; Representatives Nancy Johnson of Connecticut and Tillie Fowler of Florida, who complained bitterly that abortion was tying up huge chunks of their time because antiabortion initiatives were being written into every imaginable piece of legislation.

Finally, Greenwald presented the 1996 troupe, the newly endorsed WISH List candidates, women who had needed the group's money to succeed in primaries against opponents financed by the religious right: Sheila Frahm, appointed by the governor of Kansas to replace Bob Dole in the Senate, who was struggling to retain her seat; Janet Rzewnicki, the treasurer of Delaware, in an uphill battle for the governorship against a popular male Democrat; Cheryl Brown Henderson, daughter of the man whose lawsuit against the school board of Topeka had resulted in the historic Supreme Court desegregation decision, *Brown v. Board of Education,* running for Congress; and almost a dozen more.

The most sustained applause went to the woman who could have won the Most Embattled award, even in that embattled crowd. Sue Kelly, a freshman congresswoman from New York State, had defeated six men to win the 1994 primary and gone on to victory in the general election with 52 percent of the vote on a platform of fiscal conservatism and social moderation. One of her 1994 primary opponents, Joseph DioGuardi, had risen again, with Ralph Reed and Phyllis Schlafly at the altar beside him, and he had turned Kelly's primary race into a nasty fight. DioGuardi had thrown a fit of pique when he lost the 1994 primary to Kelly, and signed on to run against her on the Right to Life ticket. Unwilling to accept that defeat (he garnered only 10 percent of the vote) at the hands of a moderate, pro-choice woman, he was now challenging her again, and marshaling forces from all over the nation. Paul Weyrich, the conservative activist who runs the Free Congress Foundation, had endorsed him. Ultraconservative congressmen Bob Dornan of California and Chris Smith of New Jersey were helping him raise money. And Ralph Reed's minions were showing up at Kelly's rallies and campaign functions.

Kelly, a 59-year-old mother of four who sang in her local church choir before she moved to Washington, had done a little bit of everything in the workforce: rape crisis counseling, medical research, hospital administration; she'd even run a flower shop for a while. She was one of the new breed of Republican elected officials who had worked their way into office straight out of the community, through decades of volunteer work—with the local recreation department, the PTA, the League of Women Voters and the American Association of University Women.

Although she had joined the congressional women's caucus, the only Republican woman in her class to do so, Kelly was clearly no flaming liberal. She supported most of the Contract with America, a balanced budget plan and an end to the capital gains tax. When asked about women's issues, she responded, "Don't fluff us all up as gals who are in there to do something that is driven by the fact of our sex." Her only significant "liberal" credential was her support for a woman's right to choose to have an abortion.

Kelly wasn't without resources in her primary struggle—and they were not limited to the paltry sums WISH List had given her. Although New York State feminists were markedly ignoring the blatant assault on a pro-choice sister, the Republican leadership of the House of Representatives was not. "For the good of the Republican Party and the people of the 19th district, we strongly urge you to reconsider this ill-timed campaign," said a letter sent to DioGuardi signed by Newt Gingrich, House majority leader Richard Armey, majority whip Tom DeLay, Republican Conference chairman John Boehner and Representative Bill Paxon, head of the GOP House campaign committee—not exactly a liberal, pro-choice group. "Should you not withdraw your candidacy, you will be doing the party a great disservice." The rhetoric was not empty. The letter continued, "Should it become necessary, the House Republican Leadership is prepared to commit time and extensive resources to Sue Kelly's re-election efforts."

DioGuardi's supporters went on a rampage, accusing the House leadership of abandoning all principle in support of a woman who had defied them repeatedly and who was one of only five Republicans to vote against a ban on partial birth abortions. After all, DioGuardi was the national finance chairman of Gingrich's GOPAC, a loyal conservative trying to push aside "a radical, left-of-center liberal." Armey responded to the diatribes by calling potential DioGuardi contributors to ask them to withhold their money. Then Dornan and Chris Smith became involved, offering to help DioGuardi raise campaign funds. Gingrich responded by removing the congressmen from their coveted seats on the House-Senate committee negotiating the military budget bill. Boehner explained: "You don't go after other members of your team."

Dornan, with his talent for snits, turned on the House leaders. "I am an Air Force officer; I will not be punished by the likes of Newt Gingrich," he said, although he has not been in the air force for decades. He also had no choice but to accept his punishment, which was widened to include denying both him and Smith permission to travel overseas as part of official congressional delegations. The two congressmen never publicly recanted their support for DioGuardi, but they did back off on their practical assistance to him. By the time of the convention, all Sue Kelly had to worry about was Ralph Reed and the Democratic feminists who would oppose her in November.

*   *   *

NEWT'S support for Sue Kelly surprises only those who have never talked with Republican congresswomen about the Speaker of the House. To the women of America, he may be a villain, but to the Republican women of the House of Representatives, he's an unsung hero who has championed them from the moment he achieved power.

It wasn't easy being a Republican congresswoman before Newt took over the helm of the party in the House, the women say, yet Gingrich becomes surprisingly shy—almost embarrassed—when reminded of that characterization. "They deserve the credit, not me," Gingrich responded when I interviewed him for this book. "I'm just hanging out helping them . . . If you know Nancy Johnson, if you know Jennifer Dunn [congresswoman from Washington State], nobody creates them, okay? Start with this. The last thing they want is 'Gingrich Creates These People.' That's nonsense.

"So you start with the notion that these are pretty strong personalities in their own right. The difference I provided is that I have an active bias in favor of maximizing the opportunities for talent to rise. Okay?

"You have a tradition, in both parties. . . . You want to talk about an old boy network. . . . I give very high marks to Nancy Johnson, who had the courage to be openly frustrated with the system for six or seven years. It just drove her crazy. Lynn Martin was wonderful about this. . . . The party in the House eight or nine years ago was basically a bunch of male chauvinists who got together and wondered why the women were unhappy, but never invited them into the room to explain it. It just drove her nuts. . . . Lynn is one of the people who would sit down with me and say, 'You don't understand how the odds are stacked. You don't understand how the system works.' "

The situation inside the party wasn't much better than it was in the House. Women like Mary Louise Smith and Jeanie Austin, both GOP cochairs, spent years fighting to make it more attractive, and more hospitable, to women by recruiting more women to sit at the bargaining table with Johnson and Martin. But it was an uphill battle. Female candidates tended to be recruited from the ranks of the National Federation of Republican Women, and trained by its campaign school. During the 1960s, when ambitious women began pouring out of progressive organizations into the Democratic Party, and into campaigns for office, Republican women held back. Those who put themselves forward—like Senator Nancy Kassebaum of Kansas, Representative Jan Meyers of Kansas and Representative Barbara Vucanovich of Nevada—usually waited until their children were grown. The paucity of Republican women officeholders sent a loud message to ambitious women: Wrong party, wrong party.

Suddenly, after Bill Clinton was elected to his first term as president, the federation and the old female crowd were swept aside by a new attitude, and a new strategy. When Newt Gingrich was elected to lead the House Republican minority, he invited the twelve sitting GOP congresswomen to his office to vent. Week after week during 1993 and 1994, in one of only two standing appointments he made, Newt listened to the women complain.

The party already had several high-profile women, like Governor Christie Whitman and Senator Nancy Kassebaum, and the group in Gingrich's office included more who could become higher-profile, with a little effort by the party: Susan Molinari, Barbara Vucanovich, Jennifer Dunn. But their numbers were still insignificant. Gingrich worked with Molinari to identify viable female candidates for Congress and then to compile a database of activists who could advise them about public policy, about fund-raising, even about what to wear. Molinari then created a buddy system between sitting members and aspirants. Newt helped to raise money for them, and even campaigned in several of their races. He, Molinari and the other congresswomen put special effort into the races of Republican women candidates running against Democratic women. When the votes were counted in 1994, they had chalked up a record seven victories.

Few of their faces were familiar. Four of the seven had never before held elective office. Most had risen not from the ranks of the federation but from the conservative counterparts to the progressive groups which had catapulted Democratic women to power: the Eagle Forum, the Concerned Women of America and local church groups. And while their liberal counterparts campaigned as *women* concerned with *women's issues,* the new-style Republican women candidates talked about what they believed to be the new women's issues: tax cuts, downsizing government, crime and the erosion of the family.

Chenoweth and Kelly were at the opposite ends of the political spectrum of the new group, with Kelly being the odd duck on abortion. Linda Smith of Washington was swept into office by the reformist anger of 1994, winning election on a write-in bid. She was hardly the old-style Republican. Abandoned by her alcoholic father while still in diapers, she began working odd jobs in her early teens, then eschewed college as impractical and, after an unhappy stint in beauty school, wound up preparing taxes for H&R Block. An ardent conservative, she arrived in Washington with the Contract with America in hand and a commitment to campaign finance reform, beginning with the prohibition of contributions from political action committees which Smith herself never accepts.

Enid Green Waldholtz of Utah, whose first order of business in Washington was to set up a nursery in her office, was a Mormon who'd been a successful corporate attorney in Salt Lake City. Andrea Seastrand of California had been an elementary school teacher. In one campaign appearance, she suggested that California's record number of natural disasters might be a sign of God's wrath against feminism and multicultural education. And Barbara Cubin of Wyoming had prevailed against an opponent who outspent her five-to-one by campaigning against the government's "war on the West" and government regulation, which she proposed reforming by wiping out every regulation on the books and reinstating only those that could be justified.

Sue Myrick was known for invoking God's wrath on her adversaries. While mayor of Charlotte, North Carolina, she had proposed opening concentration camps for drug dealers and installing armed military police to patrol the halls of public schools. "I ran on a campaign of 'If you want pork, don't send me, because I am not going to bring home the bacon,' " she explained shortly after her arrival in Washington. "I'm there to make the decisions that need to be made. I'm going to take a lot of heat, but we've got to do it."

When the seven new members decamped on Capitol Hill, conservative pundits could barely contain their glee. "The feminist monolith on women in Congress is now broken," declared Kate O'Beirne, vice president of the Heritage Foundation.

The Republican victory gave Gingrich the Speaker's office, and he used it to continue promoting women. He appointed women to serve, for the first time, as Clerk of the House and as the House counsel. Jan Meyers of Kansas and Nancy Johnson of Connecticut became the first women to chair congressional committees in two decades. Representatives Susan Molinari of New York and Barbara Vucanovich were elected to the Republican leadership. Enid Waldholtz was named to the Rules Committee, the first freshman to serve there in eighty years. And Sue Myrick was appointed as freshman class liaison to leadership.

At the end of the first two months, Gingrich could brag without exaggeration: "We have more women chairmen, more women members in leadership than the Democrats have ever had, and that's real power. . . . These are not cosmetic changes. Ask the Democrats. Why does a Pat Schroeder leave here as the senior woman never having been a chair? How can that happen?"

Newt didn't ignore these women once they were installed. He kept up the biweekly meetings, watching over his new team, likening his role to that of a head coach. "What they needed," he said of his female colleagues, "was two things. They needed coaching. They needed somebody to say to them, You know, if you want to get on Ways and Means, here's how you do it—because what women don't tend to have in any large corporate structure is a network and a pattern of relating that allows them to teach each other to rise. The second thing they needed was a fair level of opportunity because of the mathematics of their numbers."

Newt credits his wife Marianne, his daughters and Lynn Martin and Nancy Johnson with helping him to understand the issue of a level playing field. "Marianne and I went through a long stretch of trying to sort things out because I really come out of a fairly chauvinist background. I'm an army brat. My dad was an infantry officer. This is a background that says that guys do important things like going off to fight and girls are supposed to hang around waiting for them. Neither my daughters nor my wife thought that was a rational interpretation of relationships in the late twentieth century. . . . In a funny way, it was helpful that I had two daughters because my goal for both of them has been, from birth, that they be able to survive without me, to be able to live a life that's complete and not dependent. It never occurred to me to think about designing a girl track.

"What I learned the hard way from both Marianne, to a lesser extent from Kathy and Jackie Sue [his daughters], then from people like Lynn Martin and Nancy Johnson . . . is that nondiscrimination is not the same as a level playing field. Nondiscrimination fairly well guarantees that white males will win, just because of the whole balance of the system."

Newt appointed the new, and newly anointed, Republican congresswomen as point women in the Republican assault on liberalism. "You see those two little angels," Representative Linda Smith of Washington told a reporter for the *New Republic,* pointing to photographs of her grandchildren, "I'm going to show their picture when we debate the budget. I'm having it blown up right now. I'll tell them that they're taking freedom and opportunities away from my little granddaughters. Imagine then if Pat Schroeder gets up and starts whining about killing old people and children. It's a lot different when she's fighting with a grandmother. . . ."

When President Clinton brought political consultant Dick Morris into the White House to help plot the strategy for his reelection campaign, Jennifer Dunn became the attack dog, firing off weekly press releases reminding the press of Morris's somewhat sleazy background. "Every day Dick Morris stays on the Clinton payroll is an insult to the victims of rape," read the third release, referring to Morris's polling work for the defense team of Alex Kelly,

a rich kid from Connecticut who left the country after he was accused of rap-
ing two high school girls.

The freshwomen weren't mere window dressing hung out whenever
Republican leaders needed to put a softer face on harsher proposals. The
ladies of the right were nobody's pawns. Cubin repeatedly accused the
Speaker of being too "green," too soft on environmental issues. Chenoweth
refused to play ball on the budget stalemate. And, in her first month
in office, Smith led the freshman rebellion against the balanced budget
amendment.

WHILE NEWT's gals tackled the high-profile, sexy battles on Capitol Hill, Evelyn McPhail was beating the bushes for dedicated women to refill the ranks
of the moderate women who had deserted the party. As cochair of the
Republican National Committee, the unassuming Mississippian looked with
some satisfaction at the legacy bequeathed by her predecessors. By February
1996, forty-five of the eighty-three women holding statewide executive office
in America were Republicans. The country's only female governor was a
Republican, as were eleven of the nineteen female lieutenant governors. In
the 1994 election alone, Republican women had gained eighty-five seats in
state legislatures and a 58 percent increase in the number of GOP female election winners over 1992. Things were looking good for Republican women
within the party as well, and not just at the highest levels. Twenty percent of
the state party chairs were female, and women seemed poised to rise quickly
throughout the nation. Half the state Republican committee members in
Massachusetts were female, along with 44 percent of Republican county officials in Mississippi.

But it wasn't enough. McPhail intended to see women everywhere, at
every level of the party, at every level of the nation—and she had the tenac-
ity to do it. She'd fought her way from an orphanage in Mississippi into college and a career in real estate. She'd survived the death of her husband from
leukemia, and the loss of their savings to his medical expenses. She'd
watched her grandchild born with, and die from, Down's syndrome. A gender gap favoring the Democrats didn't seem all that monumental.

With a group of Republican luminaries in tow—Arianna Huffington,
Marilyn Quayle, Betsy McCaughey Ross—Evelyn flew from state to state
facilitating workshops designed to encourage Republican women to get off
the defensive. In March 1996, they landed in Denver, where 160 women gathered at a Holiday Inn for a two-day pep rally. The old face of the party was in

clear evidence: dozens of well-coifed matrons in conservative suits with rhinestone-studded elephant pins on the lapels roamed the halls. But most of the crowd on hand to meet Betsy Ross, the lieutenant governor of New York, were a new breed, neither the old party stalwarts not the rabid ideologues who'd forced Tanya Melich to beat a retreat. Instead they were small businesswomen, PTA activists and civil servants, the kinds of women who had spent their early adult years cleaning up messes in their homes and communities and were ready to use those same skills to clean up the rest of America. They were the party's newest recruits, the grassroots activists who would face off the Christian right without turning the party back over to the country club set—at least if Evelyn McPhail had her way.

Pat Harrison, founder of the National Women's Economic Alliance and, as of 1997, McPhail's replacement as cochair of the Republican National Committee, addressed the Denver group with an upbeat presentation on the "modern" woman's route to political power. "Let me tell you about a woman who was a high school teacher with three children. There was a water issue in her community that involved an increase in taxes and she didn't like how it was handled. Her husband said, 'Do something about it.' She thought and thought and said to herself, I can do better than that.

"So she got involved and gained some visibility. Pretty soon people were encouraging her to run for a seat on the county board. She learned that she was good at communicating with people, that she liked going house to house and that she liked debating the issues." Then, in 1972, Harrison's heroine became involved with the public works commission, which didn't make the road supervisor very happy because he thought women shouldn't mess with potholes and sewage. So she turned to her family and friends and said, "I don't care how many road supervisors there are." She decided that she wanted a seat around the table and that she wanted to sit there with other women.

"Four years later," Harrison continued, "she was a member of the Illinois House of Representative. Two years after that, she was sitting in the state senate. Another two years and she was sitting in the United States House of Representatives. Then she ran for the Senate and lost. She was afraid that her political life was over, but she was suddenly appointed secretary of labor by George Bush. I'm talking about Lynn Martin, and I'm talking about you. It all began with a decision to get involved in a local issue.

"So, to paraphrase Rabbi Hillel, let me ask you: If not you, who? If not now, when?"

Harrison's presentation was a sort of old-fashioned revivalist's sermon with just a hint of consciousness-raising. The crowd hung on every word. It was just what McPhail had been looking for. "We never ceded the woman's votes to the Democrats," she said, sitting in the hotel lobby in a hot-pink suit, talking about her efforts to bring a new group of women into the party. "We just didn't know how to deal with Democratic activist women. They were strident and we didn't want to be like them. Republican women didn't want to be perceived as in your face. They put us on the defensive. We're not on the defensive anymore."

McPhail had just spent the day working an audience she knew was filled with "converts," potential converts and old-timers worried about the hijacking of the party by the religious right. "You have to become the voice of the Republican Party," she had told them during her opening remarks, as her staff handed out cards reading "Twelve Important Messages to American Women from the Republican Party."

"You are the messengers. You have to carry our message—a message that Republicans keep their promises, that we are putting women in positions of power, that we are listening to women, restoring dignity to welfare recipients, fighting for a balanced budget, protecting seniors and children and working to make health care more affordable. You have to carry that message into your homes and schools and churches, into your grocery stores, your country clubs and your rotary meetings."

Afterward, Evelyn talked about why she was willing to spend sixty hours a week in meetings, on airplanes and on the phone trying to convince Republican leaders that working from strength to weakness—concentrating your energies first on your rock-solid base, only then reaching out to the swing vote and to Democrats—could be a mistake. "It makes total sense to work from strength to weakness," she explained. "But we never seemed to get to weakness. We always stopped at the swing vote. No more.

"We partly deserve the reputation we have as the country club party. We've always had a lot of wealthy people in the party who didn't want to share what they had. I remember back in Mississippi when those people would say, 'Oh, we don't want *those people* in the party.' And we perpetuated that image by not doing anything different. But when Haley Barbour was elected chairman of this party in 1993, he declared that this was going to be a bottom-up party, and that's what we're going to make it.

"So I'm encouraging women to get active, to run for office even if they don't stand a chance of winning. It might run against conventional wisdom, but we win even if they lose. We train women volunteers, we get more women involved, we show the faces of Republican women."

During the convention in San Diego, McPhail showed those faces—almost one thousand of them—to the few media who bothered to show up at the "Celebration of Leadership," an elegant luncheon honoring Senator Nancy Kassebaum, Representative Jan Meyers and Representative Barbara Vucanovich, all of whom were retiring, and the hundreds of other Republican elected officials in the country. The "Singing Senators," led by Senator majority leader Trent Lott, entertained, with an assist from a twelve-year veteran of the *Lawrence Welk Show.* Elizabeth Dole showed up, along with Christie Todd Whitman. Newt and Marianne Gingrich sat in the audience.

Then the lights dimmed and the video projector rolled with a tribute to the three retirees: Kassebaum, the first woman elected to the United States Senate who wasn't preceded by her husband and the first woman to chair a major committee of the United States Senate; Meyers, the first woman president of the League of Kansas Municipalities, the first woman head of the Mid-American Regional Council and the first woman to head a committee in the House of Representatives in more than two decades; and Vucanovich, the first woman elected to federal office from Nevada and the first woman to hold a position in the House leadership.

Dina Butcher sat in the audience on the verge of tears. These were her heroines: ordinary, pragmatic, moderate Republican women just like her. Butcher had just been through a grueling state party convention in North Dakota. Although she was the governor's choice for commissioner of agriculture, the religious right had opposed her endorsement because of her position on abortion, and the old guys in the state joined them because they didn't much cotton to the idea of a woman mucking around in men's business. She'd emerged victorious, but she sorely needed the infusion of energy the celebration luncheon provided. She just as sorely needed to be surrounded by other moderate Republican pragmatists rather than the ideologues of the Christian right, who she believed—perhaps wishfully, she admitted—were finally on the run in her state and in the country at large. She was sick of hearing about Christian conservatives who gave nothing to her party, then packed state conventions and walked away with nominations that condemned the party to failure.

That was a common complaint at McPhail's luncheon, and the name on the tip of everyone's tongue was Ellen Craswell, the Republican candidate for governor of Washington. Craswell had lost her seat in the state senate in 1994 and then had hired a Christian—not a Republican—campaign consultant to help plot her bid for the state house. He had organized her campaign, which bore a marked resemblance to the Crusades, according to precepts he'd allegedly discovered in Exodus 18:21, in which Jethro tells Moses that he must delegate, and Moses divides his followers into groups of one thousand, one hundred, fifty and ten. So more than nine thousand volunteers were organized into teams led by forty-nine political directors. They had produced a weekly prayer-cum-campaign newsletter and sent out a children's choir called Stars & Stripes to spread the gospel. The message on the answering machine at her headquarters had chimed, "God Bless You." On Craswell's organization chart, Jesus ranked just above the candidate herself.

Craswell rejected the concept of separation of church and state. "They say you can't legislate morality," she told pastors gathered at the Northwest Graduate School of Ministry. "Every vote I took was legislating morality." Craswell had a long history of crusading against abortion and gay rights. She had proposed reducing prison sentences of sex offenders who agreed to castration, outlawing no-fault divorce and turning state prisons over to private companies. Her position on the welfare debate was succinct. "Whatever happened to 'Those who don't work, don't eat'? We need to get back to that."

Dina Butcher shuddered at the thought. Fortunately, she didn't have to deal with the Ellen Craswells, who exhibit open contempt for the party for which they are allegedly running. But she couldn't deal with the WISH List women either. Dina agreed with them on abortion, and probably most other issues, but they were too country club, and a bit too strident, for her and the hundreds of middle-class women for whom politics was a second career. But at the convention she could mingle with women like Susan Golding, the mayor of San Diego, thus the hostess of the convention. Golding, the city's second female mayor, was first elected in 1992, and reelected in March 1996 with a resounding 78 percent of the vote. She'd decentralized the city government by creating a City Neighborhood Service Center Plan, put more police on the street and turned San Diego into the safest large city in the country. She was young, pragmatic and effective, the new Republican woman's woman—Dina Butcher's kind of woman.

Dina hadn't grown up a political wannabe. Raised on a dairy farm in Princeton, New Jersey, she'd learned young from her father, a German Jewish refugee, to be suspicious of organized anything. The only exception he made for his daughter was 4-H. But in 1959, she fled the farm for Skidmore College in Saratoga Springs, New York, in those days a sort of swanky finishing school/college. Dina still laughs at how close she was to becoming June Cleaver. "We had none of the fun of the sixties, and all of the drag of the fifties. We learned to cross our legs, wear white gloves and titter instead of talking about sex. Meanwhile, the classes right behind mine were enjoying free sex and smoking funny stuff."

Like so many young people, she began college as a classic liberal, stopping just short of marching on her local Woolworth to protest segregation at the chain's southern lunch counters. (She made signs instead.) Then she went through her "socialist phase," but by 1964 had evolved politically and wound up staffing a Barry Goldwater booth—to the jeers and heckles of her liberal boyfriend.

Since she never considered the possibility of a career, Dina never wondered why in the world she was majoring in German. A job, sure; but careers seemed like something men or old maids pursued. After her marriage to an FBI agent, and their move to North Dakota, Dina was too busy raising her two daughters to think much about politics. "When feminism came along, I was out there in the wilds having kids and teaching part-time," she remembers. "It hardly seemed the time to be a radical."

Dina eased into activism in her new home state in a classic Pat Harrison-esque pattern. Beginning as a trustee of her local library, she worked her way up to state office, which led her to Bismarck, where conservative men had their hands on the purse strings. "I had to learn to schmooze those guys because they thought of libraries as a liberal concern," she says. "Then, gradually, I realized that if we were going to have money for libraries, we needed a healthy economy. In North Dakota, that means agriculture, since it is our only renewable resource."

Dina taught herself the ins and outs of agricultural dilemmas in the state: the problems of inheritance, the vagaries of federal farm programs and the challenges of running a small business dependent on the weather. She served as the female deputy commissioner of agriculture from 1981 to 1987, which was when she confronted the problem of dealing with a stubborn, suspicious breed of farmers and ranchers. "I had to learn to endear myself to the crusty old bastards who spit on their hands at cattle auctions, to fit in at ranchers' meetings where men bond by insulting each other and cope with old coots telling me that everything has gone to hell in a handbasket ever since women got the right to vote."

In the end, Dina found it was easy. She would go out drinking with the men, whether they invited her or not. She didn't play the good old boy, but she didn't expect the men to play the preacher around her either. Gradually, she says, the men accepted her for the only reason that counts: She helped them move forward. "It wasn't a woman-man thing in the end. It was could I get the job done."

Most importantly, Dina learned that farmers had fallen into the trap of promoting the myth that they were quaint vestiges of an earlier age, knowing that it would gain them public sympathy, and government benefits. "They were almost schizophrenic," she explains, "living in the world as big strong businessmen, then humbling themselves before the legislature and the public. They got trapped in their own rhetoric.

"I understood them right away because they were just like women."

As Dina grows older, she insists, she becomes less sympathetic with feminists, although "impatient" is probably a more accurate description. Enough ranting and raving, she says. Enough whining about being a victim and needing empowerment. " 'Empowerment' is an overused word. It's time to stop waving the flag, since it didn't do us much good anyway, and stop playing the victim. It's just like the farmers: no matter how much sympathy and how many programs it's gotten us, it's just not worth it. Women need to stop ranting and just do it. Plenty of women already are. I always said that women would be able to claim total equality when there were as many incompetent women in authority as there were men. Look around. We're getting close."

The race for commissioner of agriculture was one of the most hotly contested battles in the November election. In North Dakota, the agriculture commissioner isn't some powerless, faceless bureaucrat who counts cows. She's one of the state's most influential politicians, a member of the state Industrial Commission, which runs the state-owned Bank of North Dakota, the state mill and grain elevator and the North Dakota Finance Agency, and has its hands in the oil, gas and coal industries. The commissioner also sits on the Water Commission, the Board of Equalization and a dozen other bodies and commissions that chart the state's economic development.

Dina's Democratic opponent was Roger Johnson, who ran the state agricultural mediation service. He pulled in heavy hitters from the legislature. Dina, who'd been running the Wheat Growers Association, enjoyed the support of Governor Ed Schafer, for whom she worked part-time as an agriculture adviser. She and Johnson mixed it up enough to entertain the farmers of the state, with Johnson criticizing Dina's handling of a Honduran potato deal when she was deputy commissioner and Dina reminding voters that Johnson had been a leader of the effort to stop a critical water project.

Two months before the election, Dina was driving around the state nonstop, speaking at co-op meetings and dropping by ranches. Her daughter

Amanda, 23, had postponed a fellowship she'd won to Austria so that she could serve as her mother's campaign coordinator. After four years of liberal professors at the University of Minnesota, Amanda said it was a relief to come home and hear her mother being sensible. On Saturday, September 14, 1996, Amanda drove a classic Chevy truck down the main street of Alexander, a town of 150 in the far western part of the state. The Old Settlers Days parade was short. Extended families rode in the covered wagons their grandparents had built for the trip to North Dakota. Four-year-olds showed off their prowess on horseback. Dina alternately rode in back of the old Chevy waving and walked alongside handing out campaign brochures. She was in her element. "I've spent years writing other people's speeches and arranging other people's events, being the woman behind the man. It feels good to be doing it for myself."

Old Settlers Days has been an Alexander tradition for more than half a century, a celebration of the end of the fourteen-hour days of harvest, a moment of respite before the long winter, a day for farmers to remember how far they've come in less than a century. Each year a different rancher donates a cow for the festivities. The meat is cut into twelve-pound slabs, covered with three hundred pounds of onions and buried in a pit of coals overnight. The women in the community buy up every bean in the county to accompany it and bake hundreds of pies for dessert. After the parade (which is so short that it winds down the main street twice), lunch is served to whoever happens to show up, and ranchers and farmers from miles around sprawl on the lawn of the community park. The old settlers, dozens of men and women wearing badges indicating that they are over 70 or 80, sit in lawn chairs, often served by their grandchildren. Whoever wants to sing or tell a tall, or not so tall, tale mounts the steps to the gazebo and grabs the microphone. People amble back and forth to the community rodeo down the street, an event opened with a single young girl riding solemnly around the old rink carrying an American flag while "I'm Proud to Be an American" wafts out of tinny speakers.

The Republican convention seemed very far away, the wrangling over strategy and ideology lost in the closeness of community, the struggles to control the Grand Old Party irrelevant in the dust of a post-harvest drought on the plains. Dina's brand of no-nonsense, fiscally restrained pragmatism meshed seamlessly with the studied self-reliance of these pioneers in what might be the only part of America untouched by cynicism. The older women sat telling stories of homesteading that cruel land, of their mothers guiding the plows while their fathers pulled them against the rocky soil.

They had baked their own bread, hauled the water, helped split rail for the fences, loaded hay, chased cattle. "It takes two to make a go of it out here," they all said, shuddering with fondness and horror at the memory, looking forward to flying to Arizona for the winter—thus celebrating how far they had come.

Dina guided me through the crowd, making sure I understood her politics by introducing me to old women with faces mapped with wrinkles, and to their daughters: lawyers in Bismarck, engineers in Arizona, teachers in California. One old couple heard us talking about feminism. "You want to know about Women's Lip," said the old man, a farmer from north of Williston, about fifty miles away. "If the women want to do all the work so I can sit around like an Indian, that's okay by me." He chuckled. His wife gave him a withering glance. She pretended not to know much about the "issues of the day," but she did admit she was solidly behind Dole "since Elizabeth isn't running."

"Tell the lady what you think about feminism," her husband urged her. The woman pulled at the bonnet she had donned for the occasion, looked at me carefully and summed up the mood of western women of her generation: "I didn't need women's liberation to give me the right to work. I was already running a combine."

A Digression into the Strong Arms and Stronger Spirits of Frontierswomen

June Cleaver never lived in Alexander, North Dakota, and no one from Orofino, Idaho, was in Betty Friedan's graduating class at Smith College—which goes a long way toward explaining why feminism has never flourished in the soil of the rural West.

The notion that it "takes two to make a go of it out here"—a phrase repeated over and over again by older women on ranches and younger women in small towns, by educated women and women whose reading skills are limited, in Idaho, Montana, North Dakota—is more than a tired cliché on the open plains and narrow valleys of the Northwest. Whether or not it is a reality for men and women in this part of the country, it is accepted as such, literally woven into their lives and assumptions.

"Women here are hard workers," explained LaRee MacRae of Orofino, Idaho, who has been married for four decades. "We have to be, because you never know if it is going to be a bad logging year or if it is going to rain a lot in the summer. Men and women are interdependent. We have to be a team. The men work out in the woods and women have small businesses in town. We run stores, sell their crafts or do whatever. Or we drive logging trucks or skidders while our husbands log.

"Back east it's different. Men don't treat women as if they have many brains. But here women have to have equal rights, because we have to go out and work right beside their guys just to make ends meet. So here, when a woman talks, the guys listen."

LaRee talked between customers at a small stand she and her daughter had set up on the street during Lumberjack Days in Orofino. They were selling jewelry the two of them had made out of stone they dig, polish and shape. They had tried to make a living with a tattoo parlor in town, but once they'd finished covering the local bikers, the hostility of the church ladies got to them. All they had to show for their earlier efforts were intricate tattoos snaking across their own arms and legs and shoulders—and most of the unseen parts of their bodies as well, they explained, giggling. At 67, LaRee is a cross between an aging hippie, a biker moll and a militiawoman, which is not unusual in her neck of the woods. She sees no contradiction between her life membership in the National Rifle Association ("I prefer carrying a .357 magnum to a cast iron skillet, don't you?" she asks, only half joking) and her admiration for feminists who give errant men hell, between calling herself a "woman's libber" and bearing unrelenting hostility toward Bill Clinton, between her support for affirmative action and her unwavering opposition to abortion as murder.

She's a pioneer woman in nineties drag who feels entirely consistent, and is convinced that any apparent inconsistency is a measure of someone else's foolishness. Which it is, in her world. LaRee has never met a woman who is a "housewife," in the suburban sense of the word. She has never met a woman who doesn't want men to treat her like a lady. She doesn't know any women who don't carry guns.

Almost everything in America looks different from LaRee's world. I was puzzled when she and most of the other people in town complained about creeping socialism in America. Then I realized that in their corner of Idaho, the federal government exercises a degree of control over daily life inconceivable to most easterners. The government does reign supreme: it owns most of the forests they timber, it grants the permits to graze their cattle, it tells them if, and when, they can hunt the land where their parents and grandparents always found deer. Raised to be almost recklessly independent, they suddenly were butting up against federal regulations wherever they turned.

But if these women's attitude toward government is suspicious, verging on the hostile, their attitude toward the women's movement is virtually dismissive. LaRee, for example, doesn't know anyone who doesn't understand that the rules simply are different for women who live in what is still, remarkably, the Old West. "We all remember our grandmothers, who were pioneer women. They cleared the land with our grandfathers, they worked right next to them. The image of women as second-class citizens never took root here." Although LaRee would never frame the issue in these terms, she is nonetheless harking back to the argument made by Friedrich Engels a century ago, an argument long popular in the women's movement. The relationship between men and women in agrarian society was fundamentally different from what arose after industrialization, he wrote. In the agrarian world, there was no division between home and place of work. Husband and wife worked together, and that work produced a livelihood. No one thought to ask whose contribution was more valuable, since there was no clear line of separation between the contributions. In Engels's view, women's position plummeted only when the industrial revolution pulled men off their farms and into factories, leaving wives distanced from the place of labor and the source of income. Their work at home might have been socially necessary, but it had clearly, obviously, become marginal to the production of income.

In those societies, a woman's leisure became a sign of privilege—proof that her husband had "made it" to the point that his wife didn't have to find work in a shop or a mill. And, in feminist thinking, the moment women bought into that sign of privilege, they marginalized themselves from the centers of power. But a long trip through the Old West put another face on the process. What might theoretically be dangerous for women as a group is most often a dream come true for the real woman who's been breaking her back herding cows, at least according to Joyce Byerly of Watford City, North Dakota.

"Just at the point when families around here got comfortable enough that wives didn't have to milk the cows, drive combines and fix fences, the women's movement came along and starting talking about how women should work," says Joyce, sitting in her comfortable home, surrounded by photographs that testify to the changes in her life. "Well, we'd been working for almost one hundred years, the kind of work those feminist women could never have imagined. All we wanted was a chance to stop working. That was our idea of liberation."

Joyce is a notoriously pushy woman, the type of woman whom easterners would identify as a feminist and rural westerners would call a "women's libber." She's a walking almanac of female firsts: the first woman to run for the state legislature (she lost, of course, although her son won a neighboring seat in the same election); the first woman to run a grazing association; the first female member of the state beef commission; the first woman on her city council.

But mention the National Organization for Women, and the feisty 75-year-old explodes. "I'm totally impatient with them. I think they are all glory seekers. Out here, we tackle our own problems. We don't whine and complain. We don't file lawsuits or demand laws to take care of us. The men who settled this area were very chauvinistic. They had an inflated sense of themselves. But we were all in this together and that's how we solve our problem. That's very different from back east."

Joyce and her neighbors still harbor a vivid image of their mothers, who pioneered the harsh, dry hills of western North Dakota, who grew old at the age of 40 from raising ten children, from cooking supper on wood cookstoves even during scorching, hundred-degree summers, from hauling water, growing vegetables and the sheer loneliness of living ten miles from the nearest neighbor. Few women survived to old age. "If a couple celebrated their twenty-fifth anniversary, they had a long married life," Joyce says.

For their daughters, women whose hands were also callused, and for whom a store-bought dress was still a luxury, having a door opened, hearing a wolf whistle or being flirted up and flattered was hardly demeaning. It was relief from drudgery, a reminder of a softer side of life. Anyway, says Joyce, and dozens of other women in places like Alexander or Orofino, Idaho, "we don't want weak men. We don't want to be liberated from our own men."

Thirty years ago, Joyce applied for a job running her local grazing association. No way the boys were going to hire a woman, but she figured that someone had to try someday. When the man the group hired instead suddenly quit, the ranchers were stuck. They needed somebody fast, and Joyce was the only person at hand—which still didn't mean anyone was very happy about it. At first, they treated her like a secretary. She never complained. She just grinned and bore it. When she'd go out to buy fence posts and water tanks, the men would stand around refusing to help her load them. She did it herself. "I figured my job wasn't to complain, it was to earn their respect."

Joyce watched her friends and neighbors take jobs at half the pay of their male coworkers. "Equal pay for equal work is fine," she says, "but demanding it wasn't going to help anyone feed their kids. So we all worked for less money, which is what got women through the door. Then we got experience and recognition. It was a sneaky way to do it, but it was effective."

Today, in the small towns and along the back roads of North Dakota, Montana and Idaho, women are running their own businesses, their own ranches, even their own towns. Fed up with the good old boys ignoring the issues they care about, female teachers are abandoning the classroom for the state senate, housewives are expecting their husbands to make dinner while they join the town council, and church ladies are putting aside their rectory duties and seizing control over school boards. It's a breathtaking revolution in a region where women were virtually absent from public life between the days of Jeanette Rankin, the Montanan who was the first U.S. congresswoman, and the 1980s. But it is a revolution that refuses to ally itself with feminism. It is still too western to make that leap.

"You have to understand that out here even the women are ornery," says Michelle Cote. I'd heard about Michelle from women all over western North Dakota. A fugitive from New England who had been in the state for seven years, she is notorious because she is a single woman running her own ranch—all two thousand acres, 250 head of cattle and 55 ostriches—with only a single hand. "They have to be. They know how to take care of themselves. But they've learned over the years that it's better to go along than to fight, to find a way to get around the men instead of hitting them head-on.

"It's different. It's certainly not Boston. But look around," she says, pointing out her front window to an endless, empty brown landscape. "The rules have to be different."

The Ideopreneurs

For almost a decade, a small band of female intellectuals, activists and thinkers—that group that conservative writer James Pinkerton calls the ideopreneurs—have been trying to give voice to a new women's movement that they smell and sense and hear, to the frustrations of women of faith, to the disillusionment of women in the corporate chain gang, to the tension of women caught between home and work. Their work has popped up in bookstores, tomes like *Who Stole Feminism* by Clark University philosophy professor Christina Hoff Sommers and *Feminism Is Not the Story of My Life* (the sequel to *Feminism Without Illusions*) by Emory University's Elizabeth Fox-Genovese. In the months after Newt was installed in the Speaker's office, their ideas regularly graced the editorial pages of the *Wall Street Journal.* They seemed to have made it when the *New York Times Magazine* anointed Laura Ingraham, Lisa Schiffren and Danielle Crittenden as members of the nation's new "opinion elite."

These female leader–wannabes basked in the attention while high-profile feminist leaders carped that journalists were hyping this new elite with evil intent, yet another grain of proof that the media continued to be hostile to women's aspirations. Then, when the neocons got lost in a marketplace of ideas that has become a superstore, the new ideopreneurs turned the tables, whining that the "liberal media" was silencing conservative voices, while feminist leaders crowed with self-satisfaction. See, they said, Sommers and Schiffren, Ingraham, Fox-Genovese and their crowd are nothing but pretenders. Nobody wants to listen to them. They speak for no one but themselves.

Those feminist leaders aren't entirely right, and where they are, the arguments they offer are disingenuous at best. Contemporary conservative female ideopreneurs may or may not have the right stuff to become the next Elizabeth Cady Stanton or Betty Friedan, but the worth of their ideas is entirely irrelevant. Even the best ideas don't have a prayer in the waning years of the late twentieth century. Nobody in America really listens anymore.

Back in the days when communicating with "the public" was costly, Americans still had what passed for a common culture. Walter Cronkite and a handful of cronies presented the news, which was accepted as gospel. *Life, Look,* the *Saturday Evening Post* and a small handful of magazines told Americans what to think, and who to think about. And, on Sunday night, everybody watched Ed Sullivan.

Now every American cruises his or her own personal information superhighway, following an individualized course, stopping at carefully preselected destinations. Don't like the "liberal bias" of the news? Fine, tune into Rush Limbaugh or National Empowerment Television, or log on to Town Hall. Want to close yourself off from the afflictions of modern life? Keep your television on Nickelodeon or The Disney Channel, subscribe only to *USA Today* and roam the net for recipes and home remodeling tips. Too busy to keep up? Disconnect your computer, cancel your newspaper and catch snippets of gossip between courses of your evening meal. Filter out the rest as just so much extraneous noise. That's what everyone else is doing.

Imagine how much attention Thoreau or Emerson would have received if their compatriots had had the choice of turning to 250 other channels. Think about how much impact Elizabeth Cady Stanton would have made had she lived in an era in which nobody ever had to listen to anyone who disagreed. Consider how successful the women's movement might have been had Americans been as suspicious of any leader, or would-be leader, as we've become in the last three decades. Knowledge—or at least, information, which is what passes for knowledge these days—has become democratized, and leaders, religious, political or intellectual, have become villainized. The men and women who once served as the opinion elite that only the *New York Times* seems to believe still exists, the arbiters of what matters, have been condemned to oblivion. Even Andy Warhol was wrong: fifteen minutes of fame have become fifteen seconds in a chat room on the Internet.

Unless you're Madonna—or can get at least ten consecutive hours on television during a sexy trial.

Conservative women ideologues and intellectual designers weave theories and concepts contained in infrequently lively tracts about affirmative action, domestic violence and sexual harassment. When an O. J. Simpson or a John Bobbitt captures what is left of the American imagination, they jump on the bandwagon, hoping to exploit the moment. They travel to conferences where they chew on each other's fat. They have made little impact—not because American women and men prefer the voices of long-established icons like Steinem and Friedan, but because the Steinems and Friedans became icons in the old America, an America that still believed in leaders and their ideas.

The newer female voices, like the newer male voices, can't break through the wall of suspicion that has become a refusal to trust any leader, or idea, for more than five minutes. In a society in which disillusionment is almost instantaneous, they get lost in the cacophony of pundits and commentators and would-be experts who are competing for a prize that no longer exists. They might provoke some momentary discussion, but no discussion lasts very long among a populace with the collective attention span of a colony of fruit flies. Even politicians' eyes have begun to glaze over when besieged by pretenders to intellectual elitedom. They no longer need intermediaries to know if they are straying from likely reelection; their constituents have fax machines, e-mail and computer networks that link them directly to Washington. Anyway, this morning's hot idea—from the Contract with America to the Macarena—is this afternoon's old hat.

Which doesn't stop the Independent Women's Forum from trying.

FORTY women blew into the Heldref Building just off Dupont Circle in Washington on a bone-chillingly damp and gusty capital afternoon in December 1995. Lawyers and corporate executives on extended lunch breaks, journalists with reporters' notebooks in hand, regular members of the Washington conservative thought circuit and newcomers not quite sure whether they had crossed some ideological frontier stood in line before a buffet of chicken and salads—the low-fat food that has become de rigueur for women's luncheons across the nation. Mostly in their thirties and forties, they ran the gamut from no-nonsense suits to jeans and Birkenstocks. From all outward signs, they could have been gathering for a meeting of the National Organization for Women.

But Elizabeth Fox-Genovese hasn't been invited to many NOW meetings lately. The patrician professor—rail thin in a suit graced with one of those Hermès scarves that seem universal among properly dressed upscale conservative women, like the circle pins of their youths—rose after lunch to chat informally with the small crowd at the monthly luncheon meeting of the Independent Women's Forum about her new book, *Feminism Is Not the Story of*

My Life. She'd "done the impermissible," Fox-Genovese proudly declared: she'd questioned the gospel writ large by American feminists. That gospel, she explained within the first three minutes of her presentation, was "unrelentingly hostile to the ideas and the commitments American women embody."

Women in our society, she declared, grapple with complex and heart-wrenching problems—problems of family and motherhood, community and moral standards—that feminism has either created or refused to address. Fox-Genovese explained that she had arrived at that conclusion after a sort of unscientific survey of American women, a series of conversations with black women in the inner city and students on college campuses, southern belles, blue-collar workers and retirees about the relationships between men and women, the balance between home and work; about their dreams for their daughters, their reactions to abuse and their relationship to the movement which claims to speak in their voices. But it was hard not to suspect, like all too many social scientists, she had clearly arrived at that conclusion first and then conveniently found material in her interviews to bolster it.

Feminism hasn't failed American women because its ideals—equal rights, equal pay, equal opportunity—are alien to them, Fox-Genovese continued, but because the movement has been unrelentingly preoccupied with sex, with the belief (mistaken, of course) that the sexual liberation of women is the sine qua non of equality between the sexes and of women's independence from the drudgery and isolation of housewifery and motherhood. "No other society in human history has ever decided that women's sexuality is a matter of moral indifference," she insisted. "And we are only now beginning to understand the consequences. The link between women's sexuality and morality in most societies is not because of the patriarchy but because women's sexuality means the reproduction of the next generation. You cannot separate sexual freedom from children. If the first goal of feminism is to liberate women sexually, you are saying that women have the right to be liberated from children. If they do that, they are liberating themselves from society's future."

Women's sexual liberation is thus responsible, in some measure, for the breakdown of the family. (How can a family stay together if the mother is out exploring her sexual identity?) It has led to a terrifying increase in violence among youth. (The problem being that the children of mothers not closely involved in their lives tend to be deeply distrustful.) It has made feminists villains in the fight against welfare reform. ("Feminists' passionate defense of women's right to receive welfare no matter how many children they have isn't a defense of children," she said. "It's a defense of women's sexual freedom.") And it has alienated the movement from its own constituency, the vast majority of American women who, Fox-Genovese is sure, are as anxious as men about the unraveling of American society, and need society's support—in the form of IRAs for homemakers, a mommy track for professionals and respect for the role of mother—to combat this disintegration.

Fox-Genovese's paradigm is familiar cant in conservative circles, where hysteria over the possibility of a communist takeover has been replaced by fear that American civilization is on the brink of collapse because of the breakdown of the family. Feminists dismiss that fear as histrionic, as the ploy of men who want their unfettered power back, of those who believe that God means women to be subservient to men, or as the grandstanding of nouveau wannabes. But Fox-Genovese and her colleagues at the Independent Women's Forum, on whose national advisory board she serves, aren't poseurs; they sincerely believe that the ethical foundation of the nation is crumbling, and that the villain is the breakdown of the family—and they offer as evidence everything from the skyrocketing teen pregnancy rate to the intractability of poverty in large sectors of society.

Their apprehension sets women like Fox-Genovese on a collision course with feminist leaders, who not only reject the notion that they are responsible for undermining the family, but are unlikely to mourn its passing in any event. The goal of feminism is to liberate women from oppression, after all, and if the family turns out to be a casualty, so be it. Women's independence will not be sacrificed, especially not to an institution that enslaved them for millennia.

Fox-Genovese, on the other hand, is unwilling to allow what she is convinced is not just an essential institution, but one which women both cherish and need, to become the sacrificial lamb of feminist ideology. And, an avowed supporter of women's rights, she insists that there is no conflict between those rights and the social changes necessary to halt social disintegration and rebuild the family. Women, and men, can have it all—full equality and a healthy family—if feminists will only concede that women's rights are not in inevitable conflict with the interests of the very communities to which they belong. The problem, in Fox-Genovese's estimation, is the absurd contention of feminist theoreticians that the second-class citizenship of women is woven into the fabric of American family, law, politics, tradition and social norms, and that liberation can be achieved only by unraveling that fabric. "How can a women liberate herself from the fabric of her own society?" Fox-Genovese counters. "How can she disentangle those threads without leaving her own world in tatters?"

The price of doing so, she insists, is too high, for the same families and communities that feminists caricature as agents of women's oppression have also been women's protectors—from violence, from insecurity, from poverty. Look what happened when women's liberation declared sexual freedom for females: Women of means could absorb the trickle-down effects of the sexual revolution, which loosened family ties and left women free of the economic and physical protection of males. Poor women, however, could not, and were condemned by the sexual revolution to abuse, abandonment and dependence on the state. Poor women—indeed, most women—fare best when they are part of communities that respect, shelter and protect them, Fox-Genovese argues. The idea of an inevitable conflict between family and equality is a feminist fiction. Women can have both. They can be mothers and homemakers without being turned back into breeding machines or homebound drudges.

The means to that noble end is a new kind of feminism, a "family-friendly" feminism which would hold up working mothers committed to their families and society as the heroines of the movement, rather than independent career women either disinterested in family or willing to relegate it to a subsidiary place in their lives. Fox-Genovese never explains precisely how that rebalancing would occur, how society would manage to maintain, and even further, the gains of women's liberation within the confines of renewed social respect for marriage, family and motherhood. But her prescription for that renewal is abundantly clear. She advocates substantial tax deductions for having children rather than deductions for measures like child care, which reward women who don't stay home with their kids. She supports IRAs for homemakers. Her brand of "family-friendly" feminism, then, would allow women the physical and philosophical room to pursue "nontraditional" roles, but would channel society's support for women's independence into material social support for those women who opt for more traditional roles.

That "material social support" just happens to coincide with the agenda of the ultraconservative family values crowd with which Fox-Genovese claims to be in sharp disagreement. Even less surprisingly, perhaps, none of those proposals evoked much enthusiasm with her audience at the IWF luncheon, who purportedly share her values and politics. No one picked up on her comments about women as nurturers—a kind of romanticized view of women and sisterhood that she says makes her feel comfortable with the working-class Italian-American women in her husband's old neighborhood in Brooklyn because "we women recognize that we have much in common that is special to us." No one talked about "family-friendly" feminism or how to make America more respectful and supportive of motherhood. No one but Fox-Genovese even mentioned poor women, welfare or sex. Instead, the questions from the audience sounded as if they had been scripted by members of NOW rather than women with a "new agenda": how to make corporate America more friendly to women and how to motivate companies to be more flexible to accommodate working mothers.

Fox-Genovese's lecture was one in a series that the IWF has been holding for the last three years. The luncheons have become the nexus of conservative rethinking of feminism, yet another occasion on which sacred cows are slaughtered regularly and served up to a growing audience. One month Lynne Cheney, former chair of the National Endowment for the Humanities, talked about her new book, *Telling the Truth: Why Our Country and Our Culture Have Stopped Making Sense.* Another month, conservative pollster Kellyanne Fitzpatrick debunked myths about the alleged liberalism of American women and the gender gap. Abigail Thernstrom of the Manhattan Institute and her husband Steven appeared to critique affirmative action, and Barbara Bracher, chief counsel for the House Government Reform and Oversight Committee, dropped by to explain why women should support the Republican majority's attempts to improve government oversight.

The Independent Women's Forum was founded in 1992 by a group of high-powered Washington insiders who were too conservative for traditional women's organizations, too secular for conservative groups like the Eagle Forum or the Concerned Women of America and unwilling to allow their voices to be lost in the assumption that all successful, articulate, educated women were liberals. The founders first came together informally, as cheerleaders for Clarence Thomas's nomination to the Supreme Court—an act of solidarity by women for a man also socially deemed an unlikely conservative, and an act of respect and friendship from women like Ricki Silberman, who had worked with Thomas at the Equal Employment Opportunity Commission, and Laura Ingraham, who had clerked for the judge.

After Thomas's confirmation, the women called their friends, and the media, and announced the formation of a new group, a permanent organization to provide an alternative female voice in the social discussion. The new group that would, as their literature explains, "encourage women to vigorously pursue their professional lives" while also emphasizing the "great importance of family as the foundation of a thriving society and the matrix of most women's lives."

"Are you tired of the nonsense you hear from people who pretend to speak for all women?" their membership pamphlet asks. "Are you sick of being told that you are a 'victim' of the men in your life? Are you bored with the media message that strong, competent women must be feminists? Then join the INDEPENDENT WOMEN'S FORUM . . . capable, thinking women, who will bring common sense and a voice of reason to the social and political debates of our time."

"Who We Are?" the literature continues. "Some of us are professionals. Some of us are homemakers. Some of us have served in government. All of us have jobs, at home or in the workplace. All of us juggle. . . . BUT . . . while we are busy meeting our everyday responsibilities—raising our families, building our careers, working in our communities—radical feminists are un-challenged. They are influencing legislation, infiltrating our educational system, and transforming our society in ways that are destructive to our families and ourselves."

That advertisement is modest; the members of the IWF are a who's who of female highflyers in government and academia. From the first, Wendy Lee Gramm, the wife of Phil, was there licking stamps and arguing that taxes, free trade and deregulation of the economy are more critical to women's advancement than abortion rights or affirmative action. "By any objective measure, the well-being of women is more dependent on economic growth and a strong economy than on taxpayer-funded programs for child care or parental leave," wrote Gramm, an economist who taught at Texas A&M and chaired the U.S. Commodity Futures Trading Commission under Presidents Reagan and Bush, in the *Wall Street Journal*. "The best child-care program is a good family income. . . . In 1992, a broad spectrum of women were asked what they worry most about. Topping the list: jobs and the economy. Not abortion, not parental leave. These women were saying the economy is *the* women's issue."

She was joined by Christina Hoff Sommers, a professor of philosophy at Clark University, and the nation's leading attacker of sloppy research and intellectual laziness in academic women's studies programs; Diane Ravitch, one of conservative America's education experts; Lisa Schiffren, who wrote former vice president Dan Quayle's infamous diatribe against Murphy Brown; and Lynne Cheney, former chair of the National Endowment for the Humanities under Bush and a leading proponent of the abolition of that agency and its sister agency, the National Endowment for the Arts. Gradually, the advisory board has come to include Abigail Thernstrom, a sociologist at Boston University and the Manhattan Institute, who led the fight against the appointment of Lani Guinier; and Anna Kondratas, a senior fellow at the Hudson Institute, and a leading advocate of welfare reform. "The government should not be in the business of substituting for parents in the provision of aid to children unless the parents are a danger to the child," Kondratas wrote. "Otherwise, parents able to work should be assisted only in finding a job—any job."

Laura Ingraham emerged as IWF's most prominent media presence, a chic blond attorney who is conservative women's answer to Gloria Steinem. Ingraham carefully molded her image as the conservative bad girl racing around Washington in a military green Land Rover (paid for by her clients, white-collar criminals). She ran marathons, appeared on the cover of the *New York Times Magazine* in a leopard-print miniskirt, bragged about having a coat made from "baby squealing foxes" and turned up on every possible TV show—from *The McLaughlin Group* to *Politically Incorrect*—denouncing gun control, welfare abuse and affirmative action, which she dismisses with lines like "The idea that women are constantly thwarted by invisible barriers of sexism relegates them to permanent victim status." The media's ideal conservative—a conservative with a biting wit and a flair for irony— Ingraham and a friend, in 1995, organized their own version of the famed liberal Renaissance Weekend in Hilton Head, South Carolina, a regular stop for Clinton and company. Conservative America's luminaries—from Newt Gingrich to Arianna Huffington, Robert Bork and G. Gordon Liddy—showed up for Ingraham's first Dark Ages weekend in Miami, which boasted a William the Conqueror golf tournament, a Charlemagne tennis tournament and a *Canterbury Tales* banquet. The rules were simple: Number one was "No group hugs." Number three was "If you are smoking and someone approaches you and says, 'Do you mind?' answer, 'Of course not!' and offer the person a cigar or cigarette."

A slew of attorneys, government officials, academics, businesswomen and journalists bolster IWF's membership rolls, which nonetheless barely exceed five hundred. That number says little about the group's clout, or support in the fabled heartland, since IWF is not designed as a broad-based membership group. "We don't claim to represent women," says Anita Blair, a Washington attorney who is IWF's executive vice president. "It doesn't matter how many people think something. It only matters if it is intelligent and true." But IWF executive director Barbara Ledeen is quick to point out that her phone never stops ringing with calls from older women fed up with affirmative action, from younger women who think feminism is passé, from women sick of both the economic and social pressure to leave their children at home and pursue careers.

Blair and Ledeen grabbed onto one another, and the group, at one of IWF's first meetings. Blair had been looking for a political home since 1992, when she crossed the political divide by agreeing with Dan Quayle about Murphy Brown. "At first I didn't dare voice my opinion," she explains. "When I finally spoke up, people looked at me like I had told a dirty joke about the pope." Ledeen, who had resisted all pressure to leave her child rearing to someone else, was desperate to work with a group concerned with the issues confronting women who thought of themselves as part of families. "We were all in various ways saying there's a hole in the marketplace of ideas," she says.

IWF is not a newfangled version of a Republican women's club. Most of its members are as enthusiastic about the Republicans as feminists are about the Democrats. They might wind up supporting the party, but only by default. And like leftist thinkers in the 1960s, many of their leaders have a tendency to be more enamored of theory than reality, perhaps because they have had so little opportunity to test their ideas in practice.

IWF quickly evolved from a dissident conservative women's discussion group to an advocacy organization. In 1992, Blair filed an amicus brief on behalf of IWF in support of Virginia Military Institute's attempt to remain all-male, arguing that forcing the school to open its doors to women would jeopardize all single-sex education programs—including all-women programs, both public and private. The group then threw its support behind Paula Jones in her sexual harassment suit against Bill Clinton, engaging Kenneth Starr of Whitewater fame to write their legal brief.

Those acts catapulted IWF to a modest degree of celebrity. But the group achieved true infamy only when it launched a series of attacks on what members call "gender feminist laws." Their first foray was against the Gender Equity Act, a bill to channel funds into programs that increase educational opportunities for women—a bill that Anita Blair describes as a law that "authorizes millions of scarce education dollars to promote the insidious message that girls can't succeed on their own." Their second assault was aimed at the Violence Against Women Act, Title IV of Clinton's Crime Bill, which they dismiss as "feminist pork" created to protect the economic well-being of the "victimhood" industry—counseling, treatment and hotline programs—rather than to protect women from harm. Both bills passed, they insist, borrowing arguments raised by Christina Hoff Sommers, because legislators were duped by shoddy research that allegedly proved that women remain second-class citizens in the nation's classrooms and that gender-driven violence continues at epidemic proportions. Barbara Ledeen anxiously hands out her own research that proves just the opposite, her attempt to demonstrate that feminist leaders are steadfastly refusing to acknowledge how far women have come, that feminism has become a movement "whose religion is the hand-wringing of victimhood rather than the empowerment of sisterhood."

Despite its consistent attack on virtually the entire spectrum of the feminist agenda, IWF has been studiedly mute about abortion. On this single issue, most IWF members break ranks both with younger conservative women and with the women of the Christian right, who are usually their allies. "Feminists have made abortion *the* issue for women, and we're simply not buying into that," Ledeen says. "There are dozens of issues that are more important to women's lives. The women's movement was supposed to be about choice, but the only choice they're worried about is abortion. The word 'choice' is ours, not theirs. We want to give women choices: to put their kids in single-sex schools, to know whether they are HIV positive, to not put their children in day care at 6 A.M. These are the choices American women need to have, not just choice about abortion."

IWF's dramatic departure from the "expected" has garnered the group repeated flurries of publicity: a *60 Minutes* profile, coverage in major newspapers from the *Washington Post* to the *Boston Globe*. IWF leaders have become the sweethearts of the Op-Ed page of the *Wall Street Journal*, writing scathing indictments of Take Your Daughter to Work Day, the absence of mandatory testing of infants for HIV and affirmative action. They appear regularly on major news shows, pitted against feminist icons like Pat Ireland. That was the culmination of a plan most clearly articulated by Kate O'Beirne of the Heritage Foundation. "At some level, our girls have to fight their girls," she proposed in the *Washington Times*. Barbara Ledeen extends the point further. "If the male politician disagrees, then he's made to look like a misogynist. You can't have white guys saying you don't need affirmative action. We have credibility to say, 'Not all women think the way you may expect.' "

That is, in fact, the mantra of conservative and neoconservative female ideologues who are trying to reshape the nature of the debate over "women's issues" by providing female-friendly underpinnings to conservative social proposals. "It's a long, long time since the brand of feminism espoused by NOW and others did anything constructive or productive for society," Anita Blair intones at the slightest provocation. Adds Ledeen:

"When Ed Bradley interviewed me for *60 Minutes* he asked me, 'Is biology destiny?' What a stupid question. Of course it is, at least until men have babies. Those kinds of questions, those attitudes, have nothing to do with the lives of most women. Traditional feminism has burned out. We've got to get away from the idea of women as victims and whiners."

That message has been underwritten by four conservative foundations: Olin, Coors, Bradley and Carthage— but at surprisingly low levels. The IWF operation is lean. Its tiny digs are in the basement of a conservative think-tank building off Dupont Circle. Staff is minimal, and Ledeen glories in provoking her feminist opponents by comparing their meager resources to those of NOW, which has an annual budget of more than $5 million and a president who is paid more than $130,000, to Ledeen's $40,000. "The official spokeswomen of the official feminist movement are elitist," Fox-Genovese said at the IWF luncheon in a conspicuously nonaccusatory tone, as if she were merely describing their statures or hair colors. "They ignore the concerns of women less affluent than they are and with different commitments."

Her accusation, blandly delivered or not, was stunningly ironic; it is precisely the criticism hurled at Fox-Genovese by reviewers of her book, and at conservative women in general. "Fox-Genovese preaches power for the few, protection for the many," Susan Faludi wrote in the *Nation*. "What 'elitist' feminist leaders does she [Fox-Genovese] have in mind? NOW president Pat Ireland, the former stewardess? Feminist Majority Foundation president Eleanor Smeal, a former housewife from Erie, Pennsylvania, and the child of working-class Italian immigrants? Who knows? She doesn't bother to, or cannot, name a single such snooty sister in the movement."

The exchange is about par for the course in what has come to pass for intellectual discourse between feminists and their conservative female critics. What makes it downright embarrassing is that both sides are absolutely right: neither group spends much time in Watts, rural Appalachia or even amid the messy complexities of middle-class suburbia. Ireland and Smeal might have begun, respectively, as a stewardess and a housewife, but that is hardly where they wound up. Susan Faludi's pontificating on backlash earned her freedom from daily journalism and a punditry pedestal before she turned 35. And Fox-Genovese was born with a silver spoon in her mouth and a silver pen clutched between her tiny fingers. Her father, a history professor at Cornell University, was the scion of a family that landed at Plymouth Bay, and her mother was a member of one of the nation's most prominent German Jewish families. Before Bryn Mawr and Harvard, young Elizabeth studied at the kind of country boarding school where the literati shipped their kids, and, of course, spent the obligatory time in France. She now holds a chair in humanities at Emory University in Atlanta.

While the name-calling is just a sideshow in a more substantive debate, neither side is willing to acknowledge that it also serves to obscure the bitter truth that the common class status of the two warring armies has created startlingly similar mind-sets. Feminists insist that women need guidance and leadership to wage successful struggles against the patriarchy; conservative ideologues counter that they need a new, nonfeminist ideological frame-work to chart their lives. Neither side evidences the slightest sign of trust in the competence of American women to figure out what they need without any guidance from above, so to speak. The notion that American women might be perfectly capable of building successful lives without ideological assistance, from the right or the left, seems not to have occurred to women who clearly need American women much more than American women need them.

Fox-Genovese exalts the ability of poor women to resist violence without any help from feminist institutions, then turns around and presumes that those poor women need her aid to resist the excesses of feminism. Feminists revel in painting the professor as a "well-heeled, well-pedigreed" snob hold-ing forth with "lockjaw pretentiousness" about the plight of factory work-ers, then insult those same factory workers by insisting that without feminist support, they would be powerless to free themselves from the dreaded backlash.

Watching high-paid professionals in Gucci pumps argue about which of them speaks for welfare mothers might be amusing if they didn't take them-selves so seriously, if they conceded, even for a moment, that American women are too busy, and too empowered, to pay much attention to the self-anointed "opinion elite." As it stands, though, listening to successful, but childless, writers pontificate about the needs of working mothers—or to res-idents of bicoastal intellectual ghettos debating the impact of ideological conditioning on migrant farmworkers—falls somewhere between tragicom-edy and theater of the absurd performed by actresses unaware that they are playing to a half-empty house with an audience nodding off into the aisles.

DANIELLE Crittenden doesn't belong on the stage. Hers is the intellectual version of a John Hughes movie in which high school is life, and history begins with the junior prom. At 32, she is half of an almost-power couple. Her husband, David Frum, is a former editorial writer for the *Wall Street Jour-nal* and author of *Dead Right,* a blistering attack on the Reagan and Bush administrations for selling out their conservative thinkers. Crittenden—who insists she kept her maiden name only to avoid journalistic confusion—edits the IWF-sponsored *Women's Quarterly*, a would-be antidote to *Ms.*, and churns out essays making fun of natural childbirth ("Knock Me Out with a Truck"), explaining why her children's friends must call her Mrs. and meditating on whether Hillary Clinton's penchant for changing her hairstyle might be correlated with the inconsistencies in her husband's presidency. ("The voters of England would rightly have felt unnerved if their outwardly stern Iron Lady had faced the unions in a perm one week and then hammered away at Jacques Delors in a shag the next," she wrote).

Despite her age, Danielle wears her intellectual superiority with a decidedly smug air of "I invented all these ideas, aren't I entirely original?" She is, however, the mother of two. "You can't pigeonhole us," she says of the women of her generation. "We're the first group of American women who are not sectarian. We are women growing up entirely with feminist ideas. We are the living consequence of feminism, and we are talking about it." It's hard not to ask whether she might, then, be complimenting the movement she has vowed to bury. "We're saying to feminists, 'We disagree with everything you believe,' and we're saying it in their faces," she responds.

"Everything" is the type of hyperbole Danielle uses to berate the hyperbole of feminism. She concedes no ground. The most positive statement she makes about feminism is that it "brought a certain amount of dignity and respect to women." Then she quickly adds, "But most women were punished by it because it led to the breakdown of the family. The people who really benefit from feminism are men."

Not for long, since Danielle seems utterly confident that she'll be as successful tumbling the walls of feminism as Germaine Greer was in undermining the foundations of the patriarchy. To some, this might seem a bad prognosis for her work. But to Danielle, it means that she'll emerge as Gloria Steinem, Kate Millett and Erica Jong rolled into a single blond-haired package.

Crittenden breezed into the Palm restaurant on a damp Washington winter afternoon with Grace Paine Terzian, the publisher of the *Women's Quarterly*, in tow. The Palm was filled with aspiring members of the new Republican elite, an army of women and men who had captured Capitol Hill just a year earlier and were hard at work remaking America—or so they thought. Danielle had been receiving a heady amount of publicity for the *Women's Quarterly*, which was her baby, and was gushing. Articles from the small journal had been excerpted or cited by the *Wall Street Journal, USA Today* and the *Wash-*

ington Post. And Danielle herself was achieving modest fame as a sharp-tongued social critic intent on ruffling feminist feathers. She tweaked them by advertising the twelve-page magazine as "The Perfect Accessory for the Thinking Woman." ("Want something chic, trim, and in a timeless color? Something that won't make you feel too fat or plain? Something that will make passersby think you're witty and intelligent.") She slammed them head-on by running articles like "That's No White Male, That's My Husband," in which Ellen Ladowsky argued that women would kill off affirmative action; "Shrinking Violets at the Office: Why Take a Letter When You Can Take Your Boss to Court?" an attack on sexual harassment suits; and "Equal Pay for Less Work," a piece on why female lawyers constantly running home to tend sick children shouldn't be paid the same salaries as men slaving at the office for eighty hours a week.

But Crittenden's greatest titillation seemed to come from the filler columns that dot her publication and her own "Editor's Diary." To accompany a piece on the Violence Against Women Act, she ran a sidebar entitled "Annie, Get Your Gun" about the rise in violence by, rather than against, women. "He said 'No' but I knew he really wanted it" was her lead-in to a compilation of statistics on the increase in the number of women arrested for forcible rape of men. "If women earned the same as men, we wouldn't have to do it" was the caption she bestowed on a segment documenting the rise in arrests for robbery. "He danced with another girl at the prom, so I shot him" was the title that preceded the latest information on female arrests for murder and homicide.

In one of her editorial columns, Danielle tried her hand at highbrow satire, writing about the gender gap as she believed Jane Austen might have explained it on *Nightline,* dismissing the entire phenomenon as an example of female gullibility. "A man with problems is catnip to women," she wrote. "He doesn't have to be handsome or rich. All he need do is show his vulnerability and beg a woman's help for his reform." In another column she explained why she prefers that her daughters lionize Cinderella rather than *Sesame Street* characters, "who appear to regard trash recycling as the supreme human virtue." She mounted an argument about the fair princess's pluckiness, modesty and cheerfulness in the face of adversity, but it was clear that what Danielle loved most about Cinderella was that she was supposed to hate her.

Danielle wants to play in the big leagues, but she's still consigned to the minors—to parties at the house of David Brock of the *American Spectator,* where she trades quips with P. J. O'Rourke, the self-styled Hunter S. Thompson of the Newtoids. She lives, works and writes in a kind of parallel universe that never quite makes the impact on the big time. "I've been writing on these issues since 1988," she says. "But you can't be five minutes ahead of your time." She complains almost bitterly that nonfeminist women are forced into a journalistic ghetto of conservative publications. Then she turns around and observes that modern American history is now divided into two significant epochs: not pre– and post–World War II, or pre– and post–John F. Kennedy but P.N. and A.N., pre- and post-Newt. "All the intellectual ferment going on is now on the right, just as it was on the left in 1968," she opines.

Which is not to suggest that Danielle has nothing to say. Despite her penchant for banal witticism, she is often clearheaded and sharp about the limitations of feminist thinking. On the movement's affinity for defining the personal as political, she remarks, "We need to look at these issues from outside the spectrum of politics. Marriage shouldn't be about some historical patriarchal struggle." When she tackles the inescapable conundrum of the tug between career and motherhood, she speeds quickly into a discussion of the expected life span of young American women and the foolishness of setting the two possibilities up as mutually exclusive. "Have your kids early, then start your career," she says matter-of-factly. "You're not going to die in childbirth, so it would be insane not to aspire beyond motherhood after your children are grown." And she shows her unacknowledged feminist colors when she smarts over liberals who note with surprise that the women of IWF are "surprisingly savvy," branding them "patronizingly sexist."

But, like so many other conservative women ideopreneurs, she has backed herself into an intellectual and political corner by building her reputation on writings about issues that she has declared, in advance, to be nonissues. Unlike Fox-Genovese, Danielle isn't interested in family-friendly feminism. She says she isn't interested in any feminism at all. "The solution to this state of affairs, I think, is not to try to transform feminism again, nor to revert to an idealized vision of what it was in the past," she once wrote. "It is time, rather, to bury feminism entirely." But you can't bury feminism and move on to a society in which "all issues are women's issues," in which "women's issues are men's issues too," by setting up a counter–women's group, by creating a counter–Ms. magazine or becoming Susan Faludi in conservative drag. That strategy might be tempting, since it feels like a direct assault on the enemy. But it turns out to be more a ploy to replace feminists as the unofficial spokeswomen for female America than a reasonable strategy for demolishing the women's movement entirely.

"The Independent Women's Forum is a women's group for women who hate women's groups; we're out to end this way of viewing problems," Crittenden explains, seemingly without grasping the naivete, opportunism, hypocrisy or even the contradiction implicit in that statement. "We're a reactionary force, reacting against feminist positions," she adds with no hint of understanding that her stance keeps feminism in control of the agenda.

That contradiction defines the ideological circles of today's neoconservative female activism. Women like Fox-Genovese or Christina Hoff Sommers, another academic openly trying to "recapture" feminism for the masses of American women, understand that changing the terms of the debate means either advocating a reshaping of feminist thinking to accommodate a different version of "women's issues," or ignoring feminism entirely and working on those new issues within the context of the conservative movement. And as women who have built their careers in women's studies, they stand squarely in the former camp, whether for tactical or philosophical reasons. Danielle, on the other hand, like most of the younger female neocons, wants it both ways. She craves the notoriety gained by engaging "women's issues" even while insisting that such issues are feminist hype, and that Americans must move beyond gender.

But while Danielle is trapped by the hypocrisy of her position, Fox-Genovese and Sommers are similarly boxed in by their hostility to the very movement they profess to love. In 1994, Sommers declared war on the "radical feminist ideologues" she declares have seized control over the movement and transmogrified it into a bastion of male-bashing, navel-gazing and victimhood-wallowing bolstered by third-rate scholarship and anti-intellectual posturing. "In California," she told the *Boston Globe,* "there's now an explicit requirement that textbooks give equal representation to men and women. Unfortunately, history was not gender-fair. You cannot practice retroactive social justice in that way without doing historical revisionism."

In practicing her own brand of feminist revisionism, however, Sommers—like Fox-Genovese—seems more intent on destroying feminism than rehabilitating it, despite her protestations to the contrary. In fact, her view of American women would make any collective movement entirely implausible. "The thing is, we're not a tribe," she said. "We're not a class. We do not have a shared vision. We want all sorts of things. You can no more generalize about women than you can about men." Which may well be true, but is a pretty cogent argument for the obsolescence of any feminism, rather than a plea to dress the old one in new clothes.

*   *   *

IN THE END, the neofeminists and practicing antifeminists seem almost familiar to an old liberal warhorse like me. I know them, just as I know a great deal about the issues provoking them. I don't find them scary since they are still debating women's affairs on feminist terms and, in the end, don't say all that much that feminists have not been saying to one another in private for the past twenty years.

But lurking in the think tanks and conservative journals of Washington are another group of conservative ideologues who *are* saying something new, by refusing to debate anything on feminist, or even liberal, terms. These women would never be caught dead in a "women's group." They believe that feminism and women's issues are irrelevant, so they devote themselves instead to the issues they believe determine the quality of American lives. In doing so, they eschew the psychic and publicity benefits of becoming the conservative answer to feminism. They are never asked to debate Patricia Ireland or Gloria Steinem. They can never glory in the excitement of playing "bad girl" to the liberal femmes fatales.

Which makes them virtually invisible.

The "virtual" is a nod to Arianna Huffington, who has strived to emerge from invisibility for decades, and you can't blame a girl for trying. In a field overcrowded with poseurs and wannabes, Arianna is the nation's most dedicated pretender to the crown of Miss Intellectual America. She's the self-anointed Queen of Compassion, who will lead the nation back to its roots, to its very soul. She tried using her husband Michael as a surrogate voice during his 1994 California senatorial campaign, spending $30 million in the process. She bought herself airtime for her own show on National Empowerment Television. She tried for her own commercial television program (alternately titled *Beat the Press* and *Eat the Press*), created her own Center for Effective Compassion, worked up a comedy routine with Al Franken, and spent a fortune on dinners for the inside-the-Beltway crowd.

Ah, for the good old days when the committed pursuit of noblesse oblige at least bought you attention!

Arianna Stassinopoulos was born in Athens, but she moved to London, where she shined brightly—for a moment—against the backdrop of Cambridge University. She wrote a book attacking feminism. She penned a scandalous pseudo-psychological profile of Picasso; the art world swooned in disparagement. So, she moved to New York. She then worked her way through America's Most Eligible. Pineapple magnate David Murdock, politician and New Age trendoid Jerry Brown, real estate and media baron Mort Zuckerman and even est guru Werner Erhard succumbed to her charms, at least momentarily. Then Arianna found Michael Huffington, the scion of the Texas oil Huffingtons. He was rich, he was willing and he was compliant.

Until he met Arianna, Huffington didn't seem to have much ambition for anything beyond money, which he already had in abundance. Suddenly, in 1988, the couple purchased a $4.5 million estate in Santa Barbara, and entered politics. To no avail. Plan B: California offered little promise since many in the state came to see her as a manipulative harpy. Part of this stemmed from her controversial association with one of those New Age types who flourish along the Pacific coast, a would-be messiah named John Henry. She moved to Washington, D.C., and became a hostess.

Arianna is ever earnest and seemingly oblivious to the condescension of her remarks. "Many too many people go to college," she says, "but they can't get jobs without college. We have a cultural elite and a political economy that has devalued manual labor." In response to discussions about the tension women feel between career and family, she answers blithely, "I think that some significant percentage of the yuppie career women who are putting their kids in day care at a very early age are driven by some combination of the consumer culture and a misguided sense that they have to be as busy as their husbands. The necessity is more psychological than material; it's tragic."

In other words, Arianna is unlikely to make much of an impact on Main Street. Not so the conservative women who are serious policy wonks, who devote more of their time to planning than posturing. These women might have dropped by the Counter-Inaugural Ball the night conservatives were licking their wounds after Clinton's election, but few party with the IWF crowd at the home of David Brock, who still gloats over having purchased a Georgetown house down the street from the old JFK homestead with the money he made on his book attacking Anita Hill. For the most part, these conservative women don't party. They don't hang out. They aren't trying to see and be seen. They are too busy plotting the reshaping of America.

Almost all of them are Reagan's girls, members of a huge wave of women who cut their political teeth during the presidency that conservatives think of as their Bolshevik revolution. They aren't sassy or stylish. They are gluttons for policy who churn out weighty studies and tracts for the American Enterprise Institute, the Heritage Foundation and the other intellectual factories that produce the materiel that fuels the conservative state.

If you want to hear their voices and see their faces, you have to turn on National Empowerment Television, Paul Weyrich's answer to the infamous liberal bias of the mainstream media, or catch a broadcast of a Heritage Foundation press conference on C-Span. You'll probably bump into Becky Norton Dunlop, who began working for the American Conservative Union—bastion of the seriously far right—when she graduated from Miami University in Ohio in 1973 and is currently serving on that group's board of directors. Becky spent years working in the Reagan White House and then in the Justice Department and the Department of the Interior, with nary a sign that she was even aware of women's issues. These days she is busy helping Virginia governor George Allen undo environmental regulations and does not seem to concern herself with something as minor as dismantling affirmative action. Or you might read the work of Angela Antonelli, if you can get through it. Antonelli, who has degrees from Cornell and Princeton, devotes herself not to social issues like child care deductions or the Protection of Marriage Act but to the decidedly unsexy, but entirely critical, matter of government regulations, the product of her service in the White House's Office of Management and Budget.

Or, better yet, turn on CNBC when *Equal Time* is airing and listen—really listen—to the one truly conservative woman who has become a national name brand, almost replacing Phyllis Schlafly as the conservative liberals love to hate. She is the kind of tough, opinionated and uncompromising woman who would be a feminist heroine, if not for her politics. Angela "Bay" Buchanan is more than Pat Buchanan's baby sister. She is his alter ego—Pat in demure, knee-length drag and meticulously coifed hair. For a decade, she has been her brother's General MacArthur, the field marshal of his renegade campaign for the presidency, a conservative Bobby Kennedy to her brother's JFK.

But Bay Buchanan is too determined to play permanent second fiddle, even to the older brother she worships. "Bay is a hard-driving, determined woman who sets her goals and doesn't let anything get in the way," said Greg Haskin, former executive director of the Republican Party in Orange County, California, where Bay lives. "She likes a good fight. She likes the competition. She likes the challenge. She likes the opportunity to pull out a few surprises. And she has a reputation for not worrying about the mainstream or what's politically correct."

Bay came by those attributes honestly. They are the survival skills of the eighth in a family of nine scrappy children. She had to learn to fight to hold her own against seven brothers who were required to take boxing lessons, seven brothers who had little patience with their baby sister horning in on serious conversation at the dinner table. Unlike her older sister, Bay refused to retreat into traditional feminine pursuits. She became the captain of the hockey and basketball teams at Georgetown Visitation Convent School and at Rosemont College. Despite her staunch Catholic upbringing, she threw herself into a virtually all-male curriculum, studying math both at Rosemont and then in graduate school at McGill University in Montreal.

At both schools she was an ardent campus conservative. She still chuckles at the memory of how she sabotaged Rosemont antiwar demonstrations by removing the extension cords powering the loudspeakers. She was more demure at McGill, where she was surrounded by American professors she was sure were in Canada dodging the draft. When her brother launched an attack on draft dodgers from his office in Nixon's White House, Bay froze. "That's it!" she said. "I'm going to get *F*'s!" She wrote her brother a letter begging him to calm down the rhetoric.

The explosion of Watergate demoralized the young woman, who had taken a leave from McGill to work on the Nixon campaign. Torn apart by the backbiting and internecine recriminations within the Nixon camp, she left the country for Australia, where she continued her education at the University of New South Wales and worked as an accountant. More than her departure, her extracurricular activities got her into trouble with her family, especially her brother Pat. Bay began dating a Mormon businessman and gradually was pulled away from Catholicism into his church. When Bay married in the Mormon Church, all the members of her family except her brother Hank boycotted the wedding.

After she returned home from Australia, Bay threw herself back into Republican Party politics, serving as the national treasurer for Ronald Reagan's 1980 campaign. When Reagan took the White House, Bay turned to Pat for advice about her future. "What do you want?" Pat asked her. "I want to be assistant secretary of the budget," Bay responded. Pat scoffed. "Forget that. They work you night and day. Put yourself at the Treasury of the U.S., get your name on the dollar bill, get out front and do some speaking."

Bay called in her chips and was appointed Treasurer of the United States at the age of 32, the youngest Treasurer in the nation's history. She served only two years in that office, just long enough to cut the federal budget by replacing the copper in pennies with zinc. Once she got pregnant, she moved back to California and began to create her own political base. After divorcing her husband, she honed her campaigning skills with local candidates and even made her own, unsuccessful, run for treasurer of California.

Then, on the eve of the 1992 election season, she phoned her brother, whom she'd been nagging about a presidential bid since 1988. "We don't have any time for any further discussions," she said. "If you're interested in run-

ning, give me a call." Pat did, and the brother-sister team developed their
own routine, and their own rhetoric, for selling America the Buchanan
brand of right-wing populism. Pat lost that race, but Bay did not lose heart.
By 1995, she was ready again, having spent four years running American
Cause, the advocacy group that grew out of the earlier campaign. "Listen,"
she told Pat, "the stationery is already printed—'Buchanan for President'—
and if you aren't going to run, I am."

The 1996 campaign was Bay's one-woman show, the source of no end of
griping from the pretenders that she ignored, patronized or froze out. But
the disinterested were awed by the same driving skill and determination that
branded her as a shark. "She's the engine that runs the Buchanan machine,"
said Ron Robinson, president of the Young America's Foundation. "She's the
one that stays up on the conservative community, the one that has the best
grasp of practical politics." Bay, who shares her brother's slash-and-burn
style, seemed entirely unfazed by criticism. "Any idea that women are softer
in politics is certainly not true with Bay," said Democratic pollster Celinda
Lake.

Despite their political agreements, Pat and Bay are a political odd couple.
After all, he is the man who longs for the old days when women stayed home
and raised their children, intoning, "Mama bird builds the nest"; she is a
hard-driving, divorced career woman raising three boys on her own. He is
the man who argues that women don't have the "stuff" to compete in the
tough world; she is the woman he chose to front his campaign.

It's an irony Bay Buchanan won't even acknowledge, at least not in public. She reminds those who question her that she never leaves for work in the
morning until the boys are off to school, that she shows up at every basketball game and takes at least one son on the campaign trail when she travels.
"I'm a member of a very traditional church, and traditional values play a very
important role in my life," she says. "They were instilled in me by my family,
and I raise the children, attempting to instill those values in them.

"I think it is an ideal situation, which unfortunately is very difficult to
attain in today's society, where you have a parent at home with the children,
and you have a breadwinner and that they work it out together," she says,
carefully omitting the genders of the parents assigned to each role. "However, I do believe strongly that there are many very solid families who have
made the decision, because this is what's best for their family, that both work.
Maybe for economic reasons, maybe for personal reasons. I know many
women who, if they spend a lot of time at home all day long, by the end of
the week, they will not be good mothers. They'd be much better coming

home after four hours of work, or six hours, or eight hours, or whatever it is they choose to do. I think that what's very important is that we create a society that allows those choices, that a mother can stay home."

If that sounds like a paradoxical position for the nation's archetypal conservative woman, Bay Buchanan would undoubtedly suggest that paradox is in the mind of the beholder.

A Digression into
the Mind of a Femi-Newtie

Newt Gingrich on feminism: excerpts from an interview with the Speaker of the House of Representatives in December 1995:

"Feminism has become a politically correct term implying left-wing orientation. Feminism, as a modern term, means the deliberate use of state power to define people in narrowing ways, which minimizes their capacity. If you are willing to say that there is a commonsense feminist who recognizes, *a*, that women have enormous potential, and, *b*, that women and men are, in fact, different . . ."

At this point, Gingrich interrupted the flow of his answer to my question with an aside. "Many of the pure-left feminists will not accept that. They must have missed biology. There is a long pattern of the rise of women that accelerated in the industrial era and explodes with the rise of the information age. And with the decline of physical power as the primary demarcation, the normal dominance of males, which was a function partly of plowing and of physical brute strength, ceases to be societally relevant. And, in fact, is a hindrance.

"Who you are as a person, how much you want to discipline yourself, how much you want to dedicate your life to a particular ability, how much passion you want to display may be far more important than your gender. Once you accept that, by the standard of an agrarian-era language, you're a feminist—because you are now willing to say, Why wouldn't my top executive be a woman? Why wouldn't I want to have a woman chair a committee? That model simply says that who you are in terms of gender should not define your capacity as an individual."

Gingrich returned to his main point. "By any commonsense definition, I'm a feminist."

The Weary

Whitney Adams left the 1992 Republican convention in Houston madder than the mythical hatter. She'd looked forward to a gathering that would address what she thought were the burning issues: the racial strife she'd seen firsthand growing up in Alabama; the ineptitude of the government agencies she'd been forced to defend when she worked in the U.S. Attorney's Office; the record number of children killing other children; gun control that was doing nothing to stop violence; and affirmative action that cast a pall over the competence of every well-placed woman.

What did she get? Abortion. Floor fights about abortion, newspaper articles about abortion, abortion polls, abortion demonstrations, abortion amendments and abortion rhetoric. Whitney was suffering from abortion fatigue, and she didn't even care much about the issue.

That's when Whitney really became politically active. Oh, she'd dabbled in politics for years, especially in the early 1970s, when she served on the board of the National Organization for Women. But it was only after Houston that changing the nation became her crusade. Unlike Tanya Melich and other pro-choice Republican stalwarts, she didn't bolt the party. Whitney had already been a Democrat; she wasn't about to retrace her steps. Instead, she flew home to Washington, D.C., and called up a friend who was also a member of the Republican National Lawyers' Association. "We have to find women to reframe the issues," Whitney told her, almost desperate for an ally. "We have to reframe the issues and stop talking about abortion."

Whitney and her friends spent four years trying to knock abortion off its pedestal as the hot-button issue in America, as the litmus test for Republicans and Democrats, for liberals and conservatives, feminists and antifeminists. They raised money for Kay Bailey Hutchinson when she ran for the U.S. Senate from Texas. They helped out Ann Northrup, vying for a congressional seat in Kentucky. Kay happened to be pro-choice and Ann pro-life. Whitney didn't care; she only cared that both candidates were committed to women's issues, to welfare, tax reform and values—and that abortion was not an obsession with either of them. As the 1996 convention loomed, she studiously avoided throwing herself into the melee over the abortion language in the party's platform. She talked to everybody who would listen, explaining, pleading and cajoling. Abortion isn't a big issue for most Americans; why are we letting it distract us?

Sitting in an outdoor cafe at the Republican convention in San Diego in the summer of 1996, however, Whitney cannot claim victory. The day before, pro-choice Republicans mounted a flotilla in the San Diego harbor, a parade of boats decked out with banners reading YANK THE PLANK. The press has been grabbing every available female delegate and quizzing her about the politics of abortion. For weeks newspapers and magazines have been detailing every nuance of the Republican abortion debate: the abortion stance of every speaker chosen to appear on the podium, the composition of state delegations by abortion position, the anger of both the violently pro- and anti-choice crowds at their exclusion from positions of prominence. Once again, her party has become the Abortion Party.

Whitney leans back in her chair, taps her black patent leather open-toed heels—high heels, the kind actresses wore in movies in the 1950s—and tosses her hair back in the wind. She is wearing a miniskirt and a gold necklace. Men stare from across the patio; she is a dish. "They're still tearing each other apart, but it's okay now, though," she says offhandedly, almost casually. "I'm not worried about it anymore. This is the last convention where abortion will be a big deal. Technology is about to make the issue moot. Soon we'll be able to move on to the real struggles."

AMERICAN women don't agree on very much. We fight over welfare, the definition of family and the size of government. We argue over affirmative action, the ERA, pornography, how far women have come and how much further we have to go. We part company on movie stars, novelists and candidates for political office. But, despite all evidence to the contrary, something remarkably close to consensus has emerged on the topic of abortion: Like Whitney, American women are sick of it.

No poll numbers elucidate this emerging reality, since neither side has any stake in documenting the abortion fatigue women feel after twenty years of being buffeted by two implacable foes, each claiming the moral high ground. But a year of travel across America talking to women—old women and young women, wealthy women and women just getting by—made one thing abundantly clear to me: With the price of milk what it is, with the crime rate isolating Americans behind barred doors and the prospect of being forced into bankruptcy by medical costs looming over their heads, American women don't have much patience for self-righteousness that has little direct impact on their lives.

Ask them what they care about: Abortion is on the bottom of every list—after balancing family and career, crime, health care and the federal deficit. No matter how many photographs of decapitated fetuses antiabortionists display, no matter how many heart-wrenching tales of rape and incest the pro-choice produce, American women refuse to be distracted from the issues that affect their lives, day by day, hour by hour, rather than those that impinge on their existences on some lofty theoretical plane that only a philosopher can discern.

American women have already decided what they think about abortion, and moved on. The pro-choice crowd characterizes their position as a consensus that abortions should be "safe, legal and rare"—which is somewhat of an oversimplification. The truth is that the majority of Americans, male and female, believe that abortion is wrong and 40 percent go so far as to tell pollsters that it's murder. But they flounder over whether, or how, to enshrine that belief into law. If a woman's health is endangered, if there's a strong chance her baby will be born with a serious physical defect, or the pregnancy was the result of rape, the vast majority believe she should be able to obtain a legal abortion. But Americans are split evenly over whether abortion should be legal for women who want to terminate pregnancies because they can't afford more children, because they don't want to be single moms or because they simply don't want kids.

The picture is pretty clear: Americans are uncomfortable with abortion, but they are equally uncomfortable with forcing a woman to remain pregnant. They seem to have filed abortion into the broad category of socially necessary evils, or the narrower category of justifiable homicide, which is how they deal with other killings they approve of, or at least that they don't entirely disapprove of.

Despite two decades of bickering and graphic propaganda by both sides, American women have not budged from this position for almost two decades. In 1975, 40 percent told pollsters they thought abortions should be generally available, although 40 percent also thought stricter limits should be placed on them. Not even one in five wanted to outlaw the procedure entirely. Today, about 40 percent tell pollsters they think abortions should be generally available, although about 40 percent also think stricter limits should be placed on them. Not even one in five Americans wants to outlaw the procedure entirely.

That neither side in the debate has attracted many converts is the most glaring example of national abortion fatigue. No one seems to be listening to the thousands of words spoken and written and flung back and forth by the committed. And when they try to tune in, they are likely to tune out quickly and decidedly because the arguments they hear are riddled with inconsistency, contradiction and theoretical absurdities.

Listen to the pro-choice crowd talk about abortion. "I abhor abortions," declared Henry Foster, President Clinton's nominee for surgeon general; his abhorrence inexplicably did not make him oppose the practice, which led pro-lifers to oppose him enough to thwart his nomination. During his 1992 campaign, Clinton himself argued that abortion should be "safe, legal and rare." Why? If abortion is no more ethically problematic than, say, the removal of a hangnail or the extraction of a tonsil, what's to abhor? Why should abortion be rare? If fetuses are not human beings, who cares how many of them are yanked out of women's uteruses? If abortion is protected by the privacy clause of the Constitution, why should a woman need a good reason to have one? Pro-choice activists seem to be admitting that abortion is straddling an ethical line. How else can they explain their seeming ambivalence?

And then there's their problem with naming the fetus—a critical issue because the pro-choice position is rooted in a classical liberal belief that every man, and woman, has a right to own his own body. "We can get all the rights in the world, but none of them mean anything if we don't own the flesh we inhabit," abortion rights activists declaim. But how, then, do you answer the objection that a fetus is not part of a woman's body? The only real possibility is to insist, with Dr. Jane Hodgson, that it isn't. The Minnesota physician, who challenged her state's parental notification law, calls the fetus "uterine contents" or "a few embryonic cells." But too many women have followed the development of their own fetuses—watched them respond during sonograms and read all about their evolution—to swallow such rhetoric.

Consider the old pro-choice standby: that "abortions will happen, so we must keep them safe by keeping them legal." Would we ever say that about domestic violence? Poverty? Drunk driving? Trying to make something we think is bad rare because we cannot envision how to outlaw it is antithetical to the very concept of ethics and the law. Anyway, that argument comes dangerously close to suggesting that abortion is morally questionable.

The basis for pro-choice resistance to any interference with unfettered abortion rights—from parental notification for minors to the outlawing of partial birth abortion, measures which the vast majority of American women support—is no less hypocritical. Supporters trot out the tired old slippery-slope argument: once we allow any restriction, we'll slide into a total ban, which is patent nonsense. As a society, we adopt such halfway measures to deal with dozens of issues, from the dispensing of alcohol to gun control, with no slipping or sliding to speak of.

The pro-life crowd doesn't have any better record on moral and intellectual consistency. How can you be "pro-life" and support the death penalty or war, which most abortion opponents do? Sure, they make a distinction between "innocent" and "noninnocent" life, but even so, they are dancing on the head of a pin. Who are they to sort humankind into innocent and less-than-innocent? Are the Libyan children who happen to get in the way of a bomb swerving off target not innocent? Are adults conscripted to slave in Iraqi bomb factories really guilty? Pro-lifers are more accurately described as "pro-fetus." You certainly can't call many of them pro-children, since they don't seem to care much if kids go hungry or without medical attention once they've emerged from the womb—which is what the opposition of antiabortion conservatives to welfare and national health care would seem to imply.

Consider the Catholic Church, which pretends that its position on abortion is based on some deep and abiding repugnance for killing. Huh? Is that the same Catholic Church which has spent centuries offering spiritual and material support to various slaughters? Or consider the soft-core types who try to downplay any discussion of religion in regard to abortion. They say they abhor abortion because it reduces our national respect for life. Sure: the problem isn't that Americans have seen Vietnamese being murdered by their own troops, Rwandans expiring from starvation or Bosnians massacred by Serbians on the nightly news. It's not that they watch film at eleven of the murders in their towns and cities, or hear gunfire in their neighborhoods. No siree, it's abortion.

And then there are the antiabortion folks who have jumped on the "Get the government out of our lives" bandwagon, except on this issue. Does that mean they think all the bureaucrats who will be fired when they dismantle the Departments of Education and Commerce should have first preference for jobs with the Pregnancy Police? Why is it that the Food and Drug Administration is portrayed as an evil institution that needs to be abolished because it keeps our citizens from the drugs they want—*except* when the FDA is considering RU-486, the abortion pill, at which point the agency needs to be more cautious in the licensing of a dangerous drug?

The most fascinating bit of hypocrisy offered up by antiabortion activists is the support many offer to legal abortion in the case of rape or incest. That stance may make them seem reasonable and enlightened, but it's an ethical nightmare. Think it through: A fetus is an innocent life and abortion is murder. But it's okay to murder an innocent life if its mother was raped or the victim of incest?

American women know that activists on both sides are too entrenched in their positions to offer them accurate and coherent information, let alone consistent and intelligent argument. It's a life-and-death struggle, and truth was the first rhetorical casualty. How many Americans really understand how many abortions are performed in America, on whom, and why—information which would seem to be essential to the national discussion? The rhetoric of pro-choice activists makes it seem as if most women seeking abortions are in desperate straits: teens barely able to care for themselves, women desperate for children but faced with the agonizing prospect of serious genetic defects in them or women traumatized by rape and retraumatized by the discovery that their rapes left them pregnant.

But most abortions in America are the result of unwanted pregnancies that lack any such drama. Fully half of all pregnancies in this country are unintended, a startling statistic when you consider the easy availability, and general reliability, of birth control. And half of those unintended pregnancies—29 percent of all pregnancies not ending in miscarriage—are terminated by abortion, which works out to about 1.5 million annually. Recently abortion opponents have made it seem as if thousands of these are late-term partial birth abortions, a notoriously grizzly procedure. But only 10 percent of all abortions occur after the end of the first trimester of pregnancy, and only 1.2 percent of them are partial birth. Pro-choice activists like to point out that half of the women seeking abortions had been using birth control, suggesting that they are innocent victims of poor medical technology. But they are playing fast and loose with the facts. After all, most forms of birth control are more than 95 percent effective. The other 5 percent would hardly account for 5 million unintended pregnancies. The pro-choice forces include in their "using birth control" category women who say they generally use birth control but forgot on one or more occasions. And that still means that half of the women ending pregnancies didn't even pretend they had been using birth control.

Abortion rights supporters focus again and again on the plight of pregnant women caught in terrible situations: women who were raped, women whose health might be jeopardized by pregnancy or whose fetuses seem gravely ill. But only 7 percent of abortions are the result of maternal health problems, rape, incest or fetal abnormalities. The remainder—the 93 percent—are sought because a woman decides that she is unready for motherhood, because she doesn't want to be a single parent, doesn't want any more children or doesn't want anyone to know that she is sexually active.

And most of these 1.4 million women aren't crazy, irresponsible teenagers, uneducated drones or women too mired in poverty and hopelessness to organize their lives. That stereotype is the invention of pro-choice activists who don't want Americans to focus on the fact that most abortions are performed on adult women who had sex without taking precautions and don't want to bear the consequences. The truth is that four out of every five abortions in the United States is performed on a woman above the age of 19. Almost 70 percent of the women seeking abortions are employed.

What's going on? Why are so many American women getting pregnant unintentionally? Again, the explanations provided by both camps are little more than exercises in rhetorical absurdity. The real problem is all that sex, antiabortion activists argue. We need to retrain Americans to be chaste until marriage and monogamous thereafter. Right. That's certainly a practical and realistic proposal in the late twentieth century. The real problem is that the antisex fanatics are denying young women vital information about sex and access to birth control, their opponents counter, ignoring their own abortion statistics. Sure. That's the problem: millions of women, most of them over the age of 20, don't know about birth control. They didn't learn from their parents, their friends or their sexual partners that unprotected sex leads to pregnancy. They never heard about birth control—not in school, on the Internet, reading magazines or watching television. They had no idea how or where to buy condoms, since they are hidden under lock and key.

Few American women are likely to buy such absurd arguments. The problem isn't sex. Women in Europe have just as much sex as women in America, and they have dramatically fewer unwanted pregnancies, and dramatically fewer abortions. And the problem isn't information. There might be a few 20-year-old women in this country who don't know where babies come from, don't know that condoms are remarkably effective in preventing pregnancy or are incapable of figuring out how to put them on—but not 1.5 million of them annually. The problem is that Americans, male and female, are notoriously unwilling to take responsibility for their behavior. We have become so savvy about the rules of the national pastime of victimhood that we have convinced ourselves that sexual abuse is a disease, murderous instincts are a type of sugar poisoning and unwanted pregnancies are a by-product of sexism. Neither side in the abortion debate is addressing this core issue.

American women know that—and their patience is wearing thin. Listen to Rose Anderson of Miami, the kind of no-nonsense woman who never dances around controversy out of some antiquated notion of politeness, and never suffers fools, gladly or otherwise. Rose, who works as a nurse-practitioner in a clinic that serves the homeless ("If I'm going to be a servant, I'd rather be a servant for the poor than for the rich in some private hospital," she says), is simultaneously famous and infamous for enduring the first four minutes of collective intellectualizing about matters of the day, then cutting to the heart of the argument in a single sentence, thanks to a bullshit detector capable of humiliating even the most pompous physician.

"I believe that a woman should have control over her own body," she says, "but that means she also needs to accept responsibility for what she does with it. In most cases, after all, getting pregnant is a choice. If you have sex, there's always a risk of pregnancy, so if you absolutely don't want to have a kid, have oral sex or anal sex because once you're pregnant, it's no longer just your body. People need to think before they go fucking around. I'm sick of people having sex without condoms or birth control and then coming in and saying, 'Oh, my, I'm pregnant.' What do they expect?"

Rose, who is proud of being fanatical about her own ethical consistency, is opposed to abortion, in all cases, at all times. "Life begins at conception," she says. "Life that is the product of rape begins at conception, life that is the product of incest begins at conception and life that is the product of two people who are very much in love and want to have a child also begins at conception." End of discussion. Rose doesn't waste much energy in *explication de texte*.

But that belief doesn't mean she's particularly fond of most of the other people who share it. "I can't take them very seriously," says Rose. "They say they care about life but they don't fight for people's lives. They support the war in Iraq, where we went in and slaughtered people by the gadzillions. They support the death penalty. And they refuse to support things that protect life, things like prenatal care and WIC and medical things that are life-giving. After all, if someone has high blood pressure and can't afford antihypertensive meds, he's dying little by little. Those people pick and choose which life they care about. They aren't even worth talking to.

"If I could pick and choose my positions, I'd be in favor of abortion. It's easy. It's convenient. But I believe that human life is sacred and needs to be protected. I'm against killing in wars. I'm against killing in self-defense, although I understand it. I understand abortion too. I know that it's a complicated issue. But you can't design your morality just to make things less messy. If there are problems in our society that are causing women to have abortions, the solution is to fix the problems, not to kill the fetuses."

Rose rarely says any of this in public, which is more than a little out of character for a woman who is hardly shy about her beliefs. The gay men who are her closest friends know that she's a practicing Catholic. Her Catholic friends know she dismisses the church's position on homosexuality as silly and regards most of the nation's bishops with the contempt she generally reserves for the morally inept. But when abortion is mentioned, she falls into an unaccustomed silence. "Look, this issue isn't that big a deal for me. There are more important things to worry about, like changing the environment children come into so that people will have what they need to take care of children, which will go a lot further toward ending abortion than bombing clinics. Like the fact that the kids I see don't have any toys and when they're hungry their mothers feed them chips and nacho Cheez Whiz. Or that people in America go to baby showers and give pregnant mothers bottle warmers and talking toys and musical bassinets while women in Haiti give birth by squatting in their backyards, and they hope they can find a blanket when they're done.

"People love to argue about the viability of fetuses, but they won't talk about the fact that full-term infants aren't viable on their own because they need food, which too many of them don't have. Or that the adults I work with aren't viable on their own because they are poor and homeless. What are we going to do, kill them? Nobody wants to talk about the real problems because they're too hard and because people on both sides are too selfish. They want to keep their money to themselves. So they keep talking about abortion, so they can feel like they are moral and noble when they really are just avoiding their moral responsibilities. Well, I'm sick of it."

Rose pauses. She's not used to letting go on the abortion issue. "Anyway, what's the point?" she says, since all sides in the debate are too entrenched in rhetorical ethical superiority for any civilized discourse. "Nobody listens. Everybody just dismisses the people who disagree with them as Catholic crazies or anti-women or some other nonsense. There's no real discussion going on; it's just a yelling match. Do we really have time for that?"

*   *   *

No one has ever attempted to calculate the cost of America's twenty-year battle over abortion. No one has added up all the money spent in legal fees, salaries, travel, infrastructure, printing, mailing and advocacy by the hundreds of organizations devoted full- or part-time to winning the war. No one seems to have even asked what might have been accomplished—what problems might have been solved, what ills might have been ameliorated—if all the money, all the time and all the passion that have been expended on the feud had been turned in a different direction.

The price of abortion has been measured in the number of dead fetuses or the number of women who've died, or might have died, in back alleys. But what of the cost in opportunities lost because of the bitterness, the anger and the stereotyping on both sides: the money that might have been spent, the coalitions that might have been forged, the friendships that might have been formed, the recruits both feminism and its opponents might have attracted had their movements not insisted on absolute ideological purity? No one considers the dozens of issues that have been held hostage to this titanic struggle over the definition of innocence, and the millions of American women whose progress has been held captive to a fight that is, at best, marginally relevant to their lives.

The cost to the Republican Party has been high, and documented ad nauseam. The party has lost scores of female activists from its ranks, and even those who've remained under the big tent labor in terror of leaving any paper trail documenting their support for abortion. Representative Sue Kelly of New York and Senator Kay Bailey Hutchinson of Texas, both stalwart conservatives, have been censored and harassed by members of their own party because they break ranks on abortion. Pro-choice Republican women candidates have been caught between a rock and a hard place: their antiabortion flank battles them, but they receive little support from the feminist camp, which, despite their abortion politics, is deeply distrustful of Republicans.

Feminists delight at the damage to the party committed to outlawing abortion, never admitting that they, too, have sustained serious, largely undocumented, losses. Thousands of women who might support the women's movement on every other issue in their agenda—the Equal Rights Amendment, funding for programs to end violence against women, day care, enforcement of child support—have been alienated from their ranks, treated as traitors and denied the right to call themselves feminists.

Listen to the plaint of just one of them, Jenny Westberg. "Because I hold . . . 'anti-choice' ideas, I'm given to understand that I'm not allowed to be part of the feminist movement. Now, it's nothing new for me to have my ideas dismissed out of hand, but generally it's been by smug, patronizing testosterone-drunk MEN! The feminist establishment's dissent-suppressing attitude is, in my opinion, wholly patriarchal. . . . Perhaps my memory is faulty, but it seems to me that the feminist movement began as a much more inclusive entity, reaching out to Amazons and beauty queens, housewives and executives, liberals, conservatives and anarchists. All you needed to be part of the movement, as I recall, were those two X chromosomes."

Abortion has charged the atmosphere of women's politics with so much hostility and fear that both sides have been blinded to their common ground. Pro-choice activists are fed up with being caricatured as bra-burning sluts who won't be satisfied until the fetuses have been vacuumed out of every womb in the nation. They fear the vitriol rained on them by clinic protesters and live in terror that another gun-toting John Salvi will appear in Boston or Florida or Minnesota. Anti-abortion-rights activists are weary of being painted as religious fanatics blithely indifferent to the trials of women who find themselves pregnant in a world that offers all too little support to mothers. They fear that their right to protest what they are convinced is an evil is being stripped away by the very men and women who have always decried any restriction on civil liberties. They are angry that their sincere belief that abortion is murder is treated as some kind of superstition, that they—as ethical human beings—are morally dismissed.

In this climate, it has been impossible to see across the abortion divide, which is as broad as the divisions of hatred and suspicion that have thwarted peace all over the globe. Conventional wisdom has proclaimed that abortion is a kind of litmus test for where a woman stands on a wide variety of social issues. But that wisdom, as usual, is more conventional than wise. American women refuse to fit neatly into anyone's ideological boxes. Members of groups like the Independent Women's Forum, who are thoroughly and passionately conservative, nonetheless are pro-choice or, in fact, are pro-choice precisely because they are conservatives, and thus committed to barring the government from bedrooms and clinics. And the members of groups like Feminists for Life are devoted to the liberation of women and nonetheless opposed to abortion or, in fact, are antiabortion because they are devoted to the liberation of women: "Abortion does not liberate women," their position paper states. "On the contrary, abortion—and the perceived need for it— validate the patriarchal world view which holds that women, encumbered as they are by their reproductive capacity, are inferior to men.

"Abortion liberates men, not women." The guiding principle of FFL, which was founded in 1972 by two women expelled from NOW because of their pro-life views, is that abortion plays into the hands of a patriarchal society, which has set the rules that make it difficult for a woman to be both a mother and a "fully functioning adult. By settling for abortion instead of demanding the social changes that would make it possible for women to combine children and career, pro-abortion feminists collaborate with the patriarchy to keep America a man's world under a man's terms. They have betrayed the majority of working women—who want to have children." Furthermore, they say, abortion gives men an easy way to escape responsibility for their own sexual behavior, turning woman into consumer item, which if "broken" by pregnancy can be "fixed" by abortion.

"Truly liberated women reject abortion because they reject the male world view that accepts violence as a legitimate solution to conflict. Rather than settling for mere equality—the right to contribute equally to the evil of the society—prolife feminists seek to transform society to create a world that reflects true feminist ideals."

To bolster that assertion, they offer up the writings of the founding mothers of feminism, who would fit comfortably into modern-day pro-life demonstrations. "We must reach the root of the evil," Susan B. Anthony wrote of abortion. "It is practiced by those whose innermost souls revolt from the dreadful deed." Writing in Anthony's newspaper, the *Revolution*, Mattie Brinkerhoff said, "When a man steals to satisfy hunger, we may safely conclude that there is something wrong in society, so when a woman destroys the life of her unborn child, it is an evidence that either by education or circumstances she has been greatly wronged." Victoria Woodhull, the first woman to run for the presidency, insisted that "rights of children as individuals begin while yet they remain in the foetus." And Elizabeth Cady Stanton called abortion "infanticide."

Women like the members of the FFL have hardly been embraced by NOW, the Feminist Majority and other leading women's rights groups. In fact, feminists committed to ending abortion have been treated with precisely the degree of disrespect and vitriol as conservatives who dare to support laws keeping abortion legal. They are objects of suspicion and intolerance whose dilemma has been ignored by a press obsessed with their mirror images.

Consider the fate of the publisher of *Blue Stocking*, a feminist and prochoice newspaper in the Northwest. In August 1993, in the spirit of broadening discussion about women's issues, *Blue Stocking* ran an article by Jenny Westberg entitled "Apologia of a Pro-Life Feminist." The feminist establishment did not applaud the editor's desire to keep the movement from choking on its own truisms. The director of a local women's health clinic called and complained to the editors before canceling the advertising she had bought in the nascent publication and mobilizing other feminist groups in town to denounce it. The state coordinator for NOW was alerted and she too phoned in anger, insisting that the editor had no right to call *Blue Stocking* a "feminist newspaper."

Or think about what happened to Naomi Wolf, a feminist icon since the publication of her best-selling book, *The Beauty Myth.* In October 1995, Wolf committed feminist treason when she published a thoughtful article in the *New Republic* about her quandaries about abortion and, particularly, the way feminists talked about abortion. "Clinging to a rhetoric about abortion in which there is no life and no death, we entangle our beliefs in a series of self-delusions, fibs and evasions," wrote Wolf, as part of her demand that pro-choice activists find a way to discuss abortion without dipping into the "lexicon of dehumanization" of the fetus. "The fields of embryology and perinatology have been revolutionized," she continued, "but the pro-choice view of the contested fetus has remained static."

Wolf was making a plea for pro-choice activists, a group in which she still includes herself, to acknowledge—clearly and directly—the ethical gray area into which abortion falls. To those who insist that any backpedaling on abortion converts pregnant women into "fetus carriers," she responded, "A pregnant woman is in fact both a person in her body and a vessel." To those who refuse to grant fetuses any status of personhood, she argued, "So, what will it be: Wanted fetuses are charming, complex REM-dream little beings whose profile on the sonogram looks just like Daddy, but unwanted ones are mere 'uterine material'?" She drove her convictions home by talking about her own abortion, and her feelings about that act years later. "I was not so unlike those young louts who father children and run from the specter of responsibility."

Wolf's piece provoked a predictably instantaneous backlash in which she was denounced as a tool of the patriarchy, a turncoat and a weak thinker by the very journals in which her stature as a feminist heroine, a bravely independent observer and a brilliant intellect had long been proclaimed. Ann Fulredi, in *Living Marxism,* went so far as to draw a line in the sand and challenge Wolf, and millions of other women with nuanced positions on abortion: "You can no more partially support a woman's right to decide on the future of her pregnancy than you can be partially pregnant," she wrote—without explaining how she had gained that position as arbiter. "You either support a woman's right to decide on the future of her pregnancy or you do not. When the right to choose abortion becomes conditional, it is no longer a right."

Fulredi was both toeing and reinforcing the feminist party line on abortion that was pronounced most succinctly by Robin Morgan when she took over the helm of *Ms.* magazine. "The New *Ms.* Magazine will unfailingly treat a woman's right to an abortion as sacrosanct," she wrote. "There will be no dissent on that in our pages."

No dissent in a feminist magazine? "If we don't tolerate dissent," Wolf responded, "we're going to feel deeply resentful of one another because each of us becomes the intellectual jailer of the other." To those who insisted that criticizing abortion makes a woman an antifeminist, Wolf answered, "Who decides who's a feminist? What Orwellian politburo committee decides who gets to use the F-word?"

Wolf, a grande dame of young feminists, might still be trying to smash politburo control, but young women like Michelle Grothe, a recent graduate of the University of Wisconsin, don't even try. Michelle is emblematic of thousands of women who live perched uncomfortably on the bridge between feminism and the pro-life movement, a bridge leaders of both groups roundly ignore. She has virtually perfect feminist politics. She supports affirmative action because she believes racism and sexism are still firmly embedded in American society. She favors firm gun control and increased spending on education. She's against the death penalty, cuts in Medicaid and the 1996 welfare reform package. She breaks with the feminist movement only in her unwavering commitment to ending the practice of abortion in America. "We need to change the viewpoint in this country, which now denies personhood to the unborn, and denies the preciousness of life all across the board," she says. "You see it in the increase in crime, in the increase in child abuse, in every aspect of life."

Staking out that position has cost Michelle dearly. When I began to question her about the way she was treated by feminists at Wisconsin, her eyes filled with tears. When she offered her point of view in classes on that liberal campus, teachers treated her like "a person who didn't even know what an intelligent viewpoint was." Other students avoided her. When she sat behind a Rock for Life table in the student union, other young women would stop and hiss or yell "Murderer."

She tries to reason with her opponents, hoping that they will at least give her the courtesy of not dismissing the sincerity of her position. "Abortion has to matter," she says. "You can't say this person is not a person. If you do, then what stops someone else from picking out a different kind of person and saying he's not a person either." To no avail. She has some friends who are pro-choice. They protect their friendship by trying not to talk about abortion. When the issues arises in feminist circles, she pleads, "It's offensive to me as a woman that in order to succeed in this world I have to kill my child."

Nobody is swayed. Which puzzles Michelle. Pro-choice advocates, after all, decry the number of unwanted pregnancies in America and the high number of abortions. Why won't they at least work with her to deal with the underlying problems, which might help resolve their disagreement over the consequence? It is a naive question from a naive young woman, and the answer to it speaks directly to the ultimate cost of the abortion battle.

Both camps claim to be concerned about women and the issues that affect them, about teen pregnancy, about the poor and underrepresented—although neither trusts the sincerity of the other's rhetoric. For the most part, they agree that American women are trapped by the competing demands of work and motherhood, that single mothers struggle because deadbeat dads renege on their child support obligations. Imagine the coalition that could be formed—a real women's coalition joining women across the broadest possible spectrum—to work on enforcement of child support payments, improved adoption services, measures to lower the teen pregnancy rate, research on contraception for both men and women, and social and economic programs that would lift some of the burden off parents. It's a fantasy, of course, because neither side is willing to acknowledge that there is common ground.

The bitterness has made any coalition, on any issue, impossible. Abortion has so defined women's politics that even a solid, effective women's caucus in Congress, for example, is a fantasy. Conservative women refuse to join any group that endorses abortion, and liberals ask, "How can I be in a caucus with a woman who wants to force me to stay pregnant or wants to throw someone in jail for terminating a pregnancy?"—although they constantly insist that the Bosnians and Serbians, or the Israelis and Palestinians, should just sit down, talk things out and find a compromise. Antiabortion women refuse to concede that pro-choice women are individuals of integrity, even while they chafe at being morally dismissed by liberal women who refuse to grant even the sincerity, if not the truth, of their beliefs. In so doing, they isolate themselves from one another, making their own polarization seem somehow inevitable.

So American women are left caught in the vise that is abortion. Michelle Grothe, along with tens of thousands of women like her, is left to agonize over presidential elections since she can find no way to satisfy both her liberal and antiabortion commitments. In 1996, the latter demanded that she vote for Pat Buchanan, yet she understood full well that supporting him would be antithetical to her other beliefs. Contemporary America offers her no political space.

Pro-choice women have adopted a studied posture of beleaguerment, although abortion is a well-established institution subsidized by public funds, promoted as a "fundamental right" by U.S. foreign policy, required as a subject for study in medical training programs and protected by federal laws prescribing criminal penalties for those who dare to interfere with it. "Abortion today is as American as free speech," George McKenna wrote in the *Atlantic Monthly*—yet its supporters nonetheless feel so threatened that they, too, feel cramped in the political space left to them.

ABORTION has squeezed the life out of women's politics, and the only way women will regain their political space is for abortion to disappear as a political issue. That is a less fantastic possibility than it seemed when Whitney Adams mentioned it in San Diego in the summer of 1996. Technological advances have long bolstered the cause of antiabortion advocates, turning fetuses from anonymous creatures into living beings that are photographed, recorded and loved. Parents watch video sonograms of their children months before birth, making it more difficult for them, and the public, to dismiss fetuses as subhuman parasites.

But the tables are turning, as medical advances allow women to know about their pregnancies days after conception and change the very nature of the act of abortion. For more than two decades, abortion has been a public act involving physicians and clinics and insurance carriers, which is precisely what has given the antiabortion movement its power. Imagine, then, an America in which abortion truly becomes a private act. No one would be able to calculate how many pregnancies are terminated each year, and no clinics would exist that could be targeted for protests or bombings. No one would keep a list of abortion doctors because there would be no way of knowing which doctors were performing the procedure. No one could wave lurid photographs of aborted fully formed fetuses, because fetuses would be aborted before they bore any resemblance to human life. This is the America of the new nonsurgical abortions. Can the abortion wars survive such a brave new world?

It's unlikely—and America is on the cusp of just such a reality. Recent medical advances have revolutionized the options American women have for dealing with unwanted pregnancies. Worried about a missed period, they no longer have to wait to see their doctors; they can buy early pregnancy test kits at their local pharmacies. Unhappy with the results, they don't have to brave the protesters at local abortion clinics, if they are lucky enough to have them in their area. They can go to their own gynecologists and undergo chemical abortions, a procedure ob-gyns are far more willing to perform than surgical abortions.

Those doctors are supposed to report abortions to the Centers for Disease Control, so that the government can continue to track the rate of abortion. But if they use the latest abortion procedures—methotrexate and misoprostol, rather than RU-486 and misoprostol—there is no danger to noncompliance, since no one tracks why a given physician writes a specific prescription. Methotrexate has been on the market for half a century as an antitumor agent and a treatment for arthritis, lupus and psoriasis, and misoprostol is widely prescribed for patients with ulcers. Antiabortion fanatics can't root through a doctor's medical waste for telltale signs. The evidence left from an abortion induced by modern chemistry—which must be performed within the first two months of pregnancy—is a tiny speck that looks like a blood clot. The cost of the procedure? About $10 for the drugs and the physician's fee for two office visits.

The antiabortion crowd is thus far at a loss as to how to fight this new breed of abortion, abortion that lacks most of the images that have ignited their followers, from the inherent violence of surgery to aborted fetuses with recognizable features. Operation Rescue has sent threatening faxes to and picketed the offices of chemical abortion researchers, but has found no other clear targets for their wrath. Leaders of more mainstream antiabortion groups have recognized that photographs of minuscule blood clots are unlikely to whip up their followers, and that few Americans are likely to relate to fetuses as human life when they still look like they have gills. So they have begun to switch tactics from emphasizing abortion as murder to bemoaning its physical and psychological dangers.

They have paraded somewhat shaky research that might suggest a slight link between abortion and cervical cancer, twisting it into alarmist headlines. They've warned women about the dangers of hemorrhage and infection from chemically induced abortions, although both are infrequent side effects. When all else fails, they raise the specter of long-term, and still undiscovered, negative side effects from abortions. "I'm very concerned that the women of this country are going to find . . . in five or ten years that we've opened a Pandora's box as far as complications and damage to women," warned Dr. Donna Harrison, a Michigan ob-gyn. But the warning sounds empty since Harrison and her allies offer nothing tangible on which to base it.

While over the past two decades technology has undercut the positions of both the pro- and antichoice forces, the most recent changes in fact open a window of opportunity for a final truce in the abortion wars—if either side is willing to take advantage of it. At the moment, all that separates the entrenched enemies is the will to educate women about responsible sexual activity, and ten short days: the ten days between conception, thus far defined as the moment when a sperm fertilizes an egg, and pregnancy, which is the moment when the fertilized egg finishes its hazardous passage through the fallopian tubes to become implanted in the lining of the uterus, a journey about one-third of all zygotes never complete. Without that implantation, there is no pregnancy, which is how an IUD works; it makes the uterine lining inhospitable to implantation. So if a woman stops that implantation through use of the latest medical technology, she thwarts her pregnancy even before it occurs.

The technology is what physicians call emergency contraception, and it remains, incredibly, a well-kept secret. The most common method is two oral contraceptives taken within seventy-two hours of unprotected intercourse, followed twelve hours later by another two tablets. Researchers suggest that even the single dose, taken within seventy-two hours of unprotected intercourse, might be almost 100 percent effective.

Is this abortion? Well, that's the window of opportunity for members of the so-called pro-life crowd. It's clearly not termination of pregnancy, because a pregnancy never occurs. Indeed, the fertilized egg hasn't yet survived the greatest hazard of pregnancy—successful implantation in a uterus. The most steadfast literalists might argue that it is nonetheless murder, since it occurs after conception. But those same steadfast literalists would then also have to wage war against the use of IUDs. And can the pro-life crowd really argue with a procedure which could dramatically decrease the number of true abortions performed in the nation?

No truce is possible, however, without the cooperation of the pro-choice troops, who would need to put as much time, money and energy into teaching women about morning-after pills as they've devoted to protecting surgical abortions. But how could they not, when confronted with an opportunity to guarantee women control over their reproductive lives? Is it so much to say to women: Look, if you have unprotected sex and don't want to become pregnant, pop some birth control pills and you won't have to worry? Can we really not ask grown women to show that modicum of responsibility?

Such a truce is a fantasy, of course—not because the technology does not exist, and not because it poses a significant threat to the belief systems of either side. But neither side really seems to want the abortion wars to end. They have gone on so long that both sides have lost the ability to envision peace. Resolving the underlying problems seems to have become less important than scoring a win, or at least ensuring that the other side suffers a loss. The stakes are, or have been defined as, too high—morally, politically and financially. The pro-choice forces have drawn an abortion line in the sand and dared society to prove its contempt for women by crossing it, thus holding up the existence of unlimited surgical abortion services as the measure of women's liberation. And that position is reinforced by a $500-million-a-year industry of abortion providers, one of the few lobbying groups in the nation to successfully convince the population that its interests are entirely selfless. Conservatives have responded by holding up America's abortion policy as the measure of the nation's commitment to life. And that stance is similarly reinforced by a movement that understands full well that abortion, more than any other issue, swells the ranks of conservative activism and thus fuels the engine of the conservative agenda.

Which means that Whitney, Rose and Michelle will remain weary. . . .

Everything Has a Moral, If Only You Can Find It

Sue Oikle had just finished combing out a perm when I caught up with her at Curl Up and Dye in Libby, Montana. It was a perfect fall afternoon and the small salon was packed with women getting ready for the big weekend— whatever that meant in that town of five thousand. I needed to talk to women about work, their families, their friendships and their dreams. I also needed a haircut.

"Feminism?" Sue responded when I reached that obligatory question. The perky 42-year-old seemed puzzled, as if I were asking her opinion about Albanian cuisine or Rwandan geography. The salon was filled with women's magazines and Sue had been trained in Spokane, so I knew she couldn't be entirely clueless. Anyway, I'd discovered by then that everyone in America has an opinion about the women's movement. Sue considered my question thoughtfully even as she tried to make sense of my do, which had been designed for a woman who didn't own rollers. Then she laughed. "Feminism is stupid. If they want to know what it's like to live without equality, let feminists try living in Saudi Arabia for a week."

Her coworker Jeanette turned away from the pink curlers she was winding. "We agree with things like equal pay though."

"No, I don't," Sue quipped. "I think we should get more pay."

Jeanette's client didn't seem impatient when the striking young woman—a mountain woman with long, polished nails—left her station to join the conversation. By then, everyone in the shop was throwing in jokes, comments or stories. Even in Libby, a mill town in a county of seventeen thousand, feminism is ubiquitous. The union preaches enough liberal cant to keep women's issues on the local agenda. Signs advertising the Lincoln County Abuse Crisis Line are pasted on every store. A woman had just won the Republican primary for county commissioner, and the county attorney had been run out of office when he was accused of sexual abuse.

"Look, I deal with the good ole boys all the time since I'm a bow hunting instructor," said Jeanette. "Old guys are always showing up wearing T-shirts reading 'My Wife Gave Me A Choice, Her or Hunting. I'm Gonna Miss Her.' I don't mind. I tell them I want one just like that for myself.

"Feminists take things too seriously. I like to flirt, and no feminist is going to tell me I shouldn't. When we're out hunting, sometimes the men help me up the mountain. What's wrong with that? I teach my sons to do everything a woman does and everything a man does and I tell them, 'No woman will want you if can't vacuum and do a load of laundry.' So, obviously, I believe in equality. Who doesn't? But feminism is a different story entirely."

"What's the difference?" I asked, trying not to come off too much like a pushy Jewish feminist from New York. I doubt anyone was fooled.

No two women in the salon could agree. "Feminists hate men," one said, predictably. "No, they just don't know how to have fun," another added. Finally, Sue, who had fallen silent—daunted either by the conversation or by my hair—piped up. "That's not it. Feminists don't hate men. They hate women, ordinary women like us. And they can't have fun because they're sore winners. Why don't they just declare victory, go home and shut up."

Feminists as women-hating sore winners. The concept haunted me as I drove back across the United States. I felt like Alice newly emerged from Wonderland. I kept flashing back on the glory days of the women's movement, when tens of thousands of women tumbled centuries of tradition that had circumscribed women's lives, when we were brought to tears by the nomination of Geraldine Ferraro for the vice presidency, or Helen Reddy's declaration that we were strong and invincible. We had wanted to smash every barrier standing in the way of dedicated, competent women. We had fought to end every vestige of denigration, from the use of the word "broad" to sniggly comments about women suffering from PMS. We had exhorted women not to be silenced. And by 1996, women had crossed a thousand barriers, stood up against dozens of forms of denigration and were joyfully unsilent. Especially not about feminism.

Somehow during the past twenty-five years, feminism—as a movement, rather than as a set of ideals—has managed to alienate itself from its own constituency, and after I'd interviewed women like Sue for two years, the reasons became pretty clear. American women have real problems that wrack their lives—bread-and-butter issues, the tension between work and family, worries about aging parents and fears about growing children—and the National Organization for Women spends its time suing Hooters. Women's lives are intimately entwined with those of their fathers and sons and husbands, and feminists preach the kind of identity politics that separates women from men. American women want—need, in fact—to have fun, and they have fun by dressing up and making up and flirting; but too many feminists worry about *Ms.* magazine's announcing that it is okay for women to pluck their eyebrows and mock women who dream of silky underwear from Victoria's Secret.

Leaders of the women's movement gather at expositions and symposia and sing the praises of the strength and invincibility of women, then appear on the nightly news bemoaning women as weak victims. They proclaim that women can, and should, have it all, forgetting that most women are so tired, so worn out, so burdened with responsibility that the very thought of having it all is enough to engender 5 million simultaneous nervous breakdowns. They broadcast anger—for them, a delicious, exhilarating emotion—when all most American women want is a free hour to sit and enjoy Roseanne joking about being a "domestic goddess" instead of a housewife, who figures she's done her job if the kids are still alive at 5 P.M.

After all, in the late 1990s, it is Roseanne, not Gloria Steinem, who is a heroine to American women—no matter what the *New York Times* and its allied publications might think. Their ideological and spiritual guru isn't Susan Faludi or Patricia Ireland, but Oprah Winfrey, who offers them guidance on losing weight rather than lectures on fat as a feminist issue.

Feminism has discredited itself with American women because it is so intent on theory that it loses touch with reality. Women's lives are messy composites of work and relationships, responsibilities, dreams and desires that don't fit neatly into theoretical straitjackets. It's easy to create a theoretical framework that proves sisterhood across class and race lines, but few black women in urban ghettos experience solidarity with the suburban matrons whose toilets they clean. It's intellectually interesting to demonstrate how the patriarchy oppresses women and gives advantage to anyone with a penis, but such theory does little to explain Margaret Thatcher, or the shabby life of the homeless man. It's theoretically consistent to argue that men and women are natural antagonists, but such antagonism gives heterosexual women little comfort when they're lonely or sick or aging.

And when women's lives refuse to fit into these ideological superstructures created on university campuses, feminism's theoreticians don't reconsider the superstructures. They set themselves up as ideology cops and demand that women reconsider their lives. But American women have achieved enough empowerment—to use the overworked word of the nineties—to rebel against those demands, and to treat that new police force with that peculiar admixture of contempt and dismissal Americans reserve for most self-styled authority figures.

Furthermore, while feminism has convinced many men that women deserve to win the Oppression Sweepstakes, the movement has convinced fewer women, who know that their husbands have miserable jobs, that they too live in terror of being laid off. The gender card doesn't work among those who refuse to be straitjacketed by gender, and women have learned enough from feminism to shrug off any externally imposed straitjackets, no matter who is imposing them.

Ultimately, American women have rejected the feminist movement not merely because it has become the home of humorless carpers, but because they sense that the movement doesn't really like or respect women—not just the fantasy of women, not just women who follow the movement's leaders like lockstep Nazis, but that broad range of people of the female persuasion who inhabit American womanhood. The movement holds women to impossibly high, and absurdly narrow, standards and gives them no credit for being able to forge their own separate peace, treating them precisely as disapproving men have been wont to do. It disparages their choices and demeans their intelligence by bemoaning most of their decisions as still further evidence that they are victims of backlash.

In a world heavy with uncertainty, confusion and outright fear, women want and need to celebrate how far they've come, even as they need tax credits and safe streets and better math classes for their children. The last thing they want, or need, is the added burden of being asked to die on the front lines in a war they believe has been largely won.

For even while women reject feminism, the movement, they have embraced the fundamental ideals of women's liberation more thoroughly than even the most idealistic feminist of the 1960s could have imagined. Equal pay for equal work, equal educational opportunity, respect and pride—demands that seemed like dreams less than three decades ago—are assumptions, not to mention the law, in most of the land. American women know that paradise has yet to be achieved, but they also know with full certainty that they don't live in the world of their mothers, for better and for worse. They no longer have to confine their job searches to the employment section for women in their daily newspapers. They no longer have to worry that their daughters won't be admitted to graduate school in math or physics. When American women refuse to characterize themselves as feminists, they are rejecting the terminology, not the activity, because they don't like the company they'd be keeping if they put themselves in the former category.

FEMINISM reminds me of a vampy 1950s-style teenager who sashays through the halls of her high school with teased hair, pointy fingernails, dark red lipstick and plenty of attitude. Would-be studs on the football team build their status on spreading rumors about their alleged adventures with her. Cheerleaders shore up any doubts about their own propriety by trading whispers about her salacious deeds and by declaring her a social pariah. She rarely deserves her reputation, but too many others have too great a stake in it to allow her much freedom.

Like that teen, feminism has contributed its fair share to its bad reputation. The movement has degenerated into a series of all-too-public catfights over whether gender is a social or biological construct, over whether claiming victimization is a form of accepting it, over wages for housewives, comparable worth, the definition of rape and the politics of sadomasochism. It is staging its own Balkan wars, the empire having dissolved into difference feminists and dominance feminists, power feminists and victim feminists, Marxist feminists, second-wave feminists, third-wave feminists, pro-pornography feminists, anti-pornography feminists, gender feminists and separatist feminists—and no prisoners are taken by any of five dozen competing factions.

The reputation is reinforced by feminism's alternately sassy and defiant manner, a kind of teenage mien of beleaguerment mixed with a brassy insolence that dares anyone and everyone to provide proof of its status as an outcast, and becomes a self-fulfilling prophecy. Like the vampy teen, feminist leaders do their own version of stomping out of the room at the first utterance of criticism, slapping down even the most loving critics—women like Betty Friedan and Naomi Wolf—with puerile invective.

That stance, with its self-righteous, accusatory tone, doesn't let outsiders in. It offers them no glimpse of the thoughtfulness and reconsideration endemic in feminist circles, because it makes feminists loath to engage in public soul-searching, hesitant to express their reservations, reservations that bridge much of the gap between them and the self-styled antifeminists. That loss struck me indelibly during a long phone conversation with my friend Debbie about feminism and the balance between family and work. Debbie, a committed liberal feminist, is one of the heavyweight stars of print journalism and the mother of two. During her first pregnancy, she'd been almost blasé about the difficulties of juggling family and career, having accepted feminist dogma that if society—read employers—and husbands were "women-friendly," that juggling act would be as simple as tossing a ball.

Yet Debbie is constantly exhausted. The problem isn't her employer, who promotes her, encourages her and offers her every possible service, from extra pay to cover the cost of special child care during illnesses to long maternity leave and flexible work hours. Her problem isn't her husband. Bill doesn't "help out" around the house; he assumes that household responsibilities are his. But their young children lack the requisite feminist instincts. If 3-year-old Emma awakes in the middle of the night, she refuses to be comforted by Bill. When 6-month-old Adam starts screaming, Debbie's is the only voice, and only breast, that will calm him.

"Infants aren't politically correct," Debbie said to me during that phone call. "It's primal. My old feminist view of how this was going to work was a fantasy that has no basis in reality."

I wasn't shocked by Debbie's assertion. I was shocked that she had never expressed it before, that she had never written about it or broached the topic in public, and that none of my other friends who are mothers had ever done so either. I should not have been surprised. Longtime committed feminists like Debbie have given up on the debate, caught between weariness, fear and a growing sense that it simply doesn't matter. "You have to forget the utopian ideals," she said. "We're not going to get all the way there. We have to chip down our expectations and deal with the pressing issues."

Mostly, feminism's reputation suffers because it has cocooned itself in a self-protective ghetto that makes it impossible for the movement to communicate effectively with American women, and for American women to communicate back. Much of the problem is, ultimately, a matter of social class and of regionalism. But the upshot is that few feminist leaders spend enough time with anyone who fundamentally disagrees with them to be forced to confront their own inconsistencies, or their intellectual laziness. They rarely even overhear disturbing conversations, since few even live in the same neighborhoods as their antagonists.

Like all good liberals, they are dutifully aware of African-Americans, Chicanos, Puerto Ricans and Native Americans, but that is pretty much the diversity limit within the collective consciousness which underlies their politics, their cultural concerns, even their sympathies. The women on the pages of this book—women of faith, middle-class homemakers in places like

Dubuque, female farmers in Texas, beauticians in Boise and clerks in Cleveland—are pretty much absent from their radar, even from the patchwork liberals conjure up in their minds' eyes when they think about America.

The isolation is hardly unique to feminists or liberals, of course. Conservatives might know a few upscale versions of June Cleaver, but they, too, live in intellectual ghettos. Few spend much time in East Los Angeles, West Hollywood or even the Upper West Side of Manhattan. Americans of every ilk seem intent on creating our own self-reinforcing institutions, to isolate ourselves in sanctimoniously self-satisfied conformity.

Separatism has won out, no matter how frequently we all recite the mythical cant about the melting pot. Like the Arabs and the Israelis, then, women can avoid talking to one another and take comfort in our unchallenged stereotypes and hatreds. To know each other is to risk the collapse of our assumptions, after all, and in an age of uncertainty, few Americans are willing to subject that remaining security blanket to much danger. Anyway, trading caricatures and insults simply is more fun.

Despite everything feminism has done to contribute to its own bad reputation, however, like the teenager known as the tramp, she is also the victim of a bum rap created by parties who have plenty of self-interest in debunking liberal successes. Americans are suspicious of, if not downright hostile to, feminism because the movement has been blamed for everything from the breakup of the American family to skyrocketing rates of teen pregnancy and the cult of victimhood. That is a tantalizingly simple explanation, but ultimately absurd. Virtually all of these social problems are the result of forces well beyond the meager influence of feminism.

The movement arose and flourished during a moment of dizzying change, both technological and human. The American economy began reshaping itself from manufacturing and industry to service and technology, and the workforce was dragged into the shift, often kicking and screaming. Wages dropped, prices rose and families suddenly needed two incomes to finance even a middle-class living standard. At the same time, the link between sex and procreation, already weakened by the introduction of effective birth control, became increasingly strained, at least in the minds of the participants. The divorce rate, which had been rising steadily throughout most of the century, veered skyward, at the very moment that the rising number of elderly placed ever-greater demands on already shaky families.

Blowing into this dizzying mix of social and economic change came the wind of human rights, unleashed in the years after World War II. Anticolonialist movements toppled great empires, and minority groups within the seats of those empires and their sister states, brushed by the rhetoric and vision of liberation, exploded in pride and determination. In the process, the balance between individualism and community, which has shifted repeatedly throughout American history, teetered once more, as the pride and determination gradually ceded to anger and resentment that engendered, in turn, identity politics and the cult of victimhood. Those psychic changes eroded all of the nation's illusions, and a good deal of its civility. The volume was turned up on every conceivable debate as 10 million minds closed and stridency became the dominant zeitgeist of the land.

Feminism was not the least of these cosmic changes, but neither was it the greatest. Even without the movement, male-female relationships would have changed as the birthrate dropped, the institution of marriage frayed and men gained a stake in women's extrafamilial economic activities. And no movement was necessary to provoke a national schism over the nature of the family, sexual responsibility and who owes what to whom in compensation for whatever.

UNDERSTANDING all the dynamics that pushed feminism off its pedestal doesn't offer much solace to those who long for the good old days. I know because, as a woman whose identity was formed by feminism, I still thrill to the sight of women wielding jackhammers, or the sound of the voice of a woman piloting my plane when I fly to Chicago. Feminism infused me with a sense of purpose, a possibility of power that has electrified my life. Even at the age of 50, I still revel in the sense of sisterhood I felt the first time I marched down Pennsylvania Avenue as part of an all-female army. Despite the understanding I have gained in the course of my journey across America, I still have difficulty accepting women's rejection of the movement which gave them dignity.

But the reality of the evolving thinking among American women is undeniable, despite the repeated attempts of feminist leaders to indulge in contradictory fantasies. Time and time again—virtually ad nauseam—I hear young women echoing Amy Holmes, the young black woman at the Independent Women's Forum: "I don't want to be a member of a group. I wasn't raised by a group; I was raised by a family. I resent the notion that I have to owe my success to something beyond myself." I regularly listen to women of all ages repeating the sentiments of Blanquita Cullum, a conservative Hispanic radio talk show host in Washington, D.C.: "Feminists want to neuter me. I'm sick of their worrying about the lower half of my body. Tying me to the lower half of my body is like tying me to the kitchen." And I have come to understand that the bitter disappointment of Jenny Westberg is shared by thousands of women who tried, and failed, to find a place in the feminist movement. "At some point, apparently, the feminist establishment determined that they needed a great deal fewer adherents, and began systematically excommunicating one another for violating a standard of Total Philosophical Purity. Excluded (or highly suspect) groups include: prolifers; Republicans; Libertarians; conservative Democrats; members of most organized religions; stay-at-home mothers/wives; and anyone who dissents from whatever unwritten agenda is currently in force."

So the issue is no longer whether this emerging reality is an accurate reflection of women's thinking, or how it arose, but what this reality—a reality which cuts across class, race, regional and generational lines—means for American women and their politics. Dismissing it by bemoaning American women as victims of backlash, as the dupes of misogynists and a brainwashing, antifeminist media is tempting, but doing so creates a feminist nightmare, rife with contempt for women's intelligence and integrity, reeking of the sort of blithe dismissiveness with which men have traditionally treated women. And while theories about quasi-conspiracies by media, industry and political leaders against women's advancement might be deliciously fun to contemplate, ultimately, conspiracy theories are like hot fudge sundaes—not all that good for you. The time might still be ripe in America for countering unpleasant truths by casting aspersions on the sincerity and social consciousness of the truth makers. But shooting the messenger does not kill the message, or the fact that neither side in women's debates has a monopoly on integrity.

After spending two years talking to American women, I have come to realize that feminists need not bemoan, distance themselves or even wrack their brains trying to figure out how to reverse this new reality, for the rising visibility of conservative women and the mounting rebellion against the feminist movement are not signs that feminism has gone astray, as many conservative pundits, and many women, suggest. Rather, they are the clearest possible evidence that feminism has been successful, so successful that women no longer need to cling to one another in the type of solidarity which is inevitably a reflection of oppression. After all, even the most committed self-styled conservatives aren't pawns of powerful men trying to send women back into the kitchen. In fact, despite their antifeminist rhetoric, they are living up to the highest feminist ideals by seizing control over their own lives, by refusing to be confined or manipulated by anyone else's definitions of who or what they should be, by examining the choices open to them and following their own hearts and minds in selecting their path.

The initial dismay and confusion about the state of American women's politics which provoked my journey has, in fact, gradually transmogrified into pride in American women, conservative and otherwise. Sisters are doing it for themselves. After years of struggle and anguish, we don't yet have nirvana, but women finally have enough power and forbearance to splinter in a thousand directions, and still succeed. We no longer need to agree about the nature of marriage and the role of the family in reinforcing the patriarchy; women's options are now so broad that we need not speak in one voice to be heard. We no longer have to feel threatened by women who rejoice in the sacrifices of motherhood; that choice poses no threat to those of us for whom sacrifice does not connote nobility. We no longer need to worry about whether women are genetically different from men; men are no longer the gold standard against which humankind is judged. And we no longer need to fight over who owns feminism. The victory belongs to all of us: to Christian women who are running for political offices that they could never have aspired to thirty years ago, to young women who can't imagine a world without opportunity, to Republicans, Libertarians and Democrats.

Feminism's most prolific critics, women like Elizabeth Fox-Genovese and Christina Hoff Sommers, have a vested interest in blinding themselves to these overarching changes. They are poised to build their careers on declarations about how feminism is not the story of their lives, or how the movement has been stolen by dastardly demagogues with whom they disagree. But that's just malarkey. Feminism is the story of the life of every woman in the nation, whether she acknowledges it or not, and the movement can't be stolen because it is ubiquitous, residing in every household that includes a woman, in every business forced to comply with the law and on every television station that broadcasts *Roseanne* and *Murphy Brown* and *Chicago Hope.*

And all too many feminists similarly recoil from these changes, from embracing the diversity of lifestyle, political opinion and faith that has sprung from their own efforts because they refuse to own anything, or anyone, not dressed in the right outfit—or perhaps because admitting that you have been ousted from the center stage of history is simply too painful. But the truth is that without anyone realizing it, feminism got away from them; it broke loose from the feminist movement and began to grow wild across the land. Adapting itself to a dozen different soils and climates, it has mutated often into something barely recognizable. But its roots are strong and it energizes women wherever they live, work, pray and play. Feminism—not gender feminism or power feminism or any of the other self-serving subgroupings that are antithetical to the spirit of a movement that is, by definition, all-embracing—has become part of the fabric of American life. It's as American, and as diverse, as apple pie.

Signs of victory are everywhere: on the pages of the want ads of every newspaper in the country and in the gender of the commentators on the nightly news, on the basketball court and the assembly lines in Detroit, at the winners' circle of the Iditarod, the installations of female college presidents and the launchings of tens of thousands of women-owned businesses. American women aren't talking about feminism. They aren't writing about it, theorizing about it or marching for it. They're just doing it. Women's rejection of feminism, the official movement, should not be a cause for dismay. It should be a cause for celebration. American women are rewriting feminism, and, in the rewriting, they have made it their own.

Notes

Introduction: Through the Looking Glass

The seminar for incoming members of Congress mentioned in the text was held on December 10, sponsored by the Heritage Foundation and Empower America. The newly elected Republican women members were Sue Kelly (New York), Enid Waldholtz (Utah), Barbara Cubin (Wyoming), Sue Myrick (North Carolina), Helen Chenoweth (Idaho), Andrea Seastrand (California), Linda Smith (Washington).

Liberal reaction to these women is demonstrated most clearly in Hanna Rosin's "Invasion of the Church Ladies," *New Republic,* April 24, 1995.

Chenoweth's positions were articulated to me during our interview in her office in December 1995. They are also a matter of public record. See the *Albion Monitor,* June 25, 1995; the *Salt Lake Tribune,* October 27, 1996; and the continuing coverage in the Idaho press in September, October and November 1994. Especially interesting pieces appeared in the *Lewiston Morning Tribune,* October 6, 1994, and November 12, 1994.

Smith's comments on the League of Women Voters were quoted in the *New Republic,* above.

Myrick's career has been well documented by North Carolina newspapers. For her statements invoking God's wrath and proposing concentration camps for drug dealers, see the *Charlotte Observer,* December 6, 1989; April 14, 1990; April 2, 1992; and November 5, 1994.

For Cubin and the penis cookies, see Mary McGrory's column in the *Washington Post,* December 4, 1994.

Waldholtz's nursery received wide public attention. See Lisa Leiter, "Women's Work," *Insight on the News,* April 17, 1995, and the *Washington Post,* July 12 and November 11, 1995.

For information on Chenoweth's campaign, see note above.

The history of the women's movement has been written and rewritten. For some basic works, see: Kate Millett, *Sexual Politics* (Ballantine, 1970); Barbara Sinclair Deckard, *The Women's Movement* (Harper & Row, 1983); Carl Degler, *At Odds: Women and Family in America from the Revolution to the Present* (Oxford University Press, 1980); Marcia Cohen, *The Sisterhood: The Inside Story of the Woman's Movement and the Leaders Who Made It Happen* (Fawcett Columbine, 1988); Claire Knoche Fulenvider, *Feminism in American Politics* (Praeger, 1980); Flora Davis, *Moving the Mountain: The Women's Movement in America Since 1960* (Simon & Schuster, 1991); Nancy Cott, *The Grounding of Modern Feminism* (Yale University Press, 1987); Eleanor Flexner, *Century of Struggle* (Atheneum, 1974).

Friedan's *The Feminine Mystique,* first published in 1963, is available in paperback from Dell/Laurel.

The statistics on the number of women receiving degrees is from the U.S. Department of Education, National Center for Educational Statistics, Integrated Post-Secondary Education Data System, and the U.S. Department of Labor, 1993 *Handbook on Women Workers*. The figure on women at Yale is from Diana Furchtgott-Roth and Christine Stolba, "Women's Figures," Independent Women's Forum, 1996, and the figures on the numbers of female executive and senior vice presidents are from a recent Korn/Ferry study cited in that same pamphlet. The statistics on the number of workers employed by women-owned businesses is from the U.S. Department of Labor's 1993 *Handbook on Women Workers*. In 1963, there were twelve women in the House and two in the Senate. After the election of 1996, there were fifty-one women in the House and nine in the Senate. These figures are from the Center for the American Woman and Politics, Eagleton Institute of Politics, at Rutgers University.

Whatever your position on the women's movement, you are likely to be able to find support for it in someone's statistics. In *Who Stole Feminism*, Christina Hoff Sommers, for example, uses a 1992 Time/CNN poll to prove the alienation of women from the movement: while 57 percent of the respondents believed a strong women's movement was necessary, 63 percent refused to call themselves feminists. (*Time*, March 9, 1992). Sommers further bolsters her position by citing R. H. Brushkin's work, which concluded that only 16 percent of college women "definitely" consider themselves feminists (reported in the *Los Angeles Times Magazine*, February 2, 1992). In *Backlash*, Susan Faludi trots out a different set of numbers to prove women's allegiance to feminism, although most of hers speak less to women's allegiance to the movement than to the principle of equality. Indeed, she cites the same CNN/Time poll as Sommers, as well as a host of polls from Yankelovich Clancy Shulman and Roper, all of which confirm that women feel a need for a strong movement. She also cites a litany of polls proving that women supported the ERA, abortion, nationally funded child care and affirmative action in 1984. But the statistics she cites to demonstrate women's identification with feminism are similarly out of date: a 1986 Newsweek Gallup poll in which 57 percent of the respondents called themselves feminists. Indeed, in a footnote on page 465, she concedes that by 1989 only "one in three women were calling themselves feminists in the polls," although she blames the mass media for the phenomenon.

The information on and quotes from Ledeen are drawn from a series of interviews I conducted with her beginning in late 1995 and continuing throughout 1996. They were supplemented by information available in IWF publications.

Martha Burk's comment appeared in the *Washington Post*. Trish Antonucci's "expose" of IWF was written in 1995 and posted on the Internet at WLO.org. Faludi's comment about groups like IWF appeared in the March 1995 issue of *Ms.*

Faludi's book, *Backlash: The Undeclared War Against American Women*, was published by Crown in 1991.

Steinem's characterization of Hutchinson appeared in *Time*, June 14, 1993, in an article entitled "Hasta la Vista, Bobby."

PART I

The Babes

The "Merge Right" party was held on February 29, 1996.

The section on April Lassiter is based on lengthy interviews I conducted with her during the fall of 1995 and the winter and summer of 1996.

The section on Fitzpatrick is based on my interview with her in November 1995 and on profiles of her in the *National Journal,* September 16, 1995, and *George,* December 1995.

The section on Wood is based on my interviews with her in November 1995 and February 1996. For further information on the Youngbloods, see "Babes in the Pundits' Chairs," *Washington Post,* December 9, 1994.

The section on Amy Holmes is based on my interviews with her in November 1995 and February 1996.

Young conservatives received tremendous media attention in 1994 and 1995, especially in the conservative press. See Michael Crowley, "The GOP Youth Brigade," and Louis Jacobson, "Tracking the Rising Stars," both in the *National Journal,* June 17, 1995. Also, John Moore, "Right for Now," *National Journal,* March 11, 1995, and Natasha Stovall, "The GOPpies," *Village Voice,* February 27, 1996.

Gaull "Ricki" Silberman has worked closely with the Republican Party since the 1970s. She was director of communications for Senator Bob Packwood, special assistant to the federal communications commissioner and vice chairman of the U.S. Equal Employment Opportunity Commission.

The observation about the positions of younger and older women on abortion is based on my interviews with both groups before, after and during the party.

The event I am describing where Lassiter appeared was sponsored by Close-Up on January 25, 1996, at a suburban Virginia motel.

The section on Corinne Johnson is based on a long interview with her on campus in September 1996, as well as documents provided to me by her, including copies of the internal e-mail posted at Albion about her, and the coverage of her trial by the campus newspaper, the *Pleiad.* Her travails were also covered by the *Detroit Free Press* and the *Detroit News* on April 3, 1996. I also culled information from the press releases sent out by the Michigan Federation of College Republicans on April 4 and April 21, 1996, and a letter to the *Michigan Review* (April 10, 1996) by the president of that group.

The section on Adelle Kirk is based on my interview with her in January 1997.

The section on company policies toward women and working parents is from *Working Mother* magazine's special issue on the "100 Best Companies for Working Mothers," October 1996.

The material on Stephanie Herman is drawn from my interview with her at her home outside Denver in September 1996. See also her two-part article, "Feminism's Gender Gap," published on-line in CGX, May 22 and June 14, 1995.

A Digression into a Mad Hatter's Tea Party

The 1996 Libertarian Party convention was held over July 4 weekend. My description is based on my attendance, materials handed out and interviews there with—among others—delegates Jackie Bradbury, Kate O'Brien, Doris Gordon (of Libertarians for Life) and the Smiths.

Harry Browne's position on abortion was critiqued almost daily in the libertarian-feminist electronic chat group (lib.fem) between May and August 1996. For more on the controversy, see also the publication of Libertarians for Life handed out by Doris Gordon at the convention, and the discussion at the Web site of the Association of Libertarian Feminists, ALF.org.

The Karen Michaelson interview appeared in the newsletter of the Association of Libertarian Feminists, issue 57, Winter 1996, which is posted at ALF's Web site, ALF.org.

Catherine MacKinnon's position on the personal as political is embodied in her *Towards a Feminist Theory of the State* (Harvard University Press, 1989) and *Only Words* (Harvard University Press, 1993).

The McElroy quote is from her *Freedom, Feminism and the State* (Holmes and Meier, 1991).

The Jean Bethke Elshtain quote is from her piece in *Democracy,* April 1982.

The Joan Kennedy Taylor quote is from her *Reclaiming the Mainstream: Individualist Feminists Rediscovered* (Prometheus, 1992).

The Abolitionists

The section on Judy Jefferson is based on telephone interviews I conducted with her in December 1995 and March 1996 and the campaign materials she provided me.

The quotes from Frederick Douglass and Oscar DePriest appeared in the *Atlanta Constitution,* November 12, 1995, as part of an excellent history of black attitudes toward the major political parties.

For a condensed history of black attitudes toward the major political parties, see Elizabeth Wasserman, "GOP Battled Its Label as Party of White Men," *San Jose Mercury News,* March 25, 1993.

The statistics on black political attitudes, school vouchers and ideology are from a poll conducted by the Joint Center for Political and Economic Studies in Washington, D.C., printed as "Political Attitudes," by David Bositis, released in February 1996. The statistics on mandatory busing and affirmative action are from Gallup polls.

The information on Dorothy LeGrand was culled from my telephone interviews with her in February 1996 and the campaign materials she sent me. I also found background information in the *Star Tribune* (Minneapolis), September 21, September 29, October 20 and October 25, 1994.

An enormous body of literature has been devoted to both W. E. B. Du Bois and Booker T. Washington, and to the dispute between the men. For recent discussions that reflect current interpretations of the debate, see K. Humphreys and E. Hamilton, "Alternating Themes: Advocacy and Self-Reliance," *Social Policy,* Winter 1995; Sigmund Shipp, "Road Not Taken," *Journal of Economic Issues,* March 1996; Marcus Reeves, "Learning from Our Past," *Black Enterprise,* January 1996; E. Wright, B. Kauffman, and D. Beito, "Alternative Afrocentrisms," *American Enterprise,* September 1995; and T. M. Pryor, *Wealth Building Lessons of Booker T. Washington for a New Black America* (Duncan & Duncan, 1996). For books on Du Bois, see David Levering Lewis, *W. E. B. Du Bois: Biography of a Race* (Henry Holt, 1994) and Manning Marable's classic, *W. E. B. Du Bois: Black Radical Democrat* (Twayne, 1986).

The statistics comparing 1970 and 1993 and the economic progress of black Americans from 1940 to 1980 are taken from *Insight on the News,* September 27, 1993. See also Stephen Yates, "Beyond Affirmative Action," A Heartland Policy Study, September 6, 1991.

My interview with Nona Brazier was conducted by telephone in January 1996. Her campaign was well covered by the Seattle press. See, in particular, the *Seattle Post-Intelligencer,* July 17, 1996, and the *Seattle Times,* August 7, 1995.

Readers interested in Malcolm X should begin not by seeing Spike Lee's movie but by reading his autobiography, written with Alex Haley (Ballantine, 1992), and Haley's interview with Malcolm X in *Playboy,* May 1963. The quote which Judge Thomas is fond of reciting and the quote about the "beg-o-lution" appeared in K. Humphreys and E. Hamilton, "Alternating Themes: Advocacy and Self-Reliance," *Social Policy,* Winter 1995. The remaining quotes are from Benjamin Karim, *Remembering Malcolm: The Story of Malcolm X from Inside the Muslim Mosque* (Carroll & Graff, 1992). See also David Hilliard and Lewis Cole, *This Side of Glory* (Little, Brown, 1993).

The reaction to the Thomas hearings within the black community was widely covered by the black press. See also *Washington Post,* July 4 and October 12, 1991; "A House Divided," *Essence,* January 1992; *Chicago Tribune,* September 20, 1991, and the *Boston Globe,* September 8, 1991.

Anne Wortham is a professor of sociology at Illinois State University and a visiting scholar at the Hoover Institution. She is the author of *The Other Side of Racism: A Philosophical Study of Black Consciousness.*

Constance Berry Newman worked for the Department of Housing and Urban Development and was the director of VISTA. Under President Bush, she was the head of the Office of Personnel Management before being appointed the undersecretary at the Smithsonian Institution. She was an active supporter of Clarence Thomas.

Phyllis Berry Myers headed the congressional affairs division of the EEOC under Clarence Thomas. Her quote appeared in the *Washington Post,* October 12, 1992.

The section on Teresa Doggett is based on interviews I conducted with her by telephone in January 1996 and during the Republican National Convention in August 1996. She was profiled in *Headway,* February 1996.

For a history of affirmative action and a discussion of the "shackled runner" argument, read Stephen Yates, "Beyond Affirmative Action," A Heartland Policy Study, September 6, 1991. King's attitude toward affirmative action is a hotly debated issue these days. Conservatives have seized on his "I Have a Dream" speech, with its call for a color-blind society, as proof that he would be opposed to most contemporary affirmative action programs. Liberals respond with their own version of King's teachings. Both seem to ignore the fact that King's position changed over time. For guidance on this matter, turn to King himself: *Why We Can't Wait* (originally published in 1963, most recently in 1991 by NAL) and *Where Do We Go From Here* (originally published in 1967, most recently in 1989 by Beacon).

For a discussion of the improvement in the conditions of black Americans, see Yates, above, and "The Dark Side of Affirmative Action," *Destiny,* June 1995.

The cost of affirmative action per black family of four was calculated by the Center for the Study of American Business at Washington University in St. Louis.

For a discussion of which minority businesses are actually helped by affirmative action, see Timothy Bates, "Minority Business Set-Asides: Theory and Practice," in *Selected Affirmative Action Topics in Employment and Business Set-Asides,* vol. 1, 1985.

Stephen Yates provides a good summary of the compensatory justice and other arguments for affirmative action in his "Beyond Affirmative Action," A Heartland Policy Study, September 6, 1991. For the opposite perspective, see *Dissent*'s special section on affirmative action in their Fall 1995 issue.

The Virginia Held quote is from her contribution to the special section "Affirmative Action Under Fire," *Dissent,* Fall 1995.

I interviewed Faye Anderson during the Republican National Convention in San Diego, August 1996. See the profile of her by Kirk Victor in the *National Journal,* February 3, 1996, and her reaction to the convention by the same author in the *National Journal Convention Daily,* August 12, 1996. Read also her piece in *Headway,* "Television Broadcasters: The New Welfare Kings," March 1996.

The Council of 100 mobilizes support in the African-American community for the Republican Party. Further information on the group is available on its Web site, www.council100.org.

The black vote for Hutchinson was 22 percent, for Mack, 20 percent and for Voinovich, 40 percent in the 1994 election. These figures are based on exit polls done by Voters News Service.

Full information on blacks in the Republican Party—officeholders, delegates and so on—is available in David A. Bositis, "Blacks and the 1996 Republican National Convention," Joint Center for Political and Economic Studies, 1996.

Clare Alale of Little Rock was an alternate delegate to the 1996 convention.

A Digression into the World of Soccer Moms and Gender Fissures

The phenomenon of the soccer mom was reported ad nauseam in the months prior to the election of 1996. For two of the more intelligent takes on it, see the *New York Times* of October 6 and October 20, 1996.

The information on the number of children who play soccer is from the *New York Times,* October 20, 1996, and the *Los Angeles Times,* December 4, 1996.

These statements—that women hated Reagan, are more liberal and compassionate and are alienated from the Republicans because of abortion and the absence of Republican female candidates—are popular stereotypes that creep into much of the reporting on the gender gap.

For an excellent discussion of the gender gap, see Steven Stark's "What the Gender Gap Is Really About," *Atlantic Monthly,* July 1996. He provides a good analysis of the Reagan phenomenon, as does Kellyanne Fitzpatrick's "The Republican Warning," *Campaigns & Elections,* October/November 1995.

Women's most recent party and ideological identification by age and race was polled by the Polling Company in January 1996 and reported at the A Seat at the Table Conference, Denver, March 8, 1996.

In 1995 and 1996, a number of media and polling groups reported a difference in male/female values and male/female attitudes toward government, the safety net and other issues of concern. The best examples are the Washington Post/Harvard University/Kaiser poll reported in the *Washington Post,* January 30, 1996; the NYT/CBS poll reported in the *New York Times,* April 21, 1996, and the Knight-Ridder poll reported in their papers on June 18, 1996.

The statistics on the priority given to abortion show that about 10 percent of Americans consider themselves to be single-issue voters. They are evenly divided between pro- and antichoice. The source on this is a CBS poll from August 11, 1996. The one-of-850 statistic is from a poll done for *Ms.* magazine in 1992.

A discussion of the impact of female candidates on the votes of women, with the observation by Lake, appeared in the *New York Times,* April 28, 1996. See also Lisa Kalis, "What Matters More to Women Voters," *Working Woman,* April 1996.

The figures for the gaps by race, religion, income level and education were taken from "Politics Now," on-line at politicsnow.com. See also "In Control," January 29, 1996, *San Jose Mercury News.*

Wolf's suggestion to Clinton's advisers was noted by the *Washington Post,* January 24, 1996, in a column headlined "Put a Rock in the Role."

For more information on Women's Vote '96 and NOW's Fight the Right campaign, see the *Washington Post,* November 27, 1995.

Kellyanne Fitzpatrick provides a concise summary of voting patterns by gender in the presidential elections from 1952 through 1992 in her "Is There Really a Gender Gap?" presented at the RNC's A Seat at the Table in Denver, March 8, 1996.

The most thorough breakdown of women's opinions was provided by Greenberg Research and Lake Research from a six-part survey they produced for the Women's Monitor Project in October 1996.

The Outlaws

The thinking, planning and activities of the militia movement are communicated on-line, in small newspapers, via fax, audio- and videotapes, and on shortwave radio programs. Some of the major sources are: the American Patriot Fax Network in Shrinter, Texas Republic; the *Jubilee* newspaper (Midpines, California); the *New American* (Appleton, Wisconsin); *American Freedom* magazine (Johnstown, Colorado); *Taking Aim* (newsletter of the Militia of Montana), also at www.logoplex.com. For background, see the following materials available from "patriot" bookstores and/or the Militia of Montana. Videotapes: Mark Koernke, "America in Peril"; John Trochman, "Enemies: Foreign & Domestic" and "The Enemy Within." Books: Militia of Montana, *Blue Book and Executive Orders for the NWO;* Mark Anthony, *Vanishing Republic: How Can We Save the American Dream;* Rodney Stich, *Defrauding America;* Terry Cook, *The Mark of the New World Order;* Gary Kah, *En Route to Global Occupation.* The American Freedom Network broadcasts on Galaxy 6, Transponder 14, Audio 5.8 Wideband. For reporting on militias from outsiders, read John Swomley, "Armed and Dangerous," *Humanist,* November–December 1995, and Marc Cooper, "Camouflage Days, E-mail Nights," *Nation,* October 23, 1995.

The section on Kay Sheil is based on my interviews with her at her home outside St. Louis in September 1996. See also her reaction to the Oklahoma bombing in the *St. Louis Post-Dispatch,* April 22, 1995.

The Roundup was widely covered in the national press. See, for example, *Washington Post:* July 19 and August 30, 1995; and January 6, March 14 and April 2, 1996.

I garnered the information on the Laura Kuriatnyk case from my interview with Kay Sheil. The story was also recounted in the *Bullet* (the bulletin of the Western Missouri Shooters' Alliance), November 1995.

The Wendy Dalton and Darlene Donaldson quotes appeared in Serge Kovaleski's piece on women in militias, *Washington Post,* September 9, 1995.

The results of the Gallup poll were reported by Victoria Pope, "Notes from Underground," *U.S. News & World Report,* June 5, 1995.

The information on Annamarie Miller is from Jim Smolowe's "Enemies of the State," *Time,* May 8, 1995.

The woman who calls herself Kristina Sanchez was interviewed by Tony Ortega for his "Affirmative Reaction," *New Times* (Phoenix), March 28, 1996.

The section on Clara Pilchak is based on my interview with her in Detroit in September 1996. For an example of her thinking, see her "Don't Let School Control Your Child's Life," in the weekly update of the Michigan Militia Corps, September 5, 1996.

The best piece of journalism heretofore to examine the phenomenon of female participation in the militia movement, written by Serge Kovaleski, appeared in the *Washington Post,* September 9, 1995.

Although Linda Thompson is a mediaphobe, she has managed to garner enormous publicity. Her interactions with journalists have been reported in almost all profiles of her. Read Maryanne Vollter, "The White Woman from Hell," *Esquire,* July 1995; Alex Heard, "The Road to Oklahoma City," *New Republic,* May 15, 1995; Jason Vest, "Leader of the Fringe," *Progressive,* June 1995; and Jonathan Freedland, "Armed and Dangerous," *Guardian,* May 18, 1995. For a sampling of her screed, request that you be put on her electronic mailing list by sending a note to linda1@iquest.net. Also check out her postings at AEN.org. The quotes from her in this section were downloaded from these postings.

I interviewed Eva Vail at her home in Hayden Lake, Idaho, in September 1996. She died just as this book was being edited.

The figures on American pessimism are from the Washington Post/Harvard/Kaiser poll mentioned above, reported in the *Washington Post,* January 30, 1996.

The situation in the Stroudsberg school was reported both by their local press and by the *Washington Times,* May 5 and June 30, 1996.

The chemotherapy story was told to me by Clara Pilchak.

The story of the Earl family received considerable press attention, particularly in the Atlanta area. See *Atlanta Constitution,* February 12, 1996, and George Will's column, syndicated nationally, on July 16, 1995.

The story of the father in Newton, Massachusetts, was reported by Michael Chiusano, "Parents' Rights," *National Review,* September 30, 1996.

The story of the Colorado man was published in the *Rocky Mountain News,* November 3, 1996, as part of the transcript of a discussion on parental rights.

The violence of the left during the 1960s has been well documented by dozens of histories of that era. See in particular Todd Gitlin, *The Sixties: Years of Hope, Days of Rage* (Bantam, 1987), and, for the Karl Armstrong action, Tom Bates, *Rads: The 1970 Bombing of the Army Math Research Center at the University of Wisconsin and Its Aftermath* (HarperCollins, 1992). For background on SDS and the Days of Rage, see James Miller, *Democracy Is in the Streets*

(Simon & Schuster, 1987). Information on the Kathy Power case can be found in Jacob Cohen, "The Kathy Power Case," *National Review,* December 13, 1993, and *Boston Globe,* July 19, 1980. For more on the Days of Rage, see also the profile of Bill Ayers that appeared in the *Chicago Tribune,* July 8, 1993.

Clinton's comment after Oklahoma appeared in the *Nation,* June 5, 1995.

The Hayden interview was part of Nina Easton's piece on the sixties radicals and the contemporary militia movement that appeared in the *Los Angeles Times,* June 18, 1995.

There are numerous histories of the Black Panthers in which the murder of Fred Hampton figures prominently. See, for example, Elaine Brown, *A Taste of Power* (Pantheon, 1993). The events are recapped in shorter form in the *Boston Globe,* August 27, 1989, and September 15, 1995, and in a profile of Bobby Rush that appeared in the *Washington Post* on May 3, 1993.

For background on the Militia of Montana, Carolyn's group, see Marc Cooper and Lisa Westberg, "Montana's Mother of All Militias," *Nation,* May 22, 1995. MOM has a regular newsletter, *Taking Aim,* and its views of America are embodied in its *Blue Book.*

For the section on Ruby Ridge, I relied heavily on my interviews with Carolyn Trochman and an extensive collection of original documents and news accounts printed in *Massacre at Ruby Ridge: The Randy Weaver Story,* compiled by Eva Vail, available in patriot bookstores. For mainstream reporting, see Elizabeth Gleich, Cathy Free and Clay Hathorn, "Fighting to the Death," *People Weekly,* September 14, 1992; Patricia Brennan, "Overkill: The Bloody Debacle in Idaho," *Washington Post,* May 19, 1996; George Lardner, "Subcommittee Faults FBI Sniper at Ruby Ridge," *Washington Post,* December 22, 1995; George Lardner, "Sniper 'Knew What Was Going On': FBI Purposely Killed Wife at Ruby Ridge, Weaver Testifies," *Washington Post,* September 7, 1995; George Lardner, "Government Witnesses Cause Case to Collapse," *Washington Post,* September 5, 1995; George Lardner, "Standoff at Ruby Ridge," *Washington Post,* September 3, 1995; George Lardner and Pierre Thomas, "U.S. to Pay Family in FBI Idaho Raid," *Washington Post,* August 16, 1995.

A Digression into Cooking Up Trouble

The information on Chey Simonton and her letter came from my interview with her in August 1996.

Chey's letter was posted on the Internet at www.techmgmt.com/restore, a popular patriot site. The Internet and shortwave radio are the means of communication among these women.

The information on Norm Resnick came from Ward Harkavy's "Star-Spangled Banter," *Westwood* (Denver), June 15–21, 1994; Joan Veon's interview with him in *American Freedom,* July 1996; and from my interview with him in his studio in September 1996. Real-time audio of his program can be heard on-line at www.amifree.com.

The stances of Chey and Kelly are based on my interviews with them by telephone and on their on-air interviews given to Resnick during the time I was in his studio in September 1996.

The Anita Hoge story is based on my phone interview with her in August 1996 and the recounting of her struggles by B. K. Eakman in *Educating for the "New World Order,"* Halcyon House, 1991. Her position is also well explained in her testimony before the Health and Education Data Security Hearing on December 8, 1994, and her presentation, "Student Databases: For Education and For Life," at the Fifth Conference on Computers, Freedom and Privacy, March 1995. Finally, see the *Pittsburgh Post-Gazette* profile of her that ran on June 10, 1996.

The quote from Betty Mills, an elderly woman from Fort Wayne who is considered the "godmother" of the kitchen militia, is from my phone interview with her in August 1996.

Information on the CDR is available on-line from their Web site, www.logoplex.com/shops/cdr.

The education wars in Michigan, including the struggle for control over the Southfield Board of Education, were covered by the *Detroit Free Press;* see especially their piece of May 24, 1993.

The Pennsylvania battle over outcomes-based education was well analyzed by W. Boyd, C. Lugg and G. Zahorchak in "Social Traditionalists, Religious Conservatives and the Politics of Outcomes-Based Education," *Education and Urban Society,* May 1996. See also the *Philadelphia Inquirer,* September 25 and 27, 1992, and the *Pittsburgh Post-Gazette,* February 28 and March 19, 1992, and January 23, 1994.

The prayer was appended to Chey's letter, posted at www.techmgmt.com/restore.

The Apostates

The background information on Pat Millette is from a series of interviews I conducted with her in January 1996 and January 1997.

The information on female small business owners is based on Sandra Maltby, "Banks and the Woman Businessowner," *Vital Speeches,* January 1, 1996; Barbara Bronson Gray, "The Friendliest States for Women Business Owners," *Women Incorporated,* Spring 1996; publications of the Office of Women's Business Ownership of the U.S. Small Business Administration (on line at www.sbaonline.sba.gov/womeninbusiness); Stephanie Mahta, "Number of Women-Owned Businesses Surged 43% in 5 Years," *Wall Street Journal,* January 29, 1996; E. Holly Buttner, "Female Entrepreneurs," *Business Horizons,* March–April 1993; and publications of the National Association of Women Business Owners.

Nanci Mackenzie was profiled by Eric Schmuckler, "Cooking with Gas," *Working Woman,* May 1996.

Linda Alvarado has been profiled repeatedly by the *Rocky Mountain News.* See in particular their pieces on her from May 8 and June 17, 1991, and December 5, 1993, as well as the profile of her in *Women Incorporated,* Spring 1996.

The statistics on the status of women at various major corporations is from *Working Mother* magazine's special issue, "The 100 Best Companies for Working Mothers," October 1996.

For more information on Marilyn Marks, see Randall Lane's "Don't Mess with Marilyn," *Forbes,* December 4, 1995, and a profile of her in *Working Woman,* May 1992.

Ninfa's story was written by Lloyd Gite as "Steaming Safely Through Setbacks," *Working Woman,* February 1989.

For a conservative discussion of the problems of small business owners, see Susan Lee, "That 'Can't Do' Spirit," *Reason,* March 1996.

Judy Hooper's story was first reported by the *Chicago Tribune,* February 27, 1995. It then appeared in Sheila Moloney's "The Lady in Red Tape," *Policy Review,* September 1996.

The Karla Hauks and Anita Cragg stories are also from Moloney, above.

For information on the controversy around the independent contractor rules, see Peter Weaver, "Independent Contractor Rules Get Friendlier," *Nation's Business,* December 1996.

For the Kaplan story, see Moloney, above.

Details on paperwork problems are from Laura Litvan, "A Small Business Wish List," *Nation's Business,* August 1995, and Moloney, above. The statistic on the increase in the number of government regulations was given to me by the Small Business Survival Committee.

The information on the reaction of small business owners to Clinton's tax hike and health care reform proposals is from the Small Business Survival Committee, contained in a June 4, 1996, press release.

The Kellyanne Fitzpatrick quote is from her "Republican Warning," *Campaigns & Elections,* October/November 1995.

For examples of Dole's attempt to capture the votes of female business owners, see *Boston Globe,* July 25, 1996, and transcripts of PBS's *News Hour* July 25, 1996, dealing with his visit to a paper clip factory.

The Republican congresswomen newly elected in 1994 included several women with experience in small business. Sue Kelly, for example, ran a flower shop in New York, while Helen Chenoweth ran a small consulting company and Linda Smith managed an H&R Block office.

I met and interviewed Carol O'Dowd and Elaine Demery during the Seat at the Table Conference held by the Republican National Committee in Denver in March 1996. I interviewed Carol a second time in September 1996 at her home in Arvada, Colorado.

A Digression into a Posse of Pistol-Packing Mamas

I conducted my interview with Ishwari Silberman at the Libertarian Party convention over the Fourth of July weekend, 1996.

For a view of the type of accessories available to female gun owners, see the ads in *Women & Guns* magazine or the article "Handgun Accessories for Women" posted on the Internet at the site maintained by WFN (Women and Firearms Network).

Susan Whitmore's quote appeared in the *Washington Post,* January 29, 1995.

The Ellen Goodman quote is from her column in the *Boston Globe,* January 14, 1993.

Laura Ingraham's piece, "Why Feminists Should Be Trigger Happy," appeared in the *Wall Street Journal,* May 13, 1996.

The quote from Janis Cortise is from her "Left-wing, Right-wing . . . All the Same Thing," July 15, 1996, posted on her Web site, 10.com/-/cortese/resources/guns.html.

The trend toward gun ownership was well presented by Kathryn Casey in "Up in Arms (Women and Gun Ownership)," *Ladies' Home Journal,* August 1995. See also "More Women Turning to Firearms Out of Fear," *Los Angeles Times,* February 21, 1993, and "Arms and the Woman," *Boston Globe,* February 16, 1989. The statistics on the number of women who own guns were taken from the National Rifle Association's estimates, *Women & Guns* magazine, June 1995, and Gallup statistics printed in the *San Jose Mercury News,* June 16, 1992.

The insistence of antigun forces that women are not buying guns in any great numbers is from Lori Montgomery, "More Women Buying Guns? Myth," *Tallahassee Democrat,* December 4, 1994.

Bob Herbert's column containing this quote ran nationally on December 6, 1994. Tartaro's response was not printed by the *New York Times.*

The NRA campaign and the response of female legislators to it were reported in the *Washington Post,* January 29, 1994.

Marion Hammer's ascendancy at the NRA provoked a spate of media attention. See *Rolling Stone*'s profile of her in its long article on the NRA, July 1996; Deborah Kirk, "Exiles in Guyville?" *Harper's Bazaar,* November 1996; Patrick Rogers, "Top Gun," *People Weekly,* March 18, 1996; and Betsy Pisik, "NRA's New Top Gun," *Working Woman,* April 1996. Tanya caused a storm of controversy with the letter which provoked George Bush's resignation from the NRA. See for example Gail Collins, "Women in Power Who Give Women a Bad Name," *Redbook,* October 1995. For information on women in the NRA in general, see Steve Goldstein, "Women Making Presence Felt in NRA," *San Jose Mercury News,* May 22, 1995.

Details on Sylvia Daniel appeared in *Rolling Stone,* "Top Gun Folks," June 15, 1995.

Linda Mutchnick was profiled by the *Philadelphia Inquirer* on November 29, 1992, and by the *Washington Post* on December 9, 1992.

Quigley is the author of *Armed and Female* (St. Martin's Mass Market Paper, 1994) and *Not an Easy Target: Paxton Quigley's Self-Protection for Women* (Fireside, 1995).

I interviewed Callear during Lumberjack Days in Orofino, Idaho, in September 1996.

PART II

The Holy

Information on Cornerstone, an annual event held in the first week of July, is available on-line through www.jesusfreak.com.

The *Swing* survey appeared in the magazine's April 1996 issue.

I interviewed Joyce at the Crashdogs booth during Cornerstone, July 5, 1996.

I interviewed Jill during Cornerstone, July 5, 1996.

The Jesus People USA are one of a handful of remaining Christian communes that originated from the Jesus Freak movement. JPUSA's Web site is at msc.net/~jpusa/. The history of that movement and the group has been published serially in their magazine, *Cornerstone.* JPUSA offers housing for indigent elderly and runs a program for homeless families, a neighborhood ministry, a family counseling program, a recording studio, a video studio, a press, a magazine, a shelter for women with children and a community center, as well as the festival.

The information on Wendy Kaiser is based on my interview with her at Cornerstone on July 6 and on the history of JPUSA contained in *Cornerstone.*

Wendy Kaiser's seminar, entitled "Teens & Sexuality," was a four-day workshop, from July 4 through July 7.

I interviewed Linda in December 1996 and have observed and spoken with Elizabeth on numerous occasions from 1995 to the present.

For background on evangelicals and fundamentalists in U.S. history, see the PBS special *Mine Eyes Have Seen the Glory,* May 1993, and William Martin's book, *With God on Our Side: The Rise of the Religious Right in America,* (Broadway, 1996).

The information about the alternative universe created by fundamentalist Christians is drawn both from my interviews and from Doug Bandow, "Christianity's Parallel Universe," *American Enterprise*, November 1995, and John Kennedy, "Mixing Politics and Piety," *Christianity Today*, August 15, 1994.

The Fleming quote is taken from Bandow, above.

For background on the issues that began to ignite conservative Christians politically, see Garry Wills, *Under God: Religion and American Politics* (Simon & Schuster, 1990) and Erling Jorstad, *Holding Fast/Pressing On: Religion in America in the 1980s* (Greenwood, 1990).

Background information on Beverly LaHaye and CWA came from the myriad publications of CWA and my interviews with the group's legislative director. For more on both the woman and the organization, see Holler Miller's piece in the *Saturday Evening Post*, October 1985, the *Los Angeles Times* profile of LaHaye printed June 25, 1986, and the *Washington Post* profile of her, September 26, 1987. I also consulted numerous back issues of their magazine, *Family Voice*.

For a more thorough accounting of CWA's war against SIECUS, see the *Village Voice*, May 21, 1996.

Much of this information, as well as the details on Laura, result from my interview with her at CWA headquarters in December 1995.

The background on and quotes from May Ellen Miller are from Larry Witham, "Campaign Leaders Make Local Politics a Religious Pursuit," *Washington Times*, March 22, 1995.

The information on Riedemann and Smith appeared in Megan Rosenfeld's "Not NOW, Dear: The Conservative Alternative of Concerned Women for America," *Washington Post*, September 26, 1992.

The phenomenon of Christian political activity at the local level was surveyed beautifully by the *Los Angeles Times* in a two-part series entitled "Crusade for Public Office in Second Stage," published March 22 and 23, 1992. The statistics on the success of Christian candidates is contained therein. The information on the takeover of the Vista school board came from the same newspaper's continuing coverage of the event, especially articles from November 5 and November 16, 1992.

The situation in Merrimack, New Hampshire, was covered by Adele Stan in "Power Preying," *Mother Jones*, November 1995.

Joe Graybarz is currently executive director of the Connecticut Civil Liberties Union. He has worked as an organizer for the Democratic Party, the Human Rights Campaign Fund and various other liberal groups. He also served as a member of the Connecticut legislature.

Green's statistics were quoted in Larry Witham, "Campaign Leaders Make Local Politics a Religious Pursuit," *Washington Times*, March 22, 1995.

For background on the coalition that arose in New York City, see the coverage at the time of *Newsday*, April 23, May 24, June 14, November 30 and December 17, 1992. For a more current view of attempts to forge alliances of religious conservatives, see Fred Barnes, "The Orthodox Alliance," *American Enterprise*, November 1995.

The section on Kirstin Hansen includes details from the *Washington Post*, September 27, 1996.

Glendon, a professor at Harvard Law School, is a politically active Catholic. For her thinking on contemporary women's issues, see, "A Glimpse of a New Feminism," *America*, June 13, 1996.

The material on Sheldon is based on my interview with her in November 1995. Details were also taken from the *Los Angeles Times* profile of her that ran on October 1, 1995.

A Digression into Faith of a Different Fabric

The material on Reid is from my interview with her conducted in New York City in September 1996.

The chat line SisterNet is one of a number of on-line, members-only computer talk groups for Muslim women.

The material on Kim is based on my interview with her, which was conducted electronically in August 1996.

The Operators

The 1996 Republican National Convention was held in San Diego from August 12 to 15, 1996.

Melich's book, *The Republican War Against Women: An Insider's Report from Behind the Lines*, was published by Bantam in 1996. The reaction to it, from both the liberal and conservative camps, was well captured by Frank Rich in the *New York Times*, January 9, 1996; by Kate O'Beirne in the *National Review*, February 12, 1996; and by Judy Mann in the *Washington Post*, January 17, 1996.

The information on Helen Chenoweth is based on my interviews with her and pieces published in the *Albion Monitor*, June 25, 1995, and the *Salt Lake Tribune*, October 27, 1996. Her problems with the Speaker were covered in the *Washington Post*, January 11, 1996.

I interviewed Lee Ann in the stands at the community auction during Lumberjack Days in Orofino, Idaho, September 1996.

The WISH List breakfast was held at the U.S. Grant Hotel on August 14, 1996.

For the pro-choice account of the departure of moderate women, see Sidney Blumenthal, "The G.O.P. Doll's House," *New Yorker*, August 19, 1996.

Greenwald was profiled on Women's Wire, October 16, 1996. Further background on her and on WISH List are available in Connie Koenenn, "Taking a Step Off the Platform," *Los Angeles Times*, April 2, 1992; Kay Mills's interview with Patricia Goldman, *Los Angeles Times*, January 7, 1996; Jill Abramson and Gerald Seib, "Gender Specifics," *Wall Street Journal*, July 17, 1996; and Ronald Ostrow, "GOP Backs Abortion Rights," *Los Angeles Times*, March 5, 1992. See also the *WISH List News*, the newsletter of the group.

The clearest account of the abortion wars in the Republican Party is Tanya Melich's *The Republican War Against Women*, cited above.

For a contemporaneous view of women at the 1984 convention, see *Washington Post*, February 15 and August 22, 1984.

The information on Sue Kelly was provided to me by Lauren Sims of the Speaker's office. The story was covered by the *New York Times*, September 1, 1996; the *Washington Post*, June 30 and July 25, 1996; and the *Los Angeles Times*, July 25, July 31 and August 1, 1996.

The section on Gingrich's support for women is based on my interviews with Representatives Chenoweth and Seastrand, Lauren Sims of his press office and his liaison to the Republican women, Karen Feaga.

For information on Linda Smith, see Lisa Leiter, "Women's Work," *Insight on the News,* April 17, 1995; coverage of her in the *Seattle Times,* September 22 and October 1, 1994; and coverage of her in the *Seattle Post-Intelligencer,* September 7 and October 24, 1994, and October 9, 1996.

The career and professional demise of Enid Waldholtz was chronicled by Adam Platt, "Pop Goes the Waldholtz," *George,* April 1996; Ed Vulliamy in the *Observer,* May 8, 1994; and Hanna Rosin, "The Crying Game," *New Republic,* May 27, 1996.

The clearest view of Myrick comes from a regular reading of North Carolina newspapers. See in particular the *Charlotte Observer,* December 6, 1989; April 14, 1990; December 1, 1991; March 17 and April 12, 1992; and November 5, 1994.

A brief history of female officeholders and the two major political parties: The first woman elected to the House of Representatives, in 1916, was Jeanette Rankin, a Republican. In 1940, the Republicans became the first party to endorse the Equal Rights Amendment in its platform. The first female secretary of the Department of Health, Education and Welfare, Oveta Culp Hobby, was a Republican, as was the first female ambassador to a major power, Clare Boothe Luce, to Italy in 1953. The first woman to be elected to the United States Senate without being preceded by her husband was Nancy Kassebaum, Republican of Kansas. Gingrich appointed the first female clerk of the House, Robin Carle, and the first female House counsel, Cheryl Lau. When the Republicans took control of Congress in 1994, Kassebaum became the first woman ever to chair a Senate committee. Between 1976 and 1994, no woman chaired a House committee. In 1994, Jan Meyers became chair of the House Small Business Committee.

Linda Smith's quote appeared in the *New Republic* in "Invasion of the Church Ladies," April 24, 1995.

The information on Dunn's attacks on Morris is from a piece that appeared in the *New Republic,* June 24, 1996.

The statistics on Republican women in office are from "Women in Elective Office," a fact sheet from the Center for the American Woman and Politics, National Information Bank on Women in Public Office, Eagleton Institute of Politics, Rutgers University.

The material on Evelyn McPhail is based on my interview with her during the Seat at the Table Conference and on profiles of her written in the *Hill,* November 16, 1995; *Campaigns & Elections,* June 1996; and the *Commercial Dispatch* (Columbus, Mississippi), June 23, 1995.

A Seat at the Table, sponsored by the cochair of the Republican National Committee and the Colorado Federation of Republican Women, was held at the Holiday Inn in Denver, March 7–8, 1996.

Pat Harrison is a consultant in environmental public policy, a founder of the National Women's Economic Alliance and a longtime Republican Party activist. In January 1997, she was elected cochair of the RNC, succeeding McPhail. She is the author of *A Seat at the Table: An Insider's Guide for America's New Women Leaders* (National Women's Economic Alliance, 1996).

The luncheon, "Celebration of Leadership: Tribute to GOP Women Elected Officials," was sponsored by the RNC Co-Chairman's Office on August 13, 1996, at the Hyatt Regency Hotel in San Diego.

I met Dina Butcher at a cocktail party before the above-mentioned luncheon and arranged to meet her in North Dakota when she was on the campaign trail. I interviewed her and her daughter Amanda before, during and after her trip to Alexander for Old Settlers Days in September 1996.

The religiosity of Ellen Craswell's campaign was the subject of considerable media scrutiny during the campaign in 1996. See for example in the *Seattle Times:* April 10, August 28, September 10, September 20 and October 22, 1996; and in the *Seattle Post-Intelligencer:* September 19, October 10 and October 15, 1996.

Susan Golding's political career has been thoroughly covered by the *Los Angeles Times.* See in particular the pieces on her from April 16, 1985, April 9, 1989, and August 24, September 30 and November 6, 1992. *Time* also named her one of the nation's rising Republicans; see "Rising Republicans," August 19, 1996.

Alexander is in far western North Dakota, close to the Montana border. I attended the events described in September 1996.

A Digression into the Strong Arms and Stronger Spirits of Frontierswomen

I ran into, and interviewed, LaRee on the street in September 1996 during Lumberjack Days in Orofino, Idaho.

For Engels's arguments, see Friedrich Engels, The *Origins of the Family, Private Property and the State* (Pathfinder, 1972).

I interviewed Joyce at her home in Watford City, North Dakota, in September 1996.

The quotes from Michelle Cote are drawn from my interviews with her in Alexander, North Dakota, and at her ranch on the North Dakota–Montana border in September 1996.

The Ideopreneurs

Christina Hoff Sommers is the author of *Who Stole Feminism* (Touchstone, 1995).

The *New York Times Magazine* piece, published February 12, 1995, was James Atlas's "Look Who's the 'Opinion Elite' Now." This piece was, predictably, followed by a similar one in the *Boston Globe,* "The People to See," by David Shribman, January 28, 1996.

Fox-Genovese is the author of numerous scholarly works on southern women: *Feminism Is Not the Story of My Life: How Today's Feminist Elite Has Lost Touch with the Real Concerns of Women* (Doubleday, 1996); of *Feminism Without Illusions: A Critique of Individualism* (University of North Carolina, 1991); and—"It Takes a Family," *New Republic,* June 3, 1996. I also culled information about her from an interview published with her in the *Washington Times,* January 31, 1995; from a joint interview with her and her husband, Eugene Genovese, published in *American Enterprise,* September 1996; and from a profile of her in the *Chicago Tribune,* November 24, 1995.

Lynne Cheney served as chair of the National Endowment for the Humanities for seven years and is a senior fellow at the American Enterprise Institute. She is the author of *Telling the Truth* (Simon & Schuster, 1995) and, with her husband Richard, of *Kings of the Hill: How Nine Powerful Men Changed the Course of History* (Simon & Schuster, 1996).

The IWF received a barrage of publicity beginning in 1995. See "She's No Feminist, and She's Proud of It," *National Journal,* January 4, 1997; Megan Rosenfeld, "Feminist Fatales," *Washington Post,* November 30, 1995; Paul Barrett, "A New Wave of Counterfeminists," *Wall Street Journal,* October 13, 1995; Rachel Gorlin, "Angry White Females Inc.," *Boston Globe,* May 7, 1995; Mary Hancock Hinds, "Putting a New Face on Feminism," *Washington Times,* December 16, 1993; "Conservative Spotlight," *Human Events,* April 14, 1995; Jennifer Gonnerman, "Angry White Women," *Village Voice,* July 11, 1995. IWF members are well published. The pieces that have spoken for the organization include Ledeen's "Sacrificing Babies on the Altar of Privacy," *Wall Street Journal,* August 3, 1995; her "Selective Indignation over Insults to Women," *Washington Times,* April 5, 1995; Ledeen and Anita Blair, "Ten Things to Help Women, Families," *Fort Lauderdale Sun-Sentinel,* September 18, 1996; and Blair, "Shattering the Myth of the Glass Ceiling," *Los Angeles Times,* May 7, 1996.

Wendy Lee Gramm holds a Ph.D. in economics and was a member of the faculty at Texas A&M. In addition to working for the Federal Trade Commission and the Office of Management and Budget, she also chaired the U.S. Commodity Futures Trading Commission under Presidents Reagan and Bush.

Ingraham became a darling of the mainstream media in 1996. See James Ledbetter, "Laura Ingraham's Wild," *Village Voice,* December 24, 1996; Harvey Berkman, "Republican, Connected and Rising," *National Law Journal,* March 11, 1996; and Marjorie Williams, "Laura, Get Your Gun," *Vanity Fair,* January 1997. For coverage of Dark Ages weekend, see David Van Biema, "Reactionary Romp," *Time,* January 8, 1996; and Weston Kosova, "Schmoozing in the Sand," *Newsweek,* January 8, 1996.

Quotes from Anita Blair are from my interview with her in the fall of 1995 in Washington, D.C. For a profile of her, see K. C. Swanson, "She's No Feminist, and She's Proud of It," *National Journal,* January 4, 1997.

The O'Beirne quote appeared in the *Washington Times,* January 4, 1995.

Quotes from Barbara Ledeen are from my interviews with her during 1995, 1996 and 1997.

Faludi's view of Fox-Genovese is captured in her review of *Feminism Is Not the Story of My Life* in the *Nation,* January 8, 1996.

Crittenden's "Knock Me Out with a Truck" appeared in *Backward and Upward: The New Conservative Writing* (Vintage, 1995). The *Women's Quarterly* is loosely affiliated with the Independent Women's Forum. It was featured in the *Washington Times,* "No 'Angry Agenda,' No Feminists at New *Women's Quarterly,*" September 13, 1995. In addition to her "Diary" at the beginning of each issue of the *Quarterly,* Danielle is the author of "Mother Knows Best," *Ladies' Home Journal,* December 1995, and "Yes, Motherhood Lowers Pay," *New York Times,* September 22, 1995.

The Sommers quote appeared in a profile of her in the *Boston Globe,* June 16, 1994.

The section about Arianna Huffington is based on interviews with a number of Washington conservatives who prefer not to be named. It also includes information from profiles of her that appeared in the *Washington Post,* February 8, 1995; the *Rocky Mountain News,* May 26, 1996; the *New York Times,* July 17, 1996; and the *National Journal,* December 9, 1995.

Bay Buchanan was profiled extensively during the 1996 presidential campaign. Particularly helpful to my account were the following pieces: *Chicago Tribune,* March 13, 1996; *National Review,* August 14, 1995; *New Republic,* January 22, 1996; *Newsweek, U.S. News and World Report, Time* and *People,* all of March 4, 1996; *Washington Post,* February 28, 1996; and *Los Angeles Times,* March 12, 1992, and March 1, 1996.

A Digression into the Mind of the Femi-Newtie

This long quotation is from my interview with Newt Gingrich in the Speaker's office in February 1996.

The Weary

The material on Whitney Adams is from my interview with her during the Republican National Convention in San Diego, August 1996.

For polling on the relationship between women's votes and their abortion attitudes, see the *Ms.* survey, 1992, and the Wirthlin polls of July 1992 and May 1996, in which voters were asked if there was a single issue on which they cast their ballots.

For the breakdowns of the poll numbers I used about abortion attitudes, see the CBS News/New York Times poll, January 1, 1995, and the Yankelovich poll for Time and CNN, January 5, 1995. For sentiments on the morality of abortion, see Gallup poll for CNN and *USA Today*, February 24–26, 1995. For positions on government interference with women's right to abortion, see Hart/Teeter for NBC and *Wall Street Journal*, June 1994. For opinions on cases in which respondents believe abortion is justifiable, see National Opinion Research Center poll of January–May 1995. For a chart showing the history of attitudes toward abortion, see *American Enterprise*, July/August 1995.

For a review of the statistics on abortion attitudes then and now, see William Schneider, "The Battle for Saliency," *Atlantic Monthly*, October 1992.

Foster was quoted taking this position in the *Washington Post*, February 10, 1995.

The quote from Clinton appeared in George McKenna, "On Abortion: A Lincolnian Position," *Atlantic Monthly*, September 1995.

The Hodgson quote appeared in Martha Bayles, "Feminism and Abortion," *Atlantic Monthly*, April 1990.

For background on the fight against the introduction of RU-486 into the United States, see *Washington Post*, October 27, 1988, December 10, 1991, and February 13, 1997.

For a thorough discussion of who is seeking abortions and why, see "Women Who Have Abortions," by Susan Dudley, for the National Abortion Federation, 1995; A. Torres and J. D. Forrest, "Why Do Women Have Abortions?" and S. K. Henshaw and J. Silverman, "The Characteristics and Prior Contraceptive Use of U.S. Abortion Patients," *Family Planning Perspectives* (Alan Guttmacher Institute), July/August 1988.

Rose Anderson is a nurse-practitioner at Camillus Health Concern, a clinic for the homeless in Miami. The section on her is based on my interviews with her in New York, October 1996, and by telephone in January 1997.

I made the rounds of the abortion activist groups, pro and con, and the relevant federal agencies in an attempt to uncover at least the dollar figure for how much has been spent on the abortion wars: the budgets of the lobbying and organizing groups, the legal battles, the publicity, marches and the like. I was unable to find anyone who had done the math.

The quote from Susan B. Anthony appeared in the *Revolution*, July 8, 1869; Mattie Brinkerhoff, the *Revolution*, September 2, 1869; Victoria Woodhull, *Woodhull and Claffin's Weekly*, December 24, 1870; Elizabeth Cady Stanton, the *Revolution*, February 5, 1868.

Feminists for Life maintains a Web site at www.2serve.com/fem4life.

Jenny Westberg's quote is from her "Apologia of a Pro-life Feminist," in *Blue Stocking*, August 1993.

The *Blue Stocking* story was told by the publisher to Naomi Wolf during an interview published in *Blue Stocking*, December 1993.

Naomi Wolf's article, "Our Bodies, Our Souls," was published in the *New Republic* on October 15, 1995. Fulredi's response appeared in *Living Marxism* in December 1995.

The section on Michelle Grothe is based on interviews conducted with her at Cornerstone in July 1996 and by telephone to her home in Wisconsin in January 1997.

McKenna's piece, "On Abortion: A Lincolnian Position," appeared in the *Atlantic Monthly*, September 1995.

For background on RU-486, see the *Washington Post*, February 4, 1997.

Harrison's remark was made on PBS, *News Hour*, September 19, 1996.

For more details on emergency contraception, see "Abortion of the Future," *National Times*, October/November 1995; *Washington Post*, March 19, 1996; and Steve Radlauer, "A Whole New Choice," *New York* magazine, April 1, 1996.

Epilogue: Everything Has a Moral, If Only You Can Find It

I interviewed Sue and Jeanette at Curl Up and Dye in September 1996.

There is an enormous, and growing, body of literature about women's ambivalence toward the feminist movement. See in particular: Katie Roiphe, *The Morning After: Sex, Fear and Feminism on Campus* (Little, Brown, 1993); Rene Denfeld, *The New Victorians* (Warner 1995); Nan Bauer Maglin and Donna Perry, *"Bad Girls"/"Good Girls": Women, Sex and Power in the Nineties* (Rutgers University Press, 1996); Rebecca Walker, *To Be Real: Telling the Truth and Changing the Face of Feminism* (Anchor, 1995); Suzanne Gordon, *Prisoners of Men's Dreams* (Little, Brown, 1991); Maggie Humm, ed., *Modern Feminisms* (Columbia University Press, 1992); Juliet Mitchell and Ann Oakley, *What Is Feminism: A Re-examination* (Pantheon, 1986); Betty Friedan, *The Second Stage* (Summit, 1981); Gloria Steinem, *Revolution from Within: A Book of Self-Esteem* (Little, Brown, 1992); Virginia Geng, "Requiem for the Women's Movement," *Harper's*, November 1976; Friedan, "Feminism's Next Step," *New York Times Magazine*, July 5, 1981; Mary Anne Dolan, "When Feminism Failed," *New York Times Magazine*, June 26, 1988; Erica Jong, "The Awful Truth about Women's Liberation," *Vanity Fair*, April 1986; Pam Houston, "Big Sister Is Watching," *Elle*, January 1994; Claudia Wallis, "Women Face the '90s," *Time*, December 4, 1989; Kay Ebeling, "The Failure of Feminism," *Newsweek*, November 19, 1990; Sally Quinn, "Who Killed Feminism?" *Washington Post*, January 19, 1992; Eileen McNamara, "The Myth of Sisterhood," *Boston Globe Sunday Magazine*, January 5, 1992.

The Debbie story is based on my conversations with Deborah Sontag in December 1996.

Jenny Westberg's quote is from her "Apologia of a Pro-life Feminist," in *Blue Stocking*, August 1993.

Index

abortion, 19, 31, 33, 36, 64, 67, 68, 73, 124, 125, 133, 136–37, 176, 201, 212, 215, 229–47; Christian right and, 152, 153, 154, 156, 162, 168, 169; clinic murders and, 98–99, 239, 244; common ground in debate over, 243; cost of battle over, 238, 243; and decline of interest in issue, 229–31; explanations for unwanted pregnancies and, 235–36; gender gap and, 76–79; kitchen militia and, 118; libertarianism and, 47–48, 49; as litmus-test issue, 229–30, 239, 243–44; militiawomen's views on, 88, 90–91, 98; opinion polls on, 231–32; partial birth, 80, 168, 186, 233, 234; possibility of truce over, 244–47; pro-choice Republicans and, 79, 182–86, 194, 195, 229–30, 238; pro-choice rhetoric on, 232–33, 234–35; pro-life feminists and, 238–43; pro-life rhetoric on, 233–34, 235; statistics on, 234–35, 244, 245; technological advances and, 230, 244–46

Adams, Whitney, 229–30, 244, 247

affirmative action, 19, 20, 21, 31, 33, 36, 37, 50, 127, 152, 201, 229, 230; black opposition to, 56, 65–72; history of, 59, 69–70; ideopreneurs' views on, 211–15, 219, 224

African-Americans, 29, 253; civil rights movement and, 52, 58–59, 60, 84; conservatism deeply ingrained in, 55–56; Democratic Party and, 52–57, 61, 72, 77; lack of economic improvement among, 59, 60–61, 70; in Republican Party, 17, 52–74; self-help and self-reliance arguments and, 58, 59–63, 73; special diversity awards for, 37

age: voting gap and, 81

agrarian societies, 200–204

agriculture, 94, 95, 196–97

Alale, Clare, 72, 73, 74

Albion College, 36–39

Allen, George, 224

AlliedSignal, 43

Alvarado, Linda, 129

American Conservative Union, 183, 224

American Enterprise Institute, 16, 223

American Justice Federation, 90

American Patriot Network, 117

Americans with Disabilities Act, 131

Amoco, 129–30

Anderson, Faye, 72–74

Anderson, Rose, 236–37, 247

Anthony, Susan B., 50, 169, 240

antifeminism, antifeminists, 217–22, 229–30

anti-Semitism, 86

antiwar movement, 84, 97–98, 100

Antonelli, Angela, 224

Antonucci, Trish Wilson, 21

Ardizzone, Chris, 28

Armey, Dick, 68, 186

Army, U.S., 90

Aryan Nation, 84

Association of Libertarian Feminists, 48, 49

Austin, Jeanie, 187

baby boomers, 35, 36, 45

Barbour, Haley, 193

Barghouti, Kim, 173–75

Barnett Banks, 129

Bill of Rights, 97, 117, 119, 123

birth control, 234, 235, 236, 243, 246, 254

Black Panthers, 84, 97, 99, 101–2

Blair, Anita, 213, 214, 215

Blue Cross/Blue Shield of Massachusetts, 130

Blue Stocking, 240–41
Boehner, John, 186
Boston Globe, 215, 221
Bracher, Barbara, 211
Bradbury, Jackie, 45, 47, 48–49
Bradley, Ed, 216
Brazier, Nona, 59–64, 74
Break the Silence, 37, 38
Brinkerhoff, Mattie, 240
Brock, David, 219, 223
Brown, Bob, 92
Brown, Helen Gurley, 41
Brown, Jackie, 109
Browne, Harry, 46, 48
Buchanan, Angela "Bay," 224–27
Buchanan, Pat, 30, 56, 99, 153, 166, 176, 224, 225–27, 244
budget, federal, 77, 81, 179–80, 185, 191, 193, 225, 231
Bureau of Alcohol, Tobacco and Firearms (BATF), 84, 85, 91, 102, 103, 104–5
Burk, Martha, 21
Bush, George, 72, 115, 144, 192, 212, 217–18
business. *See* corporate America; small businesswomen
Butcher, Dina, 194, 195–99
Byerly, Joyce, 202

Callear, Lee Ann, 146, 181–82
Carlson, Arnie, 182
Carter, Jimmy, 76, 81
Catholicism, Catholics, 78–79, 167, 233, 237
Central Intelligence Agency (CIA), 89, 92
Chase Manhattan Bank, 42
Cheney, Lynne, 211, 212–13
Chenoweth, Helen, 15–16, 23, 134, 177–82, 188
child care, 21, 41, 43, 49, 135, 163, 173, 212, 215, 223, 238
child support, 238, 243
Christian Coalition, 150, 165
Christian Identity, 86, 102, 103
Christianity, 112; "City on the Hill" notion and, 160; decline in influence of, 160, 161
Christian right, 22, 32, 72, 149–70, 177; Cornerstone rock festival and, 149–57, 161; isolated from mainstream society, 157–61; kitchen militia and, 115–16,

118–19; liberals' denigration of women in, 167–68; parallel universe of, 160–61; stereotypes of women in, 151; women activists in, 162–70
Civil Rights Act, 72, 84
civil rights movement, 52, 58–59, 60, 84
Clark, Mark, 101–2
class, 95, 99, 250, 253; voting gap and, 78, 81
Cleveland, Ashley, 154
Clinton, Bill, 15, 77–80, 82, 93, 97, 99, 101, 133, 137, 140, 146, 167, 179, 188, 190–91, 201, 214, 223, 232
Clinton, Hillary, 90, 133, 176, 180, 218
colleges: conservatives shunned at, 36–39
communism, 93, 95, 121
community, 49, 54, 74, 255; feminism blamed for breakup of, 208, 209
Concerned Women of America (CWA), 162–66, 188, 211
condoms, 96, 161, 163, 235, 236
Congress, U.S., 18, 91–92, 99, 119, 143, 167; black Republican women running for, 17, 52–58, 67–69; Christian women lobbyists and, 162–65, 169; gender gap and, 77, 78, 82; inclusive women's caucus impossible in, 243; Republican women in, 15–16, 19, 177–91
Congressional Women's Caucus, 16
conservatism, conservatives, 76, 83, 152, 180, 254, 256–57; abortion issue and, 229, 243, 247; affirmative action and, 70–71; antifeminism and, 217–22; among blacks, 17, 52–74, 77; generation gap among, 30–31; among GenX women, 27–44; ideopreneurs and, 205–27; kitchen militia and, 118–19; religious (*see* Christian right); shunned at liberal colleges, 36–39
conspiracy theories, 93–94, 256
Constitution, U.S.: militia movement and, 85, 86, 96–97, 117–19, 123. *See also specific amendments*
Contract with America, 77, 165, 185, 188
Contract with the American Family, 165
Cornerstone, 149–57, 161
corporate America, 18, 129–30, 205, 211
Cortise, Janis, 141
Cote, Michelle, 203–4
Council of 100, 72–73

Council on Domestic Relations (CDR), 119–23
Council on Foreign Relations, 92, 95
Cragg, Anita, 131
Crashdogs, 149, 152
Craswell, Ellen, 62, 64, 194–95
creationism, 166, 169
crime, 35, 78, 80, 86, 188, 231, 242
Crime Bill, 214–15, 219
Crittenden, Danielle, 205, 217–21
Cubin, Barbara, 15, 16, 134, 189, 191
Cullum, Blanquita, 255
Cummings, Mary, 167

Dalton, Marion, 121
Dalton, Wendy, 87
Daniel, Sylvia, 144
Dark Ages weekends, 213
Darrow, Clarence, 160
Darwin, Charles, 160
day care. *See* child care
"Days of Rage," 97–98
Declaration of Independence, 97
DeCrow, Karen, 44
DeLay, Tom, 27, 32, 186
Demery, Elaine, 135, 138
democracy, 84, 85, 100, 101, 137
Democratic Party, 15, 34, 35, 59, 62, 117, 152, 187, 189, 193; abortion issue and, 229; black community's allegiance to, 52–57, 61, 72, 77; gender gap and, 76–79, 81, 82, 191; grassroots organizing neglected by, 167; gun control and, 145; libertarians' views on, 46; new female entrepreneurs and, 132, 133–38
DePreist, Oscar, 56
DioGuardi, Joseph, 185, 186
disabilities, 130, 131
discrimination, 131, 174, 190; race, 58–59, 61; sex, 50, 126, 127, 128
divorce, 18, 43, 195, 254
Dobson, James, 160
Doggett, John, 66, 67, 72
Doggett, Lloyd, 67, 69
Doggett, Teresa, 65–72
Dohrn, Bernardine, 98–99
Dole, Bob, 29, 78, 79, 80, 134, 137, 183, 185, 199

Dole, Elizabeth, 29, 176, 194, 199
domestic violence, 43, 173
Donaldson, Darlene, 87, 89
Dornan, Bob, 170, 185, 186
Douglass, Frederick, 56
drug laws, 45, 46
drugs, 16, 35, 111, 154, 161, 189
Du Bois, W. E. B., 58, 60
Dunlop, Becky Norton, 224
Dunn, Jennifer, 63, 187, 188, 190–91

Eagle Forum, 165, 188, 211
Earls family, 96
economic issues, 35, 82, 212, 254. *See also* budget, federal
EDK Associates, 142
education, 18, 21, 68, 69, 77, 78, 81, 82, 251–52; Christian right and, 157–59, 162, 163, 165–67; Gender Equity Act and, 214–15; home schooling and, 47, 87, 88, 102, 111–12, 157–59, 181; kitchen militia and, 115–18, 120–23; liberal bias on college campuses and, 36–39; libertarians' views on, 45, 47; militia-women's views on, 86–89, 93, 95–96, 111–12; multicultural, 189; outcomes-based (OBE), 120–23; single-sex programs and, 20, 21, 214, 215; special, 111; transition from Christian to secular culture and, 160; women's studies programs and, 36, 212, 221. *See also* schools
Education Department, U.S., 116, 121, 163, 233
elections: alleged tampering with, 120
Elshtain, Jean Bethke, 50
Endangered Species Act, 177, 179
Engels, Friedrich, 201–2
entrepreneurial women. *See* small business-women
environmental issues, 80, 81, 95, 110, 191, 224
equal pay, 18, 50, 203, 219, 248, 251
Equal Rights Amendment (ERA), 84, 162, 184, 230, 238
Equal Time, 224
Esquire, 89
Evans, Akwasi, 68
evolution, 160

Fair Labor Standards Act, 40

Faludi, Susan, 22, 49, 167–68, 216, 250

Falwell, Jerry, 161–62

family, 41, 49, 50, 57, 60, 79, 173, 188, 212, 230, 255, 257; Christian right and, 162, 163, 164, 167, 168; feminism blamed for breakup of, 208–10, 218, 254; tension between work and, 43, 205, 220, 223, 226–27, 231, 240, 249–50, 252–53. *See also* marriage; motherhood

"family-friendly" feminism, 210–11

Family Research Council, 165, 168

family values, 80, 82, 113, 210

Farrakhan, Louis, 73

Federal Bureau of Investigation (FBI), 84, 85, 88, 97, 101, 116; Ruby Ridge and, 104, 106–9

Federal Reserve Board, 87

Federation of Republican Women, 29

Feminine Mystique, The (Friedan), 17, 41

feminism, feminists, 21, 189; alienated from its own constituency, 19–24, 248–58; catfights among, 252; Christian right and, 150, 151, 152, 154, 156–57, 159, 162, 163, 167–69; early, government as enemy of, 50; family breakup blamed on, 208–10, 218, 254; "family-friendly," 210–11; gender gap exploited by, 79–81; GenX conservatives' views on, 31–32, 39–44; Gingrich on, 228; goals of, 17–18, 22; gun ownership and, 140–42, 145, 146; ideals of, embraced by American women, 251–52; ideopreneurs and, 205–27; Islam and, 172–75; libertarians' views on, 47, 48–51; militiawomen's views on, 112; pro-life sentiments among, 238–43; Republican congresswomen and, 16, 178, 180, 189, 197, 199; in rural West, 200–204; sacrifice notion and, 159; small businesswomen's views on, 133; successes of, 18–19, 256–58; unfairly blamed for social ills, 254–55; whining ascribed to, 63–64 (*see also* victimhood culture); as women-hating sore winners, 248–49; young women's lack of gratitude toward, 43–44; young women's lives permeated by victories of, 39, 43–44

Feminism Is Not the Story of My Life (Fox-Genovese), 205, 207–8, 216

Feminist Majority, 80, 216, 240

Feminists for Life (FFL), 239–40

51st Missouri Militia, 84, 85, 86, 96

Finley, Julie, 183

First Amendment, 47, 49

First Mounted Rangers, 87

Fish and Wildlife Service, U.S., 131

Fitzpatrick, Kellyanne, 28, 31, 33, 35, 36, 133, 211

Fleming, Thomas, 161

Focus on the Family, 179

Food and Drug Administration (FDA), 120, 233–34

Forbes, Steve, 68

Foster, Henry, 232

Fourteenth Amendment, 84, 91

Fowler, Tillie, 184

Fox-Genovese, Elizabeth, 50, 205, 207–11, 216–17, 220, 221, 257

Frahm, Sheila, 185

Freedom of Choice Act, 163

freedoms: American, gratitude for, 45; libertarianism and, 45–51

Friedan, Betty, 17, 21–22, 41, 57, 162, 164, 200, 207, 252

Frum, David, 217–18

Fulredi, Ann, 241–42

fundamentalism. *See* Christian right

Gender Equity Act, 214–15

gender gap, 75–82, 191, 211, 219; differences among women and, 81–82; exploited by feminists, 79–81

gender roles, 31–32; in information age, 228; in Islam, 172–75; in rural West, 201–2

GenX conservatives, 19, 27–44; feminism as viewed by, 31–32, 39–44; "Merge Right" party for, 27–30; schism between older conservatives and, 30–31; shunned at liberal colleges, 36–39; sixties radicals compared to, 33–36

Gilman, Charlotte Perkins, 50

Gingrich, Marianne, 190, 194

Gingrich, Newt, 19, 28, 35, 36, 77, 78, 137, 165, 191, 205, 213, 220; on feminism, 228;

Republican congresswomen and, 178, 179–80, 186–90, 194

Glendon, Mary Ann, 168

Goals 2000, 123

Golding, Susan, 195

Goldwater, Barry, 72, 161

Goodman, Ellen, 141

Good Ol' Boys events, 83–84

Gordon, Doris, 48

government: citizenry's distrust of, 19, 31, 34, 94, 97; gender gap and, 76, 77, 78; libertarians' opposition to, 45–51; militia-women's views on, 85–87, 89, 90, 94, 95, 99, 100, 110, 111; size of, 188, 230, 233

government regulation, 40, 49–50, 95, 224; in rural West, 201; small businesswomen and, 124, 125, 130–35

Gramm, Wendy Lee, 212

Grandparents for Independent Association, 121

Grant, Amy, 161

Graybarz, Joe, 167

Green, John, 167

Greenwald, Glenda, 183, 184, 185

Gritz, Bo, 92, 108–9

Grothe, Michelle, 242–43, 247

gun business: women in, 144–45

gun control, 45, 46, 49, 80, 88, 92, 140–41, 142, 144, 145, 213, 229, 233; Republican women and, 178, 179, 182

Gunn, David, 98

gun owners, female, 139–46; motivations of, 145; NRA campaign directed at, 143–44; statistics on, 141–42

gynecological examinations, 95–96

Hamer, Fannie Lou, 72–73

Hammer, Marion, 144

Hampton, Fred, 101–2

Handgun Control, 141

Hanrahan, Edward V., 101

Hansen, Kirstin, 168

Harris, Kevin, 105, 107, 108, 109

Harrison, Donna, 246

Harrison, Pat, 192–93

Harvard University, 66, 94

Haskin, Greg, 224

Hauks, Karla, 131

Hayden, Tom, 99–100, 101

health care, 77, 80, 82, 120, 133–34, 135, 193, 231, 233; parental rights and, 96

Hearst, 89

Held, Virginia, 72

Henderson, Cheryl Brown, 185

Herbert, Bob, 142–43

Heritage Foundation, 223–24

Herman, Stephanie, 44

Hill, Anita, 64–65, 67, 165, 223

Hill, Paul, 98

HIV: testing for, 215

Hodgson, Jane, 232

Hoffman, Julius, 97–98

Hoge, Anita, 118, 121, 122–23

Holliday, Deidre, 166

Holmes, Amy, 29, 39–40, 255

Holscher family, 157–60

home-based work, 21, 40, 43, 132

homeless, 170, 237, 250

homemakers, 208, 210; IRAs for, 209, 210

home schooling, 47, 87, 88, 102, 111–12, 157–58, 159, 181

homosexuality, 19, 93, 176, 195, 237; Christian right and, 161, 163, 165, 166, 167, 169

Hooper, Judy, 130–31

Hoover, J. Edgar, 101

Horiuchi, Lon, 107

Horton, Willie, 72

Howard, Susan, 144

Huffington, Arianna, 191, 213, 222–23

Huffington, Michael, 222, 223

Hutchinson, Kay Bailey, 22, 73, 182–83, 230, 238

Hyskill, Laura, 163–64

Idaho militia association, 89

ideopreneurs, 205–27; antifeminism and, 217–22, 229–30; and difficulties of communicating with public, 206–7; neofeminism and, 205–17, 221–22; and refusal to debate women's affairs on feminist terms, 222–27. *See also* Independent Women's Forum

Illuminati, 93, 95

incest, 234, 235, 236

independent contractors, 131–32

Independent Women's Forum (IWF), 20–22, 29, 30, 49, 207–21, 223, 239; abortion

Independent Women's Forum (IWF) (cont.)
    issue and, 215; advocacy actions of,
    214–15; Crittenden's antifeminismand,
    217–21; elitism charges and, 216–17;
    founding of, 211–12; Fox-Genovese's
    lecture to, 207–11; membership of,
    212–13; publicity garnered by, 215;
    "women's issues" debate reshaped by,
    215–16, 221
individualism, 49–51
industrial era, 201–2, 228
Industrial Strength Women, 63
information age, 206, 228
Ingraham, Laura, 141, 205, 211, 213
Interior Department, U.S., 178, 224
Internal Revenue Service (IRS), 15, 45, 46, 87,
    94, 100, 131–32, 180
IRAs: for homemakers, 209, 210
Ireland, Patricia, 50, 215, 216, 222, 250
Islam, 167, 171–75
IUDs, 246

Jackson, Jesse, 56
Jars of Clay, 161
Jefferson, Judy, 52–57, 58, 63, 74
Jesus People USA, 154
John Birch Society, 92
Johnson, Corinne, 36–39
Johnson, Lyndon B., 69, 70, 97
Johnson, Nancy, 184, 187, 189, 190
Johnson, Roger, 197
Jones, Paula, 214
Jorgensen, Jo, 46, 48
Judaism, Jews, 78–79, 86, 150, 151, 167
Justice Department, U.S., 106, 109, 131, 224

Kaiser, Glenn, 154, 155–56
Kaiser, Wendy, 154–57, 158
Kaiser Family Foundation, 94
Kaplan, Arlene, 131–32
Kassebaum, Nancy, 136, 182, 187, 188, 194
Kelly, Alex, 190–91
Kelly, Sue, 16, 134, 185–87, 188, 238
Kemp, Jack, 72
Kennedy, Joan Taylor, 51
Kennedy, John F., 81
Kennedy School (Harvard University), 66
King, Martin Luther, Jr., 69, 84

Kirk, Adelle, 41–43
Kirkpatrick, Jeane, 68, 177
kitchen militia, 115–23; action program of,
    119–23; prayer of, 123
Kondratas, Anna, 213
Koresh, David, 91
Ku Klux Klan, 59, 83–8
Kuriatnyk, Laura, 85
Kwanza, 60

Labor Department, U.S., 132
Ladowsky, Ellen, 219
LaHaye, Beverly, 118, 162, 163, 164–65, 169
Lake, Celinda, 78, 81–82, 226
J. T. Lambert Intermediate School, 95
Lassiter, April, 27, 30, 31–36, 150
Laurenzo, Ninfa, 130
League of Women Voters, 16, 185
Ledeen, Barbara, 20–22, 29, 30, 213–16
LeGrand, Dorothy, 57–58
Lewis, Ann, 170, 177
Lewis, Bettye, 121
liberalism, liberals, 21, 83, 152, 180, 211; abor-
    tion issue and, 229, 243–44; gender gap
    and, 76–77; gun control and, 140–41,
    145; kitchen militia's hostility toward,
    116–17; Republican assault on, 190;
    small businesswomen's desertions
    from, 124–26, 132–34, 137–38; unpre-
    pared for Christian women's activism,
    166–67
Libertarian Party, 45–51, 140; abortion feud
    in, 47–48; dearth of women in, 46–47;
    feminism as viewed by women in,
    47–51
Libertarians for Life, 48
Liddy, G. Gordon, 97, 213
Limbaugh, Rush, 15, 22, 97, 176, 206
Long, Patricia, 58
Lott, Trent, 194
Loury, Glenn, 65
Lowey, Nita, 143
Luksik, Peg, 122, 123

McElroy, Wendy, 50
Mack, Connie, 73
McKenna, George, 244
Mackenzie, Nanci, 128–29

MacKinnon, Catharine, 49
McPhail, Evelyn, 135–37, 191–94
MacRae, LaRee, 200–201
McVeigh, Timothy, 90
Magna-Trigger, 139
Malcolm X, 17, 60–61, 62, 73, 97
Manson, Charles, 99
Marks, Marilyn, 130
marriage, 21, 42, 43, 63, 168, 172, 220, 255, 257; in rural West, 200; same-sex, 37–38
Marshals Service, U.S., 104–9
Martin, Lynn, 187, 190, 192
Mason, Sarah, 154
medical care. *See* health care
Melich, Tanya, 177, 182, 192
"Merge Right" party (1996), 27–30
Metaska, Tanya, 144
methotrexate, 245
Meyers, Jan, 187, 189, 194
Michaelson, Karen, 49
Michelman, Kate, 168
Michigan Militia, 88
militia movement, 46, 83–123, 177, 178; common fears in, 93–95; desire to be left alone and, 95–96; kitchen militia and, 115–23; media-hyped concerns over, 115; paranoia and, 89–94; reasonable women in, 83–89; Ruby Ridge incident and, 86, 89, 97, 102–9, 110, 114; sixties activism compared to, 84, 97–102
Militia of Montana (MOM), 110–11
Miller, Annamarie, 87
Miller, May Ellen, 165
Millette, Pat, 124–28, 132, 137–38
Million Man March, 73
Mills, Betty, 118–19
misoprostol, 245
Molinari, Susan, 134, 176, 188, 189
morality, 56, 57, 208, 237. *See also* values
Moral Majority, 54
Morella, Connie, 184
Morgan, Robin, 242
morning-after pills, 246–47
Morris, Dick, 190–91
motherhood, 21, 168, 208, 209, 216, 220, 240, 257; feminism's lack of support for, 21, 40–42; home-based work and, 21, 40;

sacrifices associated with, 159; working mothers and, 21, 181, 210, 211, 214, 217, 226–27. *See also* family
Ms., 79, 218, 242, 250
Muslims, 167, 171–75
Mutchnick, Linda, 144–45
Myers, Phyllis Berry, 65
Myrick, Sue, 16, 68, 189

NAFTA, 92, 120, 181
Nash, Leigh, 154
Nathan, Tonie, 46
National Business League, 60
National Empowerment Television, 206, 222, 223
National Endowment for the Arts (NEA), 120, 213
National Endowment for the Humanities (NEH), 212–13
National Federation of Republican Women, 187, 188
National Organization for Women (NOW), 44, 79–80, 84, 85, 140, 146, 173, 179, 202, 207, 215, 216, 229, 250; pro-life feminists and, 239–40, 241
National Rifle Association (NRA), 141–42, 143–44, 201
Nelson, Kelly, 117–18
neofeminism, 205–17, 221–22. *See also* Independent Women's Forum
Newman, Constance, 64
New Republic, 36, 178, 190, 241
New World Order, 90, 92, 110
New Yorker, 22
New York Times, 142–43, 161, 206, 250
New York Times Magazine, 205, 213
Nixon, Richard M., 81, 225
Northrup, Ann, 230
Norton, Gale, 183

O'Beirne, Kate, 189, 215
O'Brien, Kate, 45, 47
Occupational Safety and Health Administration (OSHA), 130–31
Odd Fellows, 60
O'Dowd, Carol, 134–38
Ohio Unorganized Militia, 89
Oikle, Sue, 248, 249

Oklahoma bombing, 88, 92, 98, 99
Operation Northern Exposure, 104
Operation Rescue, 245
O'Rourke, P. J., 219–20
outcomes-based education (OBE), 120–23

parental rights, 96, 169
Parental Rights and Responsibilities Act, 118
partial birth abortion, 80, 168, 186, 233, 234
Pataki, George, 182
patriarchy, 240, 250, 257
patriot movement. *See* militia movement
Patru, Jackie, 119–20
Paxon, Bill, 186
Peretti, Frank, 161
Perot, Ross, 46
Pike, Amanda, 90
Pilchak, Clara, 87–88
Pinkerton, James, 205
pioneer spirit, 198, 200–204
pornography, 47, 49, 230
Port Huron statement, 100
poverty, 33, 124, 125, 209, 210, 211, 237, 243;
    affirmative action and, 69–72; among
    blacks, 59, 60–61, 70
Powell, Colin, 72, 74
prayer in schools, 55, 83, 117, 160, 161, 169
privatization, 117–18, 195
property rights, 120, 178, 179
Pushy Broads Association, 63

Quayle, Dan, 212, 214
Quayle, Marilyn, 176, 177, 191
Quigley, Paxton, 145

race, 229, 250; discrimination based on, 58–59,
    61; voting gap and, 78, 81
racism, 33, 34–35, 37, 55, 59, 61, 71, 83–84, 86,
    97, 124; legal fight against, 58–61; mili-
    tia movement and, 95; sixties activism
    and, 99, 100
Rand, Ayn, 28, 35, 46, 48
Rankin, Jeanette, 203
rape, 18, 219, 231, 252; abortion and, 234, 235,
    236
Ravitch, Diane, 212
Reagan, Ronald, 28, 36, 72, 76, 119, 163, 212,
    217–18, 223, 224, 225
Reed, Ralph, 165, 185, 186

Reid, Mary Ann, 171–73
religion, 19, 54, 72, 149–75; abortion issue and,
    233; school prayer and, 55, 83, 117, 160,
    161, 169; speaking publicly about,
    150–51; voting gap and, 78–79; young
    Americans' spiritual hunger and, 150.
    See also Christianity; Christian right;
    specific religions
Republican Party, 32, 34, 117, 152, 176–99, 211;
    battle for control of, 177, 183–84; black
    women in, 17, 52–74; Christian right
    and, 167, 177, 183, 194–95; congress-
    women in, 15–16, 19, 177–91; gender
    gap and, 76–79, 81, 82, 191; historic ties
    of black community to, 56; ideopre-
    neurs and, 214; libertarians' views on,
    46; moderate women recruited by,
    191–93; new female entrepreneurs
    and, 132, 133–38; 1992 convention of,
    176, 229; 1996 convention of, 176–77,
    182–85, 194, 198, 230; pro-choice
    women in, 79, 182–86, 194, 195, 229–30,
    238; young conservatives' rebellion
    against, 29–30, 34–35
Resnick, Norman, 117
Resurrection Band, 154
Ridgeview, Inc., 43
Riedemann, Fran, 165
Right to Life, 88, 90–91
Robertson, Pat, 118, 160
Robinson, Ron, 226
Roosevelt, Franklin D., 56
Roseanne, 250
Ross, Betsy McCaughey, 191, 192
RU-486, 234, 245
Ruby Ridge incident, 86, 89, 97, 102–9, 110, 114
Rzewnicki, Janet, 185

Salvi, John, 239
same-sex marriage, 37–38
Sanchez, Kristina, 87
Sanger, Margaret, 50
Schafer, Ed, 197
Scheidler, Joseph, 91
Schiffren, Lisa, 205, 212
Schlafly, Phyllis, 20, 28, 112, 118, 165, 177, 184,
    185, 224
school board elections, 165, 166
schools, 97; condoms distributed in, 96, 161;

gynecological examinations in, 95–96; prayer in, 55, 83, 117, 160, 161, 169; sex education in, 28, 87, 96, 100, 162, 166, 169, 181–82. *See also* education

school vouchers, 56

Schroeder, Pat, 170, 183, 189, 190

Scopes trial, 160

Scribner, 89

SDS, 99, 100

Seastrand, Andrea, 189

Seat at the Table, 135

Second Amendment, 140, 182

Self Haters, 30

Seventeenth Amendment, 91–92

sex, 161, 168, 211, 235, 254, 255; women's liberation and, 208–9; young Christians' views on, 154–55

sex discrimination, 50, 126, 127, 128

sex education, 28, 87, 96, 100, 162, 166, 169, 181–82

sexism, 33–35, 44, 67, 71, 100, 213, 236

sexual harassment, 146, 214, 219

Sexuality Information and Education Council of the United States (SIECUS), 163

Sheil, Kay, 83–86, 87, 96–97

Sheldon, Andrea, 169–70

Shock, Christine Krof, 48

Silberman, Ishwari, 139–40, 143–44

Silberman, Ricki, 30, 211

Simonton, Chey, 115–19

single mothers, 176, 180

single-sex education, 20, 21, 214, 215

SisterNet, 173

Sixteenth Amendment, 91

sixties radicals: GenX conservatives compared to, 33–36; militia movement compared to, 84, 97–102

60 Minutes, 215, 216

small businesswomen, 124–38, 192; changes in nature of, 128; explosion in number of, 128, 130; government regulation and, 124, 125, 130–35; in gun business, 144–45; political turnaround among, 124–26, 132–38; role models of, 128–29, 130; in rural West, 203

Smeal, Eleanor, 216

Smith, Chris, 185, 186

Smith, Judy, 165–66

Smith, Linda, 16, 62, 190, 191

Smith, Marianne, 47

Smith, Mary Louise, 187

Smith, Paul, 47

Snowe, Olympia, 182, 183, 184

soccer moms, 75, 80, 81

socialism, 47, 49

Sommers, Christina Hoff, 50, 205, 212, 214–15, 221, 257

special education, 111

Stanton, Elizabeth Cady, 206, 240

Starr, Kenneth, 214

Steinem, Gloria, 20, 21–22, 41, 44, 49, 50, 57, 207, 222, 250

Straight, Candace, 183

Supreme Court, U.S., 161; Thomas's nomination to, 60, 64–67, 165, 211

Take Your Daughter to Work Day, 215

Tartaro, Peggy, 143

taxes, 21, 45, 77, 80, 81, 87, 94, 95, 110, 117, 133, 135, 163, 180, 188, 210, 212, 230

teen pregnancy, 209, 243, 254

television: condom advertising on, 163; religious stations on, 160

Teresa, Mother, 88

terrorism, 99

Terzian, Grace Paine, 218

Thernstrom, Abigail, 211, 213

Thernstrom, Steven, 211

think tanks, 119, 120

Thomas, Clarence, 60, 64–67, 165, 211

Thompson, Bennie, 54, 55

Thompson, Linda, 89–92, 94, 97

Thrasher, Vanessa, 120–21

Time, 41, 89

Traditional Values Coalition (TVC), 165, 169–70

Trilateral Commission, 92, 95

Trochman, Carolyn, 102, 104, 106–14

Trochman, John, 103, 106, 108, 110, 113

Truth, Sojourner, 169

tuition vouchers, 118

United Citizens for Justice (UCJ), 110

United Nations (UN), 88, 93, 115, 119; Fourth World Conference on Women, 168

United States Militia Association, 87, 89

Unorganized Militia of the United States of America, 91
USAA, 42

Vail, Eva, 92–94, 97
values, 81, 230; Christian right and, 163; family, 80, 82, 113, 210; gender gap and, 76, 77; OBE and, 122, 123
victimhood culture, 21, 31, 39, 44, 45, 63, 250–52, 254, 255; gun ownership and, 143; neofeminist critique of, 212–16
Vietnam War, 85, 233; antiwar movement and, 84, 97–98, 100
violence, 161, 208, 229, 240; against women, 18, 43, 173, 176, 210, 214–15, 217, 219, 238. *See also* rape
Violence Against Women Act, 20, 214–15, 219
Virginia Military Institute (VMI), 20, 214
Voinovich, George, 73
Vucanovich, Barbara, 187, 188, 189, 194

Waco incident, 84, 91, 101, 144
Waldholtz, Enid Green, 16, 180, 189
Wall Street Journal, 141, 205, 212, 215, 218
Walters, Barbara, 162
Washington, Booker T., 58, 59, 60
Washington Post, 20, 36, 87, 89–90, 94, 166, 215, 218–19
Watts, J. C., 72
Weathermen, 97, 98–99
Weaver family, 86, 89, 97, 102–9, 110, 114
Weld, William, 182, 183
welfare, 33, 36, 55, 68, 72, 80, 81, 152, 163, 170, 181, 193, 195, 211, 213, 230, 233; feminists' defense of, 208–9
West: frontierswomen in, 200–204
Westberg, Jenny, 238–39, 240–41, 256

Weyrich, Paul, 28, 118, 185, 223
Whitman, Christine Todd, 136, 176, 182, 183, 188, 194
Whitmore, Susan, 141
Williams, Walter, 65
Williamson, Marianne, 164
Winfrey, Oprah, 250
Winthrop, John, 160
WISH List, 182–86, 195
Wittig, Sue, 134
Wolf, Naomi, 79, 241–42, 252
Women & Guns, 139, 143
women candidates: gender gap and, 76, 78, 79
women's issues: notion of, 31, 49, 63, 220; reshaping nature of debate over, 215–16, 221; voting gap and, 79–80
women's movement. *See* feminism, feminists
Women's Quarterly, 218–19
women's rights, 36, 48
women's studies programs, 36, 212, 221
Wood, Genevieve, 28–29, 32
Woodhull, Victoria, 240
work, 21, 79, 94, 172–73, 181, 251, 254; corporate America and, 18, 129–30, 205, 211; equal pay and, 50, 203, 219, 248, 251; feminism's impact on, 40–44; government regulation and, 40, 49–50, 95, 124, 125, 130–35; home-based, 21, 40, 43, 132; independent contractors and, 131–32; tension between family and, 43, 205, 220, 223, 226–27, 231, 240, 249–50, 252–53
working mothers, 21, 181, 210, 211, 214, 217, 226–27
Worldwide Christian Radio, 117
Wortham, Anne, 64